CW00547286

A Pedaller to Peking

A Pedaller to Peking

Christopher Hough

METHUEN

First published in Great Britain 1986
by Methuen London Ltd
11 New Fetter Lane, London EC4P 4EE

Copyright © 1986 Christopher Hough

British Library Cataloguing in Publication Data

Hough, Christopher
  A pedaller to Peking.
  1. Cycling—Europe   2. Europe—
  Description and travel—1971–
  3. Cycling—Asia   4. Asia—
  Description and travel—1951–
  I. Title
  914'.04558   D923

  ISBN 0-413-57980-8

Printed in Great Britain by
Richard Clay (The Chaucer Press) Ltd,
Bungay, Suffolk

Contents

List of illustrations

Acknowledgements

Of the many hundreds of people who treated me with such friendly kindness and generosity I would particularly like to thank the following: the Pigeon St Bonnet family, Ancenis; Lucille Grignon-Pumoulin, Marseilles; Peter Keneally, Florence; Nico and Nanette Moschos, Athens; Frances Melling, Tarsus; Suzanne Caplan, Bombay; Yvette Zerfas, Shirangapatnam; Jane and Willi Chan, Hong Kong; Katie Curtis, Hong Kong.

In addition, my chambers showed exceptional patience in allowing me first to cycle and subsequently to write about it all in a book, which would never have been written without the optimism and encouragement of Imogen Parker and Alex Bennion.

I would like to thank the following publishers for permission to reproduce extracts from books: Bodley Head Ltd for *Ulysses* by James Joyce, Viking for *Journey to Kars* by Philip Glazebrook, Penguin Books Ltd for *The Greeks* by H. S. F. Kitto, and Viking Penguin Incorporated for *Chinese Shadows* by Simon Leys (copyright © Union Générale d'Editions 10/18/74, English language translation copyright © Viking Penguin Incorporated, 1977).

Finally, I would like to thank my mother and Laura Longrigg, whose innumerable letters, telegrams and phone calls made it clear that at least two people cared what was happening to me despite the anguish I apparently put them through.

Prologue

'He's going to cycle to China,' said my friend, introducing me to a middle-aged man in a pub.

The man stared intently at me and, after some minutes' thought, slowly sipped his beer. Finally he asked:

'Don't you have any parents?'

It was an unusual and unexpected question.

'Yes,' I replied, a little hesitantly.

'Well, why the hell don't they stop you doing it then, you damn fool. You ever been out there?'

'No.'

'Ever been cycling before?'

'No.'

'Know anything about bikes?'

'No.'

'Don't suppose you know why you're doing it either?'

I mulled over the possible answers. It was quite untrue to say it had been a life-long ambition to cycle across Europe and Asia – the idea had occurred to me just nine months before I left, after watching Bayern Munich get knocked out of the UEFA Cup. I had cycled to the match, but apart from that there was no good reason why the occasion should have led to such a dramatic renunciation of my life in London.

'Because it's there,' sounded far too clichéd. I tried to come up with a romantic dream about crossing the world's largest land mass by bike, or how I had become obsessed by a deep craving to follow in the trail of some epic adventurer. It wouldn't work – if pressed I was forced to admit that I would be quite happy to take ferries, buses and even trains if I became bored, tired or too frightened of 'the locals'. The truth was that I hoped it would be interesting, stimulating and above all fun to cycle from London to Peking; in short, there was no good reason not to go, and every reason to go. I began to cheer up – so what if my motives sounded a little self-indulgent?

'Don't you think it will be interesting?' I demanded, feigning anger that anyone was prepared to do anything other than enthuse over my 'brilliant notion'.

'Don't be such a bloody idiot. There's nothing interesting about getting killed, you . . . you . . . pah . . . you bloody fool.'

He stomped off to stand moodily in another corner of the pub, occasionally crying out an anguished lament about 'the young' and the general decline of common sense while my friend, a little embarrassed, tried to apologise for such rude behaviour.

Unfortunately, despite the man's obvious insanity, I suspected that some of his more intelligible and coherent remarks were, in some respects, not entirely without justification. It might, for example, be a little silly to set off without any cycling experience, although there seemed little point in cycling round Britain in 'training' for cycling across France and Italy – much better to use those countries as training for the more demanding Turkish terrain, and so on through India and China.

A more convincing argument for getting some 'experience' was to find out something about bikes – I wasn't quite sure what, but my ignorance was considered by almost everyone I met to be an almost insuperable obstacle to my cycling successfully across Asia. Despite my misgivings about the value of such a journey, and really only to silence these tiresome and repetitive critics, I decided to buy a bike and cycle from John O'Groats to Land's End – about a thousand miles of pleasant villages, country lanes, friendly bed and breakfasts, spring flowers and the other delights of an Easter in Britain.

Apart from being fun, the journey proved surprisingly useful. It established that I needed a better bike if my bottom, back and knees were to survive; that I had to practise repairing punctures, learn something about dérailleurs (though again I wasn't sure what) and try and work out a route across southern Asia to include as many national parks and agreeable towns as possible.

It was all very pleasant – for the next few months I loafed around, occasionally going to court but spending most of my time in an armchair 'researching' the identity of interesting or beautiful towns, buildings or countryside. The other problems were taken out of my hands – the bicycle company F. W. Evans assured me that their standard touring bike was quite capable of getting to China and, indeed, were quite snooty that I should ever have had any doubts. My family doctor supplied me with a large sack filled wth various pills which would, if not actually cure, at least alleviate the discomfort of the numerous diseases I faced.

These efforts were wasted – abuse continued to rain down. I was 'inexperienced' (again), 'irresponsible' and 'impetuous'. Suitably encouraged, I waited for the Grand Departure, now planned for August 1984 to enable me to get to India in the winter and China in the summer. It was perhaps inevitable that, with such haphazard planning, the vicissitudes of politics and my health would all but destroy my flimsy scheme to cycle from London to Peking.

I

From here to Athens

Thoughts of the Turkish mountains, the dry and dusty plains of central India and non-English-speaking Chinese villages seemed extravagant, even slightly ludicrous, when pushing my bike from my parents' house in Blackheath to the road. Too much *Casablanca* as a boy had perhaps too narrowly defined my idea of a romantic and poignant farewell: no aeroplane stood in the mist, its propellers whirring, the captain waiting anxiously for me to get on board; no soldiers were trying desperately to prevent my departure. Absolutely nothing depended upon my leaving within the next few seconds. Indeed, nothing would happen if I didn't go at all.

I shuffled around, checking my tyre pressures, praying that I wouldn't have a puncture and generally attempting to assume an indifference to the thrills of the journey ahead.

Someone asked if I wanted them to hold the bike as I climbed on. My brother offered to demonstrate the gear-changing system, somebody pointed out that I hadn't fitted stabilisers and wanted to know how I was going to stop myself falling off – obviously my journey from John O'Groats to Land's End meant nothing to them, I sulked.

'Are you sure you can get to Portsmouth?' asked my mother, who was going to meet me in a Gosport marina before sailing me across to Cherbourg. 'You could always put your bike on the train, or maybe I could pick you up somewhere . . . what about Guildford?'

'More like Clapham,' bawled my brother.

I smiled wearily – the right reaction, I thought, for a hardened and quietly determined traveller.

'Don't worry, I'll see you in Gosport,' I announced in an appropriately grim monotone. 'And I'll see you in Athens,' to my sister, 'and you in India,' to my girlfriend, 'and the rest of you in ten months. Come on, Chris,' I declared to the friend who was cycling with me for the first three or four days. 'Let's go.'

We pedalled off, through Deptford, Stockwell, Clapham, Balham and out into the apparently endless London suburbs. At last we reached Guildford, the cause at first for some celebration until we saw a signpost claiming that there were still fifty miles to Portsmouth instead of thirty, as we had thought. In an earlier mood of expansive and quite unjustified grandeur I had dismissed the offer of a map of southern England as superfluous to my requirements, with the unhappy result that we were now forced to cycle from Guildford along the busy and unattractive A3. It was an inauspicious start, made worse by the fact that just as we arrived in Portsmouth the wind, which we had been cycling into all day, died down and we were forced to use the boat's motor all the way across the Channel.

'The last lunch' with my mother in Cherbourg was the occasion of another lengthy analysis of the tortures and disasters that I would inevitably face, portrayed with such vivid and dramatic imagery that it was only with a quite remarkable degree of willpower that I succeeded in dragging myself up the hill away from the port, and on towards the Loire valley.

Twenty miles from Cherbourg Chris and I achieved the first of my little targets — the first one hundred miles. Although for many of the round-the-world cyclists that I'd met before I left such a modest distance was an easy morning's ride, for me it represented a significant breakthrough and certainly justified a small celebration — a quiet congratulatory dinner in one of those legendary family hotels where bed, breakfast, a five-course dinner and a couple of bottles of wine cost about a fiver.

Ten miles on we found precisely the right sort of place, a little more expensive perhaps — in fact five times as expensive — but then I'd only just read in one of the colour supplements that the 'real value' of French cooking was not to be found in some cheap café, but in the more stately bourgeois country hotels. I checked that the husband worked in the bar, the wife in the kitchen and the children, supplemented by two cousins from either Paris or Provence, worked as waiters, waitresses or chambermaids. They did. Our good fortune in finding this True France so early on our travels was almost too much to bear. Oozing smug complacency we lolled about on the verandah, sipping kirs and insisting that we would eat whatever the chef recommended — another tip picked up from colour supplements.

Oysters in early August? Something wasn't quite right, but we were both fairly sure that the French would know about the right seasons — or perhaps there was an 'r' in the French for August.

Our confidence was sadly betrayed. After a terrible night suffering from oyster-poisoning, and a morning in a doctor's surgery trying to find some cure for our awful feelings of lethargy and nausea, we set off towards Granville and Avranches. Normandy suddenly seemed a dreary place – straight roads, not even lined by trees, cutting unsympathetically across the landscape and refusing to respond to the subtleties of the small brooks, copses, hills, valleys and villages. Ugly hoardings advertising restaurants, hotels and, ironically, beauty spots lined the road. In Granville, harsh loudspeakers bawled out the day's special offer – an exceptionally cheap deal on carrots.

South of Mont St Michel I was suddenly on my own as Chris, who had come along with me 'to help me get started', had to get back to work – rather thankfully, I thought. I felt totally disheartened for some reason, questioning in my less dispirited moments the whole point of leaving 'all I had' for the intangible rewards of cycling to China. In an absurd attempt to justify the trip I began the most ludicrous recording of odd phrases I found in books, magazines and inscribed on buildings. I paced solemnly about ruined castles, measuring the width of walls and the size of rooms; I tried to calculate the cubic capacity of dungeons and to sketch the developments in brick-laying between the thirteenth and fifteenth centuries 'as seen at the castle of Pouance'.

I don't know what extremes this behaviour would have ultimately reached – what collection of arcane, meaningless statistics I would have finished with, if I hadn't visited the Château de La Motte-Glain. A large sign announced that the Château was closed, an appropriate symbol of my unsuccessful attempts to discover the inner secret of France. In a weak gesture towards 'intrepid adventuring' I climbed over the gate and began to trudge morosely up and down, measuring the size of the courtyard, keeping an eye on the brickwork and trying to calculate the number of tiles on the roof.

These moronically pedantic examinations were interrupted by an angry enquiry, emanating from the stables, asking what the hell I thought I was doing. I didn't know the French for 'gathering statistics', so explained that I was cycling to China and couldn't wait for the Château to open. As I said this a man began to make his way slowly from the stables towards me, dabbing diligently at the corners of his mouth with a noticeably dirty napkin.

He quite unexpectedly turned out to be the owner of the Château, was suitably impressed by my announcement and, after making some curiously happy grunting noises over my bike, suggested that I have some lunch with him until his guide turned up, who he would get to show me around. Conversation at lunch was my first experience of the peculiarly recondite world inhabited by cycling enthusiasts, in which comparisons of dérailleurs and gear ratios assume an all-pervasive importance. It was enjoyable for two reasons – it demonstrated that, contrary to their strong reputation for arrogant unfriendliness, the French could be nice and even generous, and secondly, and perhaps of greater importance, the occasion encouraged me to abandon my austere approach to the whole business of cycling, and in future I made a practice of taking long lunches and consuming large quantities of wine. Wallowing in pleasant fantasies of rural restaurants to come, I allowed the conversation – which by then had moved on to the optimum saddle surface and the need for shaving one's legs and plastering them with vaseline – to drift gently over me and out into the courtyard.

In due course the much-promised guide appeared to whizz me around the large, rather cold rooms, half-filled with odd pieces of silver, slightly tatty Louis Quinze furniture, some tapestries, portraits of the owner's predecessors, children, horses and dogs and a room filled with an exhibition of his own paintings. The guide ended his tour with an invitation to stay at his parents' Napoleonic château overlooking the Loire at Ancenis. Naturally I accepted, and left Ancenis the next day convinced of the charms of the French character, and feeling optimistically that however gloomy things appeared to be, something or someone would always come along to cheer me up.

My good mood continued as I cycled through the Loire vineyards, taking full advantage of the free *dégustation* offered, and even collecting two bottles as presents 'pour le cycliste'. I slowed down, bought a beret and a token onion and began to fantasise about my empathy with the French way of life. At La Roche-sur-Yon, quite happy to conform to a caricature of cheap French living, I bought some rough bread, some cheese and a bottle of suitably unpleasant red wine and headed off to a *gîte d'étape*, situated at the side of a lake just to the north of the town.

So long as I remained alone in the *gîte d'étape*, a satisfactorily simple form of accommodation and, by chance, unsupervised and unoccupied by anyone else, I was able to indulge freely in these absurd fantasies. Fortunately, though, they were interrupted by the arrival of thirteen elderly cyclists, laden down with food and cases of wine donated by the mayor of La Roche. All the cyclists were old-age pensioners and were following, at a fairly gentle pace, the route of the Tour de France. Half, on arrival, showed an extraordinary concern for the condition of their dérailleurs, the other half an equally extraordinary concern for the vicissitudes of seduction.

Unfortunately, but a little predictably, the number of elderly women who wanted to cycle around France was insufficient to allow for even numbers in this game, which meant that the three women on the tour were besieged by admirers. One of the women found the whole thing highly distasteful and particularly objected to the rather smarmy methods employed, heavily reliant on wandering hands and exaggerated declarations of eternal love. Another, a seventy-year-old Parisienne, was boycotted by everyone as her bikini – which was the smallest I have ever seen – was supposedly giving the group a bad name in the French media. The last woman, from Alpes-Maritime, found herself constantly surrounded by groping pensioners led by a man from Marseilles but with strong support from the rest of France.

Too unmechanical, and in any case too uninterested, to plod about comparing bike components and far too young to join in the unpleasant mauling of 'Alpes-Maritime', I was brought in as a chaperon to try and embarrass the seducers into some alleviation of their torrid pursuits. 'Marseilles' thought my acceptance of this role a sad symbol of the modern decline in manhood and told me, with great sadness, of the fundamental importance of maintaining an exclusively sexual relationship with women. His views, which sounded desperately old-fashioned, almost medieval, for one brought up in the New Age of Equality, strengthened my commitment to the cause of protecting women – more specifically, 'Alpes-Maritime' – and I prowled about trying to prevent the attempted acts of debauchery with ever-increasing vigilance.

Sixty or seventy years of dodging Marseilles matriarchs, however, had perfected the old man's ability to escape from unwanted attentions, particularly my amateurish attempts to act as policeman. 'Marseilles' and 'Alpes-Maritime' disappeared within about five minutes of my appointment as chaperon and re-established themselves, with the benefit of an Italian lookout, at the bottom of the garden. When I finally found them it was obvious from their disgraceful conduct that I had completely failed in my duties. I panicked – what should I do? The position I had been assigned required me to interrupt immediately, loudly and forcefully by denouncing their astonishing behaviour, but the parties' age and shrieks of laughter and pleasure suggested that such an intrusion would be at best quietly waved away, at worst considered impertinent, even contemptible. Resigning my position on the spot, I went off to join the Italian lookout who I found secretly smoking a cigarette, an activity he claimed was forbidden by the tour leader.

At first I was confused by this – nothing in anyone's conduct up until now had suggested they might hold any responsibility over the party and, if such an unexpected person really existed, it was obvious that he wasn't treated with any respect. This was borne out by my subsequent identification of 'the leader', who turned out to be an ex-professor of physics and chemistry at the University of Rennes. When I was introduced to him he was busy attempting to prove that a glass could be held in an ex-policeman's rolls of stomach-fat; this he proved could be done, and indeed that as much as half a glass of wine could be added before the glass popped out.

Once he had determined the results of this experiment to his satisfaction, the professor turned to me and asked, with a voice laden with unbearable despair, 'Why, please tell me, why do English drivers wish all cyclists to be in the ditch?'

After just a week's cycling, I had no idea what he was talking about, though the murmurs of agreement and gloomy nodding demonstrated that it was an issue felt deeply by at least one section of the French public. The reason soon became clear after I had left the *gîte*; south of La Roche I entered a great belt of English colonisation spreading south from La Rochelle, through the Dordogne and parts of the Cévennes and reaching down to the Mediterranean coast. For the next fortnight, as I travelled towards the Mediterranean, every second car that passed seemed to be a British right-hand drive, laden down with fat paperback romances and sulky children contemplating when to sick up the excessive amounts of ice cream allowed them by their indulgent parents. These, the real villains of the piece, drove their cars in the unjustified belief that French roads were incapable of taking two cars unless the wheels touched the kerb and, more importantly, that cyclists in France not only had eyes in the back of their head but were able to fly to safety if necessary.

Another British driving characteristic, though of a quite different nature and on the whole confined to the Dordogne, was the widespread pose of buying beaten-up old Citroen 2CVs, filling the back seat with bales of hay, trussed-up chickens and other evidence of rural existence, and wearing scruffy overalls, clogs, neckerchiefs and an extinguished Gauloise hanging damply from the lower lip.

These people – whose British nationality was given away by the copies of the *Financial Times*, *Euromoney* and their daughters' *Cosmopolitan* strewn upon the hay – drove in a manner which successfully emulated a particularly absent-minded French peasant; they would drift haphazardly across the road, parking at perverse angles and refusing above all to travel at more than thirty kilometres per hour, which at times caused even me to brake. Worse, they refused to give directions in either French or English but would mutter in some incomprehensible Dordogne argot, possibly invented by the members of this transient and migrant population themselves. If they could be persuaded to speak in any recognisable language they would punctuate their instructions with aggravating references to their intimate connection with the area – to turn left at Madame Mirouet's, or right at the end of Monsieur Minoret's farm.

My entry into this British colony was the signal for everyone I met to refuse to speak to me in French, and claim to be quite unable to understand my own efforts. Suddenly, after perfectly adequate conversations with, for example, the old-age pensioners and the Château-owner, nothing I said was understood, and not just by English bankers and stockbrokers masquerading as peasants, but by genuinely French café-owners, shop-keepers and hoteliers.

In Les Eyzies I asked a waiter for, 'Un kir, s'il vous plaît.' The waiter stared at me as if I was quite demented, before slowly analysing the request in an exaggerated attempt to extract some meaning from the words. He turned to the occupants of the other tables and appealed for their assistance in establishing what it was I wanted. To a large audience of drinkers, I repeated my simple request. There was a stunned silence, as people studied their thighs, the backs of their hands and rolled their lips together. In due course the silence was broken, but only by an anguished sigh, a suggestion perhaps that their incomprehension was genuine. I tried again.

'Un kir, s'il vous plaît. C'est vin blanc et cassis.'

'Aaaarrhh. Un kir. L'homme désire un kir. Mon dieu. Il a dit "un kir". C'est incroyable. Ooeeurr . . .'

The most disconcerting aspect of this absolute refusal to understand what I was trying to say was found in restaurants in the busiest towns, where a single person, as well as being incomprehensible, seemed to be considered a danger to the health of other customers. The result was that, having finally managed to convey that I was alone and therefore wanted a table for one, I would immediately be thrown out. At best I was informed that if I returned after midnight they might be able to find a few scraps for me.

My vigorous complaints that I'd come to France to experience the sensation of 'la cuisine' and to attend the performance of an opera, as Paul Bocuse described his meals, were rudely dismissed.

'Après minuit. Peut-être.'

Hadn't they read Escoffier, I cried. 'In cooking there are no principles except the need to satisfy the person one is serving.'

'Après minuit.'

The predominance of Britons did not, fortunately, stretch over the whole of south-western France, and a few miles south of the highly anglicised Dordogne I found myself cycling in the virtually undiscovered Lot valley and on into the Cévennes national park, where I went for two days without seeing a British numberplate. Quite coincidentally, it happened to be the most enjoyable cycling since leaving London – quiet roads, beautiful scenery, exhilarating descents and satisfying climbs up into the mountains. With alarm, I realised that I was beginning to prefer cycling in the mountains to cycling on the much simpler flat country of the north-west – the first sign, I thought, that I was on the road to discussing gear differentials and dérailleur models with as much avidity as the 'serious' cyclists I had come across.

Anxious to delay that moment for as long as possible, I paused for a couple of days in Marseilles and tried to banish my athleticism in the discos of Marseilles and Cassis. The attempt was unsuccessful. Crawling out of bed at seven-thirty after an hour's sleep, I stared into my whisky-stained eyes and concluded that the pleasures of cycling in beautiful country, the sensation of tired but fit muscles and the joy of swooping up and down hills under my own coordinated propulsion was preferable to the abject, hungover condition caused by late-night dancing and drinking.

These priggish thoughts remained with me to the Italian border, where the sudden change in atmosphere from the rather prim decorum of Nice, and particularly Menton, to the relatively anarchic chaos of peeling stucco, speeding motorcyclists with pretty girls clinging on to the back and an ever-present backdrop of noisy chatter, car and scooter klaxons and the squelches and gurgles of the very public young lovers, encouraged a return to alcohol.

My serious approach to cycling was further jolted by the mushrooming of racing cyclists wearing the most sensationally garish clothes, covered in chequered patches emblazoned with the names of bike companies, and made of some shiny material supposedly highly efficient at keeping out the cold, the heat, the rain and all other unpleasant phenomena, and designed to reduce significantly wind resistance, perspiration and baldness. Despite the obvious advantage of this clothing when compared with my baggy rugby shorts, old tennis shirt and training shoes (as well as the contrast between my load of panniers, saddle-bag and handlebar-bag with their spare inner tube tucked neatly under their saddle), several of these exotic cyclists offered to pace me along the Via Aurelia. This entailed a grimly relentless pounding along the road, in which it was considered a sign of failure to get off and push one's bike up a hill and a waste of an opportunity to break one's speed record not to pedal downhill.

Cycling in these dedicated groups had two consequences. Firstly, I began to use my water bottle instead of stopping off at cafés every time I wanted a drink, which saved me quite a lot of money and increased my credibility as a cyclist, and secondly I became so used to cycling amongst groups of garish racers that, at Genoa, I failed to notice that the road had been closed to all traffic and that I had become involved in a cycle road-race. The only thing that made me at all suspicious was that none of the cyclists who raced past me ever bothered to stop for a chat, but that could be attributed to cities being generally less friendly than the countryside.

In any case, none of the policemen who lined the route attempted to stop me, and it was only when I heard the enthusiastic applause of a crowd ahead of me, gathered around two small vans with poles propped up on their roofs and a banner announcing 'Finito' suspended between the poles, that I realised what had happened. I turned round and began to cycle in the opposite direction, before it occurred to me that I was then going the wrong way and would probably get hopelessly lost trying to find a way through the Genoese suburbs. The best thing, I felt, would be to walk my bike along the pavement, but that too proved impossible as the race stewards had thoughtfully put up crash barriers to prevent the excited crowd from mobbing the winner.

After some deliberation, I simply carried on towards the finishing line and the applause of the crowd, who were impressed by what they thought had been a particularly extravagant victory gesture. Some of the onlookers, obviously unfamiliar with what a real racing cyclist should look like, even crouched down and began to make strange bellowing noises at me, rhythmically clapping their hands in encouragement.

Slowly, however, the more informed sections of the crowd – those close to the finishing line and wearing the same shiny material complete with advertisements and funny hats as the racers – saw that I had gatecrashed their race. With rare good humour they applauded me across the line, while I, still unused to these gregarious Italian ways, managed only to wave and grin in a pathetically embarrassed manner.

Those impromptu races and fraudulent victories were timely, as without the encouragement of my fellow cyclists it is unlikely that I would have succeeded in cycling from Marseilles to Florence in just five days. The reason behind this need for haste was that I had been invited to a party in Florence given by an Irish philosopher and his flatulent dog. Ostensibly, he and other equally incongruous couples were exploring the various implications of 'European integration', an activity pursued in the none-too-arduous environment of a large villa near Fiesole.

By an extraordinary piece of good fortune my arrival coincided with a fairly slack period in the academic year, and picnics, soirées, cocktails and parties of every variety seemed to flow into each other, creating an impression of infinite pleasure broken only by epic stories of theses lost and found, partners swapped or pinched and drinks consumed.

'It's not always like this,' I was assured, to be presented with photographs of someone sitting in a deckchair with an academic document of some sort in their hand. Such a contemplative existence seemed far removed, almost indecently so, from the sweaty effort involved in cycling to China and represented an existence which, in truth, I thought infinitely preferable to staying alone in dismal hotels, pleading for tables for one in restaurants and crawling painfully up the Apennines.

The Italians were unanimous in supporting this change of plan, the thought of cycling alone to China representing the most perverse abandonment of family and friends, and showing a reckless disregard for security and comfort. In the end, though, I was driven out of Florence a week later by the uncivilised combination of the flatulent dog, rampant mosquitoes and the mounting chorus of sarcasm from the academics that I hadn't already reached Greece. So, one cold and drizzly morning, I set off for Arrezzo.

Staying with the Irish philosopher, being driven wildly about Tuscany and Umbria and remaining throughout my stay slightly mesmerised by the extraordinary legends of the academic institute had blinded me to the vast crowds of tourists that filled practically every town, and particularly those agreeable Renaissance hill-towns. Not only were hotel beds and restaurant tables at a premium, but space in which to admire the very real attractions was almost impossible to find. Huge camera lenses clattered over my shoulder, bulky walking boots crushed my feet and 'day-packs' whacked me in the face. I retreated to the hills, cycling down the Apennines and into the isolation of the Abruzzo national park.

The effect of cycling quickly through mountains was a gradual decline in my control over my fingers, caused by constantly maintaining a tight grip on the handlebars. At first I merely found it difficult, even slightly painful, to write, but the condition increased to the point where it was impossible to use a knife and fork, turn book pages or do anything other than the most basic, brutish activities. Stupidly, instead of stopping for a rest to allow my fingers time to get their movement back, I carried on cycling – if anything even faster and covering higher and higher mileages.

I began to chase increasingly meaningless targets. Could I cycle 100 miles in a day? I discovered I could. Could I get from X to Y in three days? I discovered I could – but even at my most mindlessly enthusiastic I knew that such 'achievements' were of no consequence. Fortunately, I had already committed myself to the ferry between Brindisi and the small Greek port of Igoumenitsa, an essential break from the pursuit of stupid targets and a time, albeit brief, to reflect on the wisdom of racing my way to China when a more languid method might prove infinitely more enjoyable.

Having broken this crazy pursuit of records, I began a new policy of drifting about the country, idling south of Igoumenitsa towards Messolongi and the ferry across to the Peloponnese. It was a journey which did little but emphasise just how ugly modern Greek architecture could be – rows of concrete boxes which succeeded in looking simultaneously unfinished and dilapidated, jumbled up in uncoordinated developments around a bus station or ferry-crossing. In England, as well as most of Europe, such small villages would have served an agricultural community, probably holding a market and providing a church, some sort of pub and the usual range of small shops. Indeed, I had cycled through many such villages in my journey from John O'Groats to Land's End and during the six or seven weeks I had spent cycling through France and Italy.

In north-west Greece, however, there was no sign of any agricultural activity and the absence of even the most general of shops supported the impression that it was still an ancient 'gathering society' – living by hunting and fishing; collecting plants, fruits and olives; and milking and occasionally killing the odd goat. Such an existence is of course far from unpleasant, allowing plenty of time for sitting underneath an olive tree or grape-vine, reflecting on the passing world.

The most surprising thing was that south of the Patras Straits, without any particular change in agricultural techniques or 'way of life', I was able to prowl around Olympia, Epidaurus, Mycenae, Tiryns and Corinth – the classical cities of a people who, in the words of Professor Kitto, 'had a totally new conception of what human life was for, and showed for the first time what the human mind was for'. No guide at any of these sites was able to explain how this civilisation developed from such an unpromising background, preferring to dwell on more sensational stories such as the exclusion of women from the Olympic Games, the successful contravention of that rule by Pherenice or the snake-filled pit at Asclepius's sanctuary at Epidaurus. Alternatively, they would talk about more technical matters – the architectural technique, for example, behind the Tomb of Agamemnon at Mycenae; this was the sort of information which in northern France would have reduced me to an ecstatic lump of jelly, but now left me totally apathetic.

Such complaints seemed trivial when I reached Athens – the smog, the Athenian rudeness and the disgracefully bad driving forming an entirely appropriate background to my miserable tour of the various Middle Eastern embassies in an attempt to obtain visas for Syria or Iran so I could get across to Pakistan. Fortunately, I had friends who were prepared to put me up and, more importantly, let me use their balcony and deckchair as a refuge from the hustle and bustle of modern city life. Slumped in the sun, flicking idly through old copies of *Wisden*, I suffered another of my 'questioning moods' – was it really worth missing the Delhi and Bombay Tests for Isfahan and Shiraz?

In normal times probably yes, but 'normality' seemed far removed from an Islamic fundamentalist country run by Revolutionary Guards, particularly when my time there would coincide with an English tour of India. Support for boycotting Iran was prompted by the behaviour of the Iranian consul, who seemed to take a perverse pleasure in creating difficulties with my visa – it would take three to four weeks to process, would be valid for just four weeks and would allow me only two weeks in the actual country. If I waited, apart from definitely missing the Test matches, I would have to cycle about 3000 miles in six weeks. It seemed ridiculous – a denial of the New Spirit of cycling I'd settled on since the rejection of targets and time trials. The consul seemed to share my view, smiling contentedly as, day after day, I presented him with reasons for not just a faster processing of my application, but a doubling of the time limits he considered reasonable.

It was clearly a waste of time. The dates of the cricket tour had begun to dominate my future plans, and even seemed to provide sufficient justification for the trip itself. I began to explore other routes, which inevitably entailed either flying or sailing part of the way to India. The Syrians quizzed me anxiously about whether I'd been to Israel, and the Jordanians and Egyptians laid down their own conditions. I heard about an incredibly protracted technique of crossing from

Jordan into Israel, which I've now forgotten, but it was seemingly impossible to do on a bicycle.

Meanwhile, the Iranian consul continued to smile at my discomfort, agreeing fully with me that it was absurd to wait in Athens for up to four weeks for such a restricting visa, but remaining firm in his rejection of my pleas. After a week I tired of it all. It was clearly going to be impossible to go through Iran, and if I couldn't go to Iran there seemed little point in going to Pakistan – there was nothing I really wanted to see there. The Syrian embassy had offered me a visa within twenty-four hours, and had even advised me to buy a cheap ticket to India in an Athenian bucket-shop unless I was prepared to pay the full scheduled air-fare in Damascus. Such consideration for my impecuniosity suggested a pleasant and civilised national character far removed from the haughty disdain of the Iranian consul – so I decided to take the 'Syrian option'.

I telephoned England to confirm the dates of the tour and to announce, to a strange mixture of relief and porcine squeals of protest, my dramatic change of plans. For me the careless, almost frivolous, manner in which I had abandoned cycling 'the whole way' seemed unnecessary to justify – I would cycle through Turkey and Syria before returning to Athens for the flight to Bombay and the Second Test. Although I did have some regrets, and even felt a little foolish, my main emotion as I boarded the ferry to Samos, the Greek island just three miles off the Turkish coast, was one of absolute delight.

2

Of soothsayers and sun-hats

Pestilence, floods, earthquakes, Tartars and Turks were, in the Middle Ages, the traditional punishments reserved by the Almighty for sinners. In the sixteenth century, Martin Luther prayed to be delivered from 'the world, the flesh, the Turk and the Devil'. In the twentieth century, anyone planning to cycle through Turkey will never stop hearing of Turkish atrocities, of the number of murders that have occurred in the last few months and how *Midnight Express* failed to convey fully the horrors of a tourist's life in Turkey.

The French had been less alarmist about the country than the British, but found the whole subject slightly academic as they were sure that I would either have my bike stolen in Italy or be involved in an accident. The Italians found it so puzzling that I wanted to go further east than Otranto that they dismissed me as a philistine lunatic. The Greeks enthusiastically took the British line, and added several embellishments.

Guides at Olympia, Mycenae and Nafplion spoke with unbearable sadness of the destruction of the Hellenistic civilisation in Asia Minor by the ignorant hordes who had invaded from the brutal east. For centuries these dour, warlike people had occupied the central Turkish plateau, remaining within the Taurus mountain range and leaving the western and southern coasts to the maritime and commercial Greeks, until, at the beginning of this century, Turkish nationalism had led to the savage expulsion of the Greeks and Armenians.

On Samos I climbed the hill overlooking the port and sat disconsolately at the summit, staring across the narrow stretch of water at the Turkish coastline and wondering whether I should after all go ahead with my ride around the southern coast into Syria. The price of the ferry had been set at a level which required serious examination of one's motives in visiting the country, and made a swift return almost unaffordable. The least unattractive fate I faced would be a mauling by the huge and lethal mountain dogs which, as I sat gloomily on this last

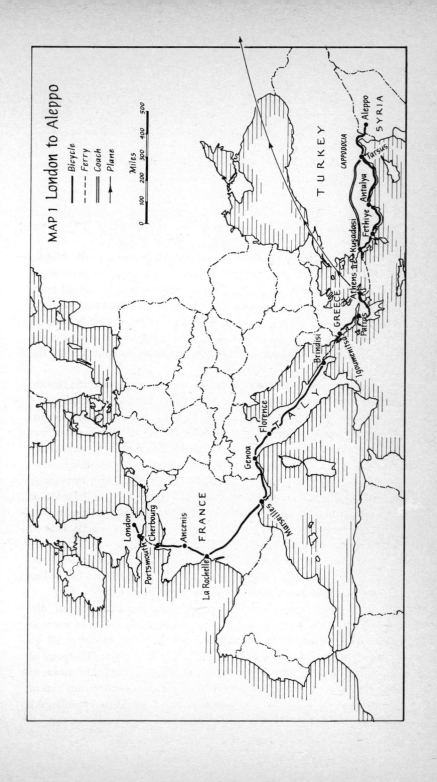

MAP 1 London to Aleppo

——— Bicycle
- - - - Ferry
——— Coach
———➤ Plane

Miles
0 100 200 300 400 500

London
Portsmouth
Cherbourg
Ancenis
La Rochelle
FRANCE
Marseilles
Genoa
Florence
ITALY
Brindisi
Igoumenitsa
Patras
GREECE
Athens
Kusadasi
Fethiye
Antalya
CAPPODOCIA
TURKEY
Tarsus
Aleppo
SYRIA

Greek mountain top before Turkey, I was almost sure I could hear howling in greedy anticipation.

My mercenary nature eventually prevailed, however, and I decided that having bought my ticket across to Kusadasi in the relaxed environment of Athens it would be a sad waste of money if I threw it away to face another long journey back across Europe to my detractors in London who had guaranteed that I wouldn't make it to China. With some trepidation, I concluded that I had already compromised my original plans enough and that I should go into this awful place.

Kusadasi was a bit of a disappointment to me in my new role as intrepid, brave and even foolhardy traveller. Expensive carpet and souvenir shops, their windows filled with every conceivable credit-card sticker, lined the well-finished road leading from the small dock to the impressive caravanserai. Huge, garish American cars, built between the late forties and early sixties, stood in front of the shops, their drivers asking $40 to take passengers to Ephesus. Their demands fell on stony ground – two South African girls, a destitute English-woman returning to her Turkish holiday romance and two Americans had been my only companions on the ferry, and all fervently hoped that the sum asked for would easily cover two weeks in Turkey.

An army of hotel proprietors descended on us, and we haggled over the price of a room until one agreed to take us all for approximately 27p each. Happily recalculating our budgets, we agreed to the pleasantly exotic idea of cramming together into whatever room the man provided. In fact we were given two rooms, one with four beds pushed side by side and allowing no space for luggage or bikes; the other – an almost elegant room containing just two beds – was quickly claimed by the destitute Englishwoman, who, predictably, had been stood up and the American woman, who, it transpired, was very keen to disassociate herself from the American man. Having been included in this strange sleeping arrangement I ended up with the South Africans and the undesirable American, an arrangement which lasted for two nights until the South Africans and I decided that the American was justifiably being ostracised by his ex-girlfriend, and we abandoned the crowded dormitory for more expensive comfort.

Initially, the rather unpleasant architecture of the town had a certain interest, being the first typically Asian town I had seen. Much of it looked as if it had only recently been built, and pieces of old wire and excess piping stuck out of concrete at obscure angles. Some of these pipes were used as impromptu hanging rails for the souvenir costumes, which emphasised the general impression of unplanned and rather scruffy development. Outside most of the shops there were huddles of men, almost unanimously gloomy, peering intently at the small glasses of tea which seemed to be an ever-present feature of Turkish life. The shops themselves were mainly one-storey buildings, with a strange half floor above, presumably used as a store. Behind these shops the ugly concrete boxes, so familiar after Athens, led up the side of the hill to the south of the town or stretched haphazardly northwards, unchecked by anything as mundane as aesthetics or planning controls.

Within the central tourist, souvenir-shop area a phoney local colour was attempted by loud recordings of the most awful wailing and scraping sound, a sort of cross between a ruler being scraped across a blackboard, a pig being slaughtered and a badly tuned radio. The noise helped explain the terrible hopeless air shared by the unhappy shop-owners who declared that, although they themselves hated it, tourists apparently expected to hear this local din and would even produce tape-recorders – presumably to show the folks back home just how ghastly Turkey was.

After a day most of the shop-owners had invited me in for a cup of tea and a fairly unenthusiastic demonstration of their goods. Rather than embark on a long exposition of how improved my home would be with, for example, a finely knotted and coloured rug, they appeared almost bewildered that anyone could want such a backward artefact. All were of the opinion that I would get a much better price further inland, away from the Ephesian tourist route, although they grudgingly conceded that Kusadasi did have a particularly wide selection of *kilims* and carpets. Most seemed pleased that I had already decided not to buy anything on the grounds that it would be difficult to cycle with a couple of carpets draped over the crossbar – an objection I later disproved by wobbling along with five carpets suspended from various points of my bike.

A different breed of salesman inhabited the small parade of stalls which stood outside the entrance to Ephesus, sneering unpleasantly as they calculated how extensive my capital was, before embarking on the classic hard sell. Groups of numbed tourists stood unhappily around clutching some foul, over-priced piece of onyx, or a plastic model of the Temple of Artemis. Occasionally they stared at the object in disbelief that they had been made to buy such rubbish while coachloads of Americans, Japanese and Scandinavians queued up to outspend each other.

I had arranged to meet the South Africans at the theatre, and to join the tour promised them by two Turkish shop-owners in Kusadasi. The two girls were clearly unimpressed by the men's conversation, and were standing at the back of the theatre screaming 'Coo-ee' at the hapless Turks, or desperately scurrying about attempting to use the automatic shutter release on their camera. The Turks were terribly upset by such behaviour, having assumed that the girls would want to explore the Library of Celsus and hear about Herostratus's burning of the Temple of Artemis and St Paul's conversion of the Ephesians to Christianity. Their only partial success was that the girls began periodically chanting 'Diana is great', a sorry reference to the mob organised by Demetrius to riot against the said conversion, who swarmed down the marble road towards the theatre crying 'Great is Diana of the Ephesians'.

Every few minutes a party led by a megaphone-wielding guide would barge into the theatre and solemnly listen to their guide's impressive collection of statistics:

'Here we are in the Great Theatre of Ephesus. The building was begun in the reign of Emperor Claudius and completed in the reign of Emperor Trajan (AD 117). The capacity was 24,000 and the audience sat up to 30 metres above the orchestra. The façade of the three-storied proscenium was richly decorated with columns, reliefs and statues. The first two storeys were built in the reign of Emperor Nero (AD 54–68), while the third was added in the reign of Septimus Severus (AD 193–211). Now we go on to the Library of Celsus . . .'

I trudged off to the Library, the shouts of 'Coo-ee' and 'Diana is great' slowly subsiding as I went further from the theatre. At the Library I watched incredulously as elderly people clambered up rocks and through brambles and gorse to try and get the right camera angle to avoid the large banner advertising an Austrian lager company who were sponsoring the 'restoration' of the façade, and the scaffolding used to carry out the repositioning of the suspiciously immaculate marble columns and statues. In the words of Philip Glazebrook: 'Archaeological excavation has evidently struck a bargain with speculative building, to produce as much of a town as the Turks judge the tourists want to see. . . . Where ruins mouldering into the earth pluck faintly at your sleeve, these marble buildings shout in your ear.'

I went back to the theatre to announce my departure. The South Africans had been joined at the top of the theatre by half of a Norwegian tour party. To the Turks' absolute horror, the half that remained in the orchestra then began to sing some Scandinavian carol, to be joined for the chorus by the other half. We fled, the South Africans rushing down to take advantage of the Turks' car, while I cycled back to the hotel.

There were further horrors awaiting me. Simpering madly, the South Africans asked if I would escort them to a disco that evening, as they didn't feel entirely confident about the Turks' intentions. Unfortunately, I had only recently been reading of the Islamic view of women, and two quotes from the Koran had stuck in my mind: 'men have authority over women because God has made the one superior to the other ... so good women are obedient', and the more general guiding note that 'women are your tillage'. Though I instinctively felt that my services were unlikely to be necessary, I vaguely felt the stirrings of Crusading chivalry in protecting these Christian maidens from 'the horrors of the Turk'. Less worthily, I was anxious to disprove the implication that I would happily sit on the sidelines watching the four of them dance away with a general brief that I should judge when things had gone far enough.

For the first hour I astonished the girls, the barman and the one other couple at the disco by the sheer energy, vitality and imagination of my frenzied leaps and shakings. The Turks sat impasssively at the bar, occasionally bawling across the floor that another gin and tonic was waiting on the counter. At midnight one of them sidled over to the disc-jockey, passed over an instruction of some sort, and the two of them, straightening their trousers and undoing another shirt button, eased up to the South Africans to announce that for the rest of the evening the four of them would be dancing romantically together. Almost simultaneously, the silken sound of Frank Sinatra's 'Strangers in the Night' boomed out, the couples formed, each partner clinging desperately to the other before lurching around the floor. Feeling decidedly put out, I sat on a bench overlooking the sea and thought of Hellenism. The evening wore on, the couples' activities growing more and more distressing and my thoughts obsessively narrowing on to more specialised, even arcane, realms of academia.

The combination of the commercialisation of Ephesus and the seduction of the South Africans persuaded me that it was the right moment to head off along the coast towards Syria. My three days in Kusadasi had been worthwhile if only for one thing – I was now reasonably confident that the unpleasant reputation the Turks had gained was, at least so far, undeserved. Nervously, I adopted a particularly asinine grin to persuade everyone that I was a friendly sort of fellow and pedalled off towards Soke.

My view of Kusadasi as a rather dreary, run-down place, although not invalidated by Soke was at least put in perspective. Soke achieved the not inconsiderable feat of making a small town in the centre of beautiful mountains, cooled by breezes from the Mediterranean and seen on a particularly fine autumn day, look like an abandoned cotton mill somewhere in Lancashire on a miserably rainy day. The predominant colours were grey, dark brown and a dirty navy blue. Despite the obvious lack of rain the gutters contained ominously black puddles, shimmering under the sun with oily circles. A few horse-drawn carts wheezed through the town, laden down with sacks of, appropriately, cotton. Balanced on top of these enormous loads were anything up to a dozen women, who introduced a rare dash of colour with their chintzy printed clothing – although nothing like the garishly vivid garments sold as typical peasant wear in Kusadasi, let alone the Turkish costume described by Joyce: 'Opulent curves fill out her scarlet trousers and jacket slashed with gold. A wide yellow cummerbund girdles her. A white yashmak, violent in the night, covers her face, leaving free only her dark eyes and raven hair.'

In Soke, such sensual, exotic creatures were reduced to the worn-out women in their faded clothes, slumped on top of the cotton they had just picked and driven off to sort it by a morose man in a de-mob suit. Strangely, the population seemed to be divided between those under about ten, and those over a rather haggard fifty, an impression possibly misleading because the unceasing hardship of cotton-picking seemed to age prematurely all those who were caught up in it. Groups of small boys occupied themselves by systematically picking at the foam handlebar covers on my bike, while I drank fruit juice and half a dozen glasses of tea with a couple of old men. Our conversation was minimal, my Turkish not stretching beyond replying 'Evet' to the offer of 'Chai?' In some ways I felt that little else would have been said had I been fluent – we sat staring at the bleak scene, in silent contemplation of the uglier side of life, until finally, in despair, I decided to move on to Miletus and Didyma.

An enormous theatre dominates the old site of Miletus, which, unlike Ephesus, has not yet been redeveloped or restored. Six other people were there on the day I visited it: two French tourists trying to work out how to get back to Milas and four English eagerly scouring the theatre for inscriptions. The English enthusiasm was watched a little sceptically by three men leaning against a donkey, who found the excited squeals emerging from these sun-hatted, sandalled and red-faced people somewhat alarming. I watched the whole scene from the top of the theatre, looking down over the city trying to identify the old perimeters of the town and trying to imagine how this scrubby scene was once a grandiose classical city about which Abbé Barthélemy wrote: 'Never within so narrow a space, did Nature produce so great a number of men of destiny, talents and sublime genius.'

I was interrupted by a great roar from one of the Englishwomen, standing a few seats down from me, waving her pale blue sun-hat to attract my attention.

'Do you speak English?' she yelled. I told her I did.

'Do you read Greek?' I told her I didn't.

'Well, come here anyway.'

I obeyed and shuffled down to examine the inscription she had found on one of the stone seats; some of these were marked to identify areas in which certain categories of people should sit. She hoped it read 'lovers', in which case I was to take a photograph of her and her husband. She cried out:

'Here it is, darling. Oh, do come quickly. We've found it. Oh come on.'

A man in a pink sun-hat wearily climbed up to join us, muttering about the frivolous and stupid nature of his wife's search and furious, almost demented, to discover that neither she nor I had realised that the letters were nothing to do with 'lovers', but said 'politicians'.

'Don't you speak Greek?' he thundered, scarcely believing that anyone could live in a state of such abject ignorance.

'Not ancient Greek,' I replied, a little disingenuously as my modern Greek was limited to a few items on menus.

'Well, you jolly well should,' he barked and stomped off to continue his own more serious searches, followed by his wife, complaining about such rude behaviour.

Anxious to avoid getting myself involved in a domestic argument, I dashed quickly round the Faustina Baths and pedalled off to Didyma, where I was assured by the three men with their donkey that I would find somewhere to stay. This information was correct, but failed to mention that at least one of the Didyma *pansiyones* stood in the shadow of the remains of the vast Temple of Apollo. A great marble platform remains, a staircase leading up to the portico of the Temple where a columned hall gives on to two marble corridors, each so narrow that only one person can pass through at a time. Three sides of the temple were flanked with double ranks of columns, of which just two remain standing, more than sixty feet high but, including the platform, nearly a hundred feet off the ground. Dozens of fallen columns lie on the ground beside heads of the winged Medusa, victims of the earthquake which destroyed the temple at the end of the fifteenth century.

Modern Didyma huddles around these majestic ruins, a few flimsy and ramshackle buildings providing accommodation and meals for tourists. The one souvenir shop had a collection of hubble-bubbles, old teapots and three filthy carpets, none of which the shop-owner seemed in the least interested in selling. My *pansiyone* had a spectacular position, and I was able to get a bedroom overlooking the temple from which I watched the sun set through the two remaining columns. I lay contentedly on my bed, happily reflecting on how pleasant my first day's cycling in Turkey had been. Only the foam-handlebar pickers had marred the day, and a bottle of particularly pleasant red wine soon removed any lingering sense of irritation.

The next morning I jumped eagerly out of bed, anxious to resume my tour of these superbly impressive sites, and optimistically decided that I would have breakfast at Euromos, some twenty miles away. Enthusiastically, I set off along a road described on my map as being unfit for vehicles but felt by the *pansiyone*-owner to be perfectly adequate for bicyclists. The owner was wrong, and at about half past eleven, after nearly four hours' cycling, I had fallen from a great state of elation into an awful depression. Far from breakfasting on yoghurt and honey sitting on ancient Greek steps and admiring the mountainous countryside, I found myself cycling wearily through flat marshland chewing at a piece of bread I'd found in my pannier that was left over from a packed lunch given to me in Athens.

About two-thirds of the way from Didyma to the main road to Milas (and Euromos), perhaps the most bizarre sight of my whole trip emerged from the bleak landscape – a modern housing estate of five blocks of six-storey buildings standing in this isolated position. I could see no sign either of any older housing or of any shop, factory or other suggestion of how people lived in this almost surreal development. Appropriately, only one old man accompanied by a large dog appeared to live on the estate – I saw no one else, nor even any cars, washing, smoke or any of the other indications of human activity.

The road connecting this place with the comparatively picturesque towns and villages of the rest of that south-western corner of Turkey was, instead of the smart dual-carriageway that should have existed, a dirt track weaving its way through an infertile bog. Unfortunately, my intention of exploring the estate and trying to establish why it had been built was dashed when the old man's dog began to run at me aggressively, apparently with the intention of ripping my leg open. As the awful condition of the road prevented a speedy escape, and the old man was obviously not going to do anything to help, I had to face the challenge armed with my bicycle pump, and desperately scrabbling in my saddle bag for my steel lock.

Strangely, despite the obsession dogs have with cyclists – possibly a reaction to the bike wheels producing a high-pitched hum which only dogs can hear, or possibly because dogs just don't like seeing human knees pumping up and down – I had not previously had to face a dog clearly determined to bite me. In France and Italy, the uniformly savage brutes kept in people's gardens were, quite rightly, kept either on a length of chain or behind high walls. The only problem these north-western European animals posed was the shock of their demented barking catching me unawares, and the difficulty of asking for water as I climbed mountains in high temperatures when the only taps were guarded by killers. The Greeks either don't have dogs, or keep them looking after sheep and well away from humans. Naturally, all three countries had several owners of toy dogs, like poodles and pekineses, but few have taken their threats seriously.

Turkish dogs, on the other hand, are the stuff that horror stories and nightmares are made of. I had been warned about them not just in Greece, where anti-Turkish feeling sometimes leads to an exaggerated view of how evil the Turks really are, but also from one of the shopkeepers in Kusadasi who described with a classically gloomy relish the size of the dogs that were known to attack cars and motorbikes. It therefore came as a very pleasant surprise to discover that a well-aimed blow from my pump, combined with some fairly innocuous swearing, terrified the dog; it ran feebly back to the old man, who was watching the whole event with a complete lack of interest.

My supposedly friendly wave was obviously misinterpreted as a victory salute, because the old man immediately began to mutter, in a manner reminiscent of his dog, and advance towards me. Fairly sure that if I hit him on the head with my pump I would end up in trouble, I decided that retreat was the best option and carried on with my struggles across the stony track.

Two miles on, massive earth-moving equipment was grinding and howling away beside a small village of just four houses constructed out of mud, thatch and a few stones in a design virtually identical to the igloo. Low entrances, perhaps four feet high, revealed the width of the walls to be at least two and a half feet, with no windows or any obvious method of lighting the interior other than by fires, the smoke from which escaped through a hole in the centre of the roof. Outside one of these huts, a woman was crushing grain with a pestle and mortar while just yards away an enormous bulldozer was shoving heaps of mud about. It was a timely reminder that there was more to south-western Turkey than exploring ancient Greek theatres, stadiums and temples.

After the most cursory inspection of the Temple of Zeus at Euromos, where I bumped into more English people peering at inscriptions, I moved on to Milas, where I thought I might spend a night in a run-of-the-mill Turkish town, undistracted by the classical world. My heart sank, however, when I saw the town, dominated by great aqueducts, columns, marble platforms and what looked ominously like a theatre. This clearly wasn't modern Turkish architecture. I checked my Penguin edition of Arrian's life of Alexander and, sure enough, Milas was mentioned. Suspiciously, I kicked at the undergrowth to find the remains of a mosaic floor. For a short time I debated whether to stay anyway, and simply ignore these un-Turkish architectural features, but a closer inspection of the contemporary Turkish buildings was too depressing to allow such a course. I would spend the night in Yatagan Goktepe, about thirty miles east of Milas and without any classical background that I could find.

Yatagan was just how I imagined a dingy, industrial Turkish town to be. Factories lined the approach road, pouring out great black clouds of polluting smoke and almost shaking from the loud noise of the machines within. Outside every gate the heavy lorries had dragged mud from the untarmaced factory yards on to the main road, which naturally caused everyone to drive in the middle of the road, leaving the muddy edges for me and the pedestrians. The town was built around what was in effect a crescent stuck on to the main road – one of the few instances of a bypass being built before the town. Large, square concrete buildings were occupied by banks, the post office and bleak government offices, beyond which a crossroads provided the social centre of the town. Unfortunately, the authorities were busy digging up the road for some purpose, and one crossed the centre of Yatagan balancing on planks which had been laid across the various ditches, holes and piles of earth.

At the crossroads a sign announced the presence of an 'Oteli', run by two men who were almost desperate for me to stay somewhere else. Neither of them could speak any English, and the only other language that any of their friends or other customers spoke was Polish. The bank-workers were widely rumoured to be able to speak French but they had gone home. Despite my basic understanding that they didn't really want me to stay, I settled down on a chair and smiled wearily at them, trying to make it clear that I was too tired to move. Eventually,

I was led up to a tiny room – measuring at most eight feet by five feet – in which the owners had somehow succeeded in placing a bed, a stool and a wooden clothes rail.

The bed was about six inches shorter than me, a difference made more apparent by its resemblance to a sagged hammock and a sack of potatoes, although its lack of comfort was, on the whole, less trying than its particularly energetic and hungry fleas. For a while I thought about the strange places fleas choose to occupy, when, for example, the other rooms appeared to be less crowded than my own, could not possibly have had less comfortable beds and were all filled with a wide selection of Turkish males happily listening to two radios, both vying to be the loudest. They also seemed quite unconcerned by flea-bites, whereas I constantly swatted and sprayed and rubbed foul-smelling lotions all over myself in a vain attempt to banish them. It might be that I have always underestimated the bravery and sense of adventure in fleas, and that nothing is duller for the upstanding flea than to bite furiously away at someone who doesn't really mind. Whatever the case, the fleas won their contest with me, and I crept out to try and find a bar where I hoped to get drunk enough to be able to sleep through the night's attacks. Even that was beyond me. The Polish-speaker had never abandoned his desire to practise his second language on me, and even though I assured him that I would be quite unable to follow or contribute anything he launched into a long story, told in Polish and accompanied by letters posted from Wroclaw and blurred photographs of people standing in front of unidentifiable churches.

This absurd conversation attracted quite a crowd, who I suppose were not offered many options for entertainment – and watching someone speak a funny language has its amusements. Eventually, with the crowd growing a little restless, I announced my intention to drink beer, a statement which I could say in both Polish and Turkish. Ostentatiously I used both languages, which somewhat confused the Polish-speaker and delighted some of the crowd, who led me off to an unexpectedly modern bar. Red lights, pine benches, loud music and a large television which, on full volume, could just about be heard over the music were features I hadn't expected in Yatagan, and although I would not normally have relished the sleazy atmosphere I settled into a corner table and ordered the first of what I hoped would be quite a number of beers.

The people who had accompanied me then presented me with a bottle of West German lager, soon followed by plates of peanuts, sliced apple and tangerines. Such generous behaviour was quite typical of the

Turks, and every day some equally undeserved present would arrive, even in the so-called tourist trap of Kusadasi. Still unfamiliar with the nature of their hospitality, however, I asked if I could buy them a drink. With anguished cries they ordered the barman to provide me with another bottle, obviously insulted that I should imagine I would have to buy a thing. An hour later this lavish treatment had become an embarrassment, as I was so aware that I was giving nothing in return – not even conversation, as the providers stood in a huddle at the bar, while I sat in solitary splendour at my corner table. There seemed little alternative but to leave, which, in Yatagan Goktepe, unfortunately meant that I either had to walk the streets or go back to the flea-ridden hotel room. As I left the bar, I saw the Polish-speaker clutching another wad of letters and skulking in the shadows of a general store, presumably intending to resume our conversation. I sneaked past him and into the hotel.

My earlier inspection of the hotel room had concentrated on the fittings and had largely ignored the fixtures, beyond the most cursory dismissal of the room as too small. Returning fairly late at night, I realised that the walls were made of the most flimsy hardboard and were little more than partitions, as they left a gap of at least two feet between the top and the ceiling. This was made obvious by the great cacophony of snores, expectoration, flatulence and other groans and moans caused by sleeping on potatoes with your feet and head about eighteen inches above your bottom. The effect of the partitions was to amplify the horrible sound, which in combination with the still-active fleas guaranteed a sleepless night.

Just as I was about to fall into an exhausted and itchy doze, the various factories emitted great blasts on their klaxons and the noisy inhabitants of the other rooms began to make peculiar revving-up sounds before stomping about the landing as they waited to use the cold water tap, not so much to wash as to gargle loudly. The last of them had plodded downstairs, and a rare peace was established, when the sun rose up above the next-door building and illuminated the room. My attempts to suspend my towel and trousers over the window were unsuccessful, and in any case the sun had woken the fleas, who had finally abandoned tormenting me at slightly after four o'clock. There was little point in not making what others called 'an early start'.

Normally, I took a fairly relaxed attitude towards getting up in the morning, not particularly worried if I didn't start cycling until as late as half past ten, or even eleven o'clock. As my schedule only required me to cycle an average of thirty miles a day, I was quite able to finish by mid-afternoon as I always hoped to be able to do. It was therefore fairly ironic that my earliest start since leaving London should end 105 miles on in Fethiye, two hours after nightfall.

Yatagan Goktepe, though undoubtedly an interesting experience, provided a level of privacy, comfort and general availability of facilities that I was quite anxious to see improved. Mugla, the first town I came to, would probably – perhaps even certainly – have represented an improvement, but it was much too early to stop for what looked a fairly dull place. This was a mistake, as Ula and Dalaman were virtually identical to Yatagan, and though the position of Koycegiz suggested that it should be full of lovely places to stay, I had lost a bit of confidence in my ability to rough it, and didn't want to waste precious time trailing round the lake looking for a *pansiyone*.

The shortage of reasonable accommodation was surprising, as the scenery was particularly beautiful and the south-western corner of Turkey the most popular area amongst tourists. Several people had rather sneeringly referred to the herd-like rush to Marmaris and Bodrum, and the resolute refusal of these 'sheep' to move out of the safe, sanitised resort atmosphere. Others spoke of the unimaginative development which has led to the few resorts becoming indistinguishable from their Spanish, Greek and (to some extent) Italian equivalents. A great convention of these observers of international tourism had gathered in Fethiye, and more particularly at Ulu Deniz, a beach some ten miles away. Although I didn't then know it, those attending the convention were exactly the same as other groups I was to come across on Goan and Keralan beaches, in Mahabillpuram in India, Koi Samui in Thailand and Cantonese dormitories. Membership was confined to those away from their own country for at least a year, if not two years, who were prepared to spend months in the same place getting to know the 'real' a) Turkey, b) India or c) China. It was a solemn moment, as their presence was the first real confirmation that I had arrived in the exotic East and was no longer a tourist but a 'traveller', even an adventurer.

At last, then, the Orient of Chateaubriand and Nerval, a place of romance, exotic beings, haunting memories and landscapes, of remarkable experiences and adventures. Appropriately, this important change came in a town which in classical times, under the name of Telmessus, was renowned for its supremacy in divination and boasted a college of soothsayers. Croesus, King of Lydia, consulted the college at the outset of his campaign against the Persians, Alexander asked the secret of his future after the siege of Halicarnassus, and I met a man in a bar who told me what would happen when I reached Syria.

'Where you go?'

'Syria.'

'Souria? Ha, ha, ha. Horrible. Ha, ha, ha. Very dirty, ha, ha, ha. Boom, boom, ha, ha, ha.'

I wondered what 'Boom, boom' meant – was this a prediction and, if so, of what?

3

Don't shoot me,
I'm only the cyclist

My impression that Europe was behind me and that I was now in the exotic Orient was quickly tarnished. Up until now, southern Turkey had been too similar to both Greece and parts of southern Italy for me to feel a great sense of change, and whilst the standard of accommodation (both private and in hotels) had significantly worsened it hadn't, with the exception of Yatagan Goktepe, been too unbearable. The bizarre blocks of flats and the mud igloos outside Didyma were untypical of most private houses, which varied from fairly boring concrete boxes to really very attractive brick houses with sophisticated wooden lattices on the upper storey.

The reputation the Turks had for latent, if not explicit, aggression was wholly unfounded – at least in their reaction to me. My monosyllabic grunts when ordering food and drink were such that their patience must have been sorely tested, yet they treated me with a basically friendly, though somewhat dour, amusement and continually showed extraordinary generosity.

Generosity apart, the most significant change in behaviour had been the level of interest shown in my bike, which had been little more than polite in France, Italy and Greece. The crowd of boys in Soke were behaving quite typically in their desire to pick the foam off my handlebars, play with my gear levers and generally fiddle with the various moving parts. The only surprising thing about this was that, although my bike was enormously advanced compared to the normal Turkish bike, there were at the same time as me at least twenty-five other Britons cycling through Turkey on their way to India, and one would have thought that the novelty value of yet another sweaty person wearing shorts, busily pedalling through the Taurus mountains, would have not just worn off but become rather boring, even slightly contemptible. But the fiddling of the boys and, as I cycled further east, the men encouraged a certain feeling that, despite all the evidence that large numbers of people had either done or were doing the same as me, it was still fairly unusual, and I began to feel quite heroic.

It was also a good way of quickly establishing some contact with the local people. This contact ranged from long-distance yelling and waving from the top of some mountain top; to shaking hands grimly with someone met at a café, visibly moved by seeing yet another British cyclist; and on to lengthy conversations about the condition of the Turkish economy, political prisoners and the westernisation process begun by Ataturk. Such conversations were rare, and usually uncritical of the regime – the economy was doing splendidly, there were no political prisoners, torture was never resorted to, and the Armenians and Kurds deserved all they got.

The almost doctrinaire beliefs of the Turks with whom I was able to speak in English meant that I began to prefer the solemn smiling and grunting that I managed with non-English-speaking villagers and café-owners. These meetings were affected by a strange and overwhelming poignancy which appears to be central to the Turkish character, a fatalistic belief that we would never meet again, and that I should be sent on my way refreshed and heartened by their friendship.

The solemnity of their attitude was matched by the typical Turkish appearance, so consistently alike that one almost began to wonder what government forces were insisting upon it. With few exceptions the men wore dark, rather baggy, suits – generally a murky grey but occasionally brown and always with wide lapels and slightly flared trousers. Underneath, a wider range of shirts could be seen, in that about half wore lumberjack-style checks and the other half a variety of white striped with a single colour. The typical Turkish face revealed the mountainous background – weatherbeaten, with clenched brown eyes peering into the distance for goats or sheep somewhere on the horizon, and short, cropped hair because the next visit to the barber might not be for some time. Everyone had a moustache. At Antalya, I decided that I would award myself three days' holiday for every Turkish man I saw who was cleanshaven. I reached the Syrian border claiming a morning off, on the basis that one person had little more than a pencil moustache, which I didn't think qualified as a 'Turkish moustache' – great bushy things which reached out on to their permanently stubbly cheeks.

Women's clothes showed a potentially greater variety than one would normally find in the West, because although there are some veiled women in, say, London, few wear the voluminous trousers which drape down to mid-calf length that women in Turkey prefer when working in the fields or smashing grain with their pestle and mortar. Western fashion, which appears particularly ridiculous when imagined in the scruffy mountain villages, was, if not actually worn, certainly available if anyone could be bothered to risk the religious disapproval that such clothes would incur, and face the bus journey from their village to Antalya. I never came across anybody who had bothered, although as I only ever saw women when involved in some tiring work either in or connected with the fields, this may simply have been because I didn't get along to the Kas Young Farmers' dinner-dance, where such clothes would have been more appropriate.

Presumably the Antalyan shopkeepers bought their whizzy silk dresses and swanky blouses to sell either to amazed tourists or to Antalyans. It would have been interesting to have heard the sales talk when they were selling to the local people, as the observant would immediately have noticed that these 'Western clothes' bore no relation to what the Western people actually in Antalya were wearing, which ranged from very little to the sun-hat-and-sandals brigade, resplendent in 'functional' lightweight cotton outfits.

There were further examples of both sun-hats and the half-naked on my ride from Fethiye to Kas, a small fishing village opposite the Greek island of Megiste and a popular haunt of the 'Asian travellers' who found its restaurants, cheap *pansiyones* and, of course, its position on the sea conducive to a lengthy stay. The sun-hats, who referred to Kas as the Antiphellus of Strabo, scurried enthusiastically about the Hellenistic theatre and the Lycian tomb about a hundred yards west of the village, and anxiously tried to gather enough people to get a *dolmus* (a small mini-bus) to the nearby sites at Patara, Xanthos, Letoon and Myra. The half-naked felt such obvious tourism to be quite the most distasteful thing they had ever heard and sank back in their chairs, pulling on, in an affirmation of their Turkish credibility, some brightly coloured scarf lined with small mirrors or hoisting up their navy blue baggy trousers.

Most of the half-naked had changed the few Western clothes they had for the more colourful and traditional local clothes, on the possibly reasonable basis that these would be more comfortable – having been designed for use in that climate, atmosphere and altitude. However, few went for the coarse black wool or the faded cotton colours which most Turkish women wore, preferring the more expensive variety, still only sold in one colour but slightly better cut and of infinitely superior material. And none of the men, who solemnly supported the women's line on the inherent superiority of local fashions, went so far as to travel around in a de-mob suit, and most relied on an amalgam of African and Asian garments, each of which had a long and intrepid history which the wearer would tell in the dull monotone adopted by the group.

The Turks looked on rather gloomily, obviously unhappy to live so close to the sea and so far from their mountains and sheep or whatever it was they dreamt of. The son of my *pansiyone*-owner revealed that something in the atmosphere was causing his hair to fall out, a sad indictment of the sea air, and desperately asked for the name of a Western remedy for his predicament, refusing to accept my opinion that none existed. Perhaps a little condescendingly, I urged him to accept that baldness was not unattractive. This led to the unexpected production of some letters from a German girl with whom he had had a holiday affair, and who filled her letters with anxious enquiries about his hairline. For some reason she had decided to correspond in English, which she wrote badly and which he was practically incapable of understanding.

The passion with which the Turk had acted out the relationship was sadly absent in the general tone of the letters, which spoke rather seriously of the Greens in Germany, and little of love in Turkey. Fortunately, the Turk hadn't realised the discrepancy in their feelings, possibly imagining that 'the Greens' was a term of the fondest endearment. I was asked to respond to these letters, and to write in English a description of the Turk's behaviour. No sooner had I agreed than he began to make peculiar squelching noises on his wrist, which I eventually identified as particularly soggy kisses. The seduction continued until, sweating with excitement, the Turk flopped into an armchair and repeated 'It's good' a number of times. I did my best to convey the ardour of his passion and asked him if he wished to end the letter with 'all my love' or some similar affectionate term. He scurried through his dictionary and began to wail loudly about, I think, the soppy, overromantic way I had approached the letter. I assumed that this was just shyness, and that Islam discourages an honest assessment of what might be perceived as unmanly feelings, so I left him with the letter, to do with it what he wanted, and went off to dinner.

The next morning, the lover invited me to a 'Turkish breakfast' to thank me for writing the letter. The breakfast consisted of yoghurt, honey, cheese and several glasses of tea, and was served to us as we sat on the family's balcony overlooking the port by the lover's mother and sister, who obviously approved of signing letters 'with love'. The only drawback was that Hassan, as I discovered his name was when his sister offered him a plate of cheese, had told his family that he could speak English, so instead of using a dictionary and gestures as we had done the night before, he insisted on relying solely upon the little English he knew. This consisted of a series of questions which would undoubtedly be useful when trying to let a room, but did not generate the most interesting conversation: 'what was my nationality?', 'how long was I staying in Kas?' and 'did I know that the water was hot in the afternoon?' We struggled on, reciting these questions and my answers for about half an hour, until I began to suspect that Hassan's family would recognise the fraud. It was interrupted by two sun-hats shouting from the street that they had managed to persuade a sailor to take them across to Megiste, not to land but 'just to have a look'. Did I want to go across with them? Hassan, who obviously hadn't understood a word, replied that he did, while I refused on the basis that I was going to Myra that day, and on to Finike. The sun-hats loudly discussed the political implications of smuggling young Turks across to Greek territory, while Hassan dangled over the balcony and, continuing to repeat his questions, eventually drove them away. His mother then ordered his sister to clear up, and a little peremptorily ushered Hassan and me downstairs.

I packed and began to push my bike up the enormous hill above Kas. The road was being repaired and had been reduced to a stony, bumpy mess, churned up by the various construction vehicles and the coaches on their way to Antalya. My lengthy breakfast meant that, on top of the great dust storms that blew up whenever a vehicle drove past, I had the added discomfort of having all the dust stick to me because the sun was so high and I was revoltingly sweaty. Fortunately, the Turks have installed a series of water pipes along the road, which presumably supply water from a mountain stream. One of the few luxuries I had allowed myself was a sponge, which proved ideal for removing the crust of dust that formed on me. To begin with I had cycled past these pipes, wishing nervously to keep my exposure to potential germs as low as possible. Until I started to sponge myself down, it had been quite easy to operate a policy of only drinking tea, fruit juice or my sterilised water. But once I began to cool myself, to dip my head under the water and see the dirt peel off me, I lost completely my sense of danger and began to drink from these streams, unconcerned about the possible uses for them in villages higher up the mountain. Within a week I was to regret this recklessness.

By an incredible stroke of good fortune, the roadworks ended at the brow of the hill, and I was able to coast down the old road into Kale.

Possibly when the new road is completed more traffic will start to use it, but when I cycled along the coast road there was practically none. On the whole that was a good thing. The Turks were kind, friendly people when I met them in cafés, hotels and even at ancient sites, but when put behind a wheel most of them jettisoned their consideration, respect for life and general lack of urgency to adopt an unattractive aggression towards – indeed domination of – all others on the road. With traffic so light I was able to minimise the risk of an accident by getting off my bike whenever I heard a growling motor coming towards me, and retreat on to the hillside until the lorry or coach had gone past.

Apart from the safety of this method, it had the great advantage that I was able to rest a lot, read and generally remain moderately well informed about where I was and whether there was anything I should look out for. This was possible not because I carried a great rack of guide books, but because I had carefully annotated my map with brief outlines of the whereabouts of particular temples, theatres and other 'places of interest'. It had been a time-consuming activity which had just about proved worthwhile, though not nearly as interesting or reliable as a decent guide book.

The necessity for brevity, if I was also to be able to use the map for cycling purposes, meant that I was frequently more confused than enlightened by my notes. Kale was such an occasion. My note read: 'Virgins, pawnbrokers and Christmas,' but Kale, when seen from the top of the hill, gave no clue as to what this might mean. In the foreground I could see a large factory, which I suppose provided some employment but was otherwise a particularly horrible object, belching out smoke and dominating the small coastal plain. The town itself was nothing much when seen from above, a fairly haphazard pattern of two-storey houses built in a mixture of wood and concrete. A few classical remains could just be made out – a small hill with the outline of a building visible on it, and lots of overgrown walls in fields between the town and the factory – but little that, at least compared with other remains in Turkey, one could become terribly excited about. I had long abandoned my old pacing-out of remains and anxious calculations about the size of their ancient settlement.

For no particular reason I had decided that I was going to cycle to Finike that day, so I gave up trying to decipher my note and pushed on, to my relief along a flat road, until I reached Finike – an almost completely unmemorable town. Only one incident of consequence occurred, which by coincidence solved the problem of my unintelligible note and provided me with a lift to the mountainous site of classical Termessus. Slumped in a café over a glass of beer, I was approached by the most unlikely Turk, wearing a dapper leather jacket, jeans and a stylish haircut, who asked me in French if I was the cyclist. If so, did I want to join his party for dinner because they had seen me at Fethiye, Xanthos, and Kas, and had on three occasions passed me in their coach. At that moment a party of about twenty-five Swiss walked into the restaurant, of which it was reassuring to see that nearly half wore sun-hats.

Kale, they told me, was the birthplace of St Nicholas, perhaps better known as Father Christmas, but in addition the patron saint of sailors, pawnbrokers, Imperial Russia, virgins and children. Had I remembered, I was asked, a port near Xanthos called Patara? If so, did I know that St Nicholas gave three purses of gold to serve as dowries for three virgin daughters of an impoverished Pataran nobleman to save them from prostitution, and that he had almost certainly followed the route I had just cycled?

I had never heard such a detailed account of St Nicholas's activities; having read in London the shocking statement that Father Christmas was born in Patara and not in some snowy waste, and had probably never even heard of reindeer, I had decided not to destroy any further the legends of my childhood. The Swiss didn't share my dismay at all, and spoke cheerfully of the vicissitudes of the cult of St Nicholas – the persecution by Diocletian, the assault by the Saracens, the looters from Bari, Venice and St Petersburg, and the Turkish prohibition of bell-ringing, which meant that the call to evening service was sounded by a small boy hammering at a plank.

There was something a little tiring about the depth of their knowledge. Whereas I was going to Antalya, they were going to Attaleia, the second-century BC city founded by Attalus Philadelphus, the King of Pergamum. The maps they carried were about fifteen hundred years out of date – Termessus, Perge, Aspendus and Side were the only towns marked, which they were visiting in unclassical haste over the next two days. My hints about how difficult I might find it to get to Termessus were readily taken up, and it was agreed that if I was able to be at their hotel in Antalya (or Attaleia) the next day I could have a lift up to the mountainous site.

Unfortunately, nobody was quite sure why Termessus was built in such an inaccessible place, or in such grandeur. An agora, with elaborate vaulted cisterns; a Roman palace; two Doric ruins; a complex aqueduct and a stunning Roman theatre were strewn between the three peaks of

Gulluk Dag, the Rose Mountain. The whole site is overgrown now with arbutus, myrtle and bay which added to the extraordinary thrill of locating the theatre, poised on the brink of an abyss and reinforced by the walls and buttresses of Roman engineers with, beyond the auditorium, a spectacular natural panorama – looking through the crags and ridges of rocky mountains to the distant sea.

I was reminded of Philip Glazebrook's reservations about Ephesus, his preference for ancient sites 'where ruins mouldering into the earth pluck faintly at your sleeve'. In Termessus, more than anywhere else that I visited in Turkey, the ruins tugged at my sleeve in humble recognition of the confidence and nobility of enterprise that had built such a theatre in such a spot – remote, inaccessible and really only suited for a fortress.

Termessus spoilt the other sites for me: from Perge, Aspendus and Side I looked back to the Gulluk Dag and remembered the view from the theatre. Though the theatre at Aspendus was larger and in better repair, fronted by an intact proscenium complete with ranks of columns and pediments from which only the statues are missing, it lacked the imaginative genius suggested by Termessus. Perge too epitomised a solid colonial efficiency, the drum-like theatre looming over the stadium which once seated 12,000.

Nothing had replaced these old sites. Like Ephesus, Miletus and Xanthos, the towns had died with the fall of the Romans and the Turks had turned back towards the mountains. Strangely, tourism has begun to revive building on the coast of the Bay of Antalya, and pockets of modern hotel blocks suddenly appear in a peculiar isolation from contemporary Turkish life. Only in Side is there any evidence of fairly constant occupation, the small village huddled under the remains of the theatre, and its main streets roughly following the course of Roman times.

There are some pleasant aspects of living within the ruins – in the back garden of my *pansiyone* in Kas an old marble bench is used for breakfast. In other parts of the village an elegant, vaulted hall is now used as a garage for two tractors, and elsewhere a marble column is used partly as a support for a washing line and partly as a nice place to put an old metal can, now used as a flower pot. At the east of the town, the columns of a temple are used to form a verandah to a house, part of which had been built using a metal Singer sewing-machine advertisement.

In the theatre some sort of Ephesian re-building appears to be taking place – possibly the restoration of the proscenium. A museum in the restored baths waxes lyrical about the splendour of the past, omitting the fact that the wealth of the town was built on the slave trade, first by Cilician pirates and continued by the Romans. East of Side this robust history was more evident. Castles in various states of repair stand on virtually every high point along the coast, some – like Alanya, Anamur and Corycus – in good condition, others just battered shells. From Gasipaza to Tasucu the main attraction for me was the coastline, which was as beautiful and impressive as anything I have seen. The steep slopes of the Taurus mountains plunged into the sea – a constant succession of wooded headlands, fiords and small river plains which were used to eke out an existence from bananas, forestry and, to a surprisingly small extent, fishing.

The only drawback to the whole cycle ride through this idyllic scenery was my health, which was bad in Side and became progressively worse. In Side my landlady took control of my food, after she found me sitting on the marble bench slowly working my way through a bag of pears. She forced me on to a dreary diet of tea, dried cake, bananas and some unpleasant yellow tablets called 'Dioralex'. Fortunately, my next point of collapse was supervised by the waiter in the main restaurant of the town, Anamur. He insisted that the only proper cure was large amounts of raki. His interest in my stomach reached quite absurd proportions, and his anxious enquiries were always accompanied by a bottle of raki, and a strange incantation of 'Earlandy. Boom, boom.'

This arose from a broadcast on the restaurant's television about a recent IRA bombing campaign, which he recognised as something to do with me. Faced with the daunting prospect of explaining that not all of Britain faced the problems of Northern Ireland, I reduced the entire conflict to the three words 'Earlandy. Boom, boom.' From then on, he would greet me with a great bellow of *'Earlandy!'* and I would reply 'Boom, boom', whereupon he would ply me with raki. Steadily our drinking sessions became less and less restrained, ending on the first night with a slow and sombre waltz around the restaurant in an attempt to dramatise the poignancy of Northern Ireland for the other diners. The dilemma about such occasions is that on subsequent meetings one is expected to behave in a similarly unrestrained way, in fact preferably to become even more outrageous. This 'behavioural pattern', as some call it, is as true in Turkey as in England, and on the second night we extended the physical limits of our dance-floor, and toured the various establishments surrounding the main square, concentrating on the *baclava* shop and a rival restaurant.

The unexpected consequence of these two dances was an invitation to sit on the 'Mayor's Balcony' for the parade celebrating the anniversary of the birth of the Turkish republic. For no apparent reason I was asked to arrive at the Hotel Bulvar at seven-thirty in the morning, where a balcony had been lined with a few pieces of red cotton, and contained a pile of six interlocking chairs in a corner. I helped place these around the balcony and waited. At that time in the morning the repetition of 'Earlandy', 'Boom, boom' had lost much of its charm, and I wasn't quite ready for another raki session. The waiter and I sat alone on the balcony staring gloomily out into the empty streets. Finally, at about eight-fifteen we heard bands in the distance, and an astonishing number of school children marched into the square, followed by their loving families. Then a few local dignitaries deposited wreaths in front of a statue of Ataturk and some military bands marched in and played some horribly discordant music, before we launched into an hour and a half of speeches.

My position on the Mayor's Balcony prevented me from escaping. Though the waiter and I had eventually been joined by others, and indeed had given up our seats, there were never more than ten people at a time and we occupied the prime position for viewing the interminable praising of Ataturk and the westernisation of Turkey. The boredom appeared to be confined to our balcony, as at the end of every speech – which were all delivered with tremendous flamboyance – a great roar of approval came from the school children and the others in the packed crowds. My own overwhelming reaction was that this was a particularly harsh penalty for two nights' relatively indecorous behaviour. Slowly, my clapping became less enthusiastic (having only ever been polite) as we heard speeches from representatives of the schools, the armed forces, the Anamur Chamber of Commerce and every other conceivable organisation. At last, the Mayor left the balcony and, to an almost hysterical response from the crowd, delivered the final speech.

Worse was to come. A group of teenagers wearing goblin costumes sidled into the square and began a performance of Turkish folk-dances. From then on things moved in slow motion. I heard and saw virtually nothing, just stood staring with glassy eyes at the sky. At some stage I was asked to wave to the parade of children as they marched back to their schools. Had I been able to face it, a celebratory lunch followed, but my stomach decided that food was unacceptable. I drank two glasses of raki, and went back to bed with what felt like a high temperature, a savage headache and stomach cramps.

It might have been a complete coincidence that the speeches and dances immediately preceded my rapid physical decline. My illness in Side had been bad food poisoning, not much worse than the oyster-poisoning I had had in northern France, but from Anamur I began coughing up blood, suffering almost constant diarrhoea and vomiting and generally succumbing to the most abject lethargy. The result was that I walked from Anamur to Tarsus, too tired to pedal along even the flat ground that exists east of Tasucu. The hundred miles I walked took me five days, an impressive average achieved by coasting down the hills between Anamur and Tasucu. Throughout that time I was looking for somewhere pleasant to stay and recover from what I was sure was a temporary setback. Sadly, however, the *pansiyones* were designed for those in a tougher condition than I was; lying on metal beds in uncarpeted rooms which had never been swept and had in-adequate lighting and heating wasn't going to help me recover, par-ticularly when any food I ate was immediately and violently expelled.

Nearly all my hopes were pinned on Mersin, perhaps the ideal town to make a recovery in. Its exalted status as the largest Turkish Medi-terranean port guaranteed a number of smart hotels to accommodate the various fat-cats who collect for the purpose of international trade, and it offered absolutely nothing to attract tourists – no monuments, parks, museums, art galleries or pleasant sea-side walks, indeed nothing to tempt one outside the comfortable precincts of one's hotel.

Understandably, the hoteliers were reluctant for their rooms to be filled with mewling and puking Western tourists suffering from stomach problems, so they charged nightly rates which required the resources of a large and successful multinational. A few less glamorous hotels existed, and I found a double room in one of these and crawled into bed, determined not to get out again until I was better. It was a policy which failed to take into account the Turkish predilection for sitting inside hotel rooms and gloomily staring at a tape-recorder or radio, played as loudly as possible and regardless of content. The result was usually an irritating mix of terrible versions of Western rock music, hideous Turkish music and a long-running contest to find the most unpleasant voice in Turkey.

My room was between three of these noisy parties and none of them would turn down, let alone turn off, their radios or cassettes; these were much grander and shinier models than those I'd suffered in cheaper hotels, but unfortunately my hotel wasn't expensive enough to have reasonable sound-proofing. A little sheepishly I went down to reception to ask for another room, and found the receptionist and about twenty of his friends all watching a very loud television featuring a singer, dressed in an extraordinary sequined dress, belting out Tamla Motown hits.

Wearily I abandoned Mersin and walked on to Tarsus, a town with a long and illustrious history: the birthplace of St Paul, the rendezvous for Cleopatra and Marc Antony and the whole series of great commanders who had marched through – Alexander the Great, Pompey, Hadrian, Tigranes the Great, Sultan Selim the Grim. Only one aspect of that history interested me – whether any of those great leaders had suggested to Tarsusians that a decent hotel would be a good idea.

I cycled past the Gate of the Bitch, hardly giving it a second glance, and charged into the two hotels I found. One was full, the other too expensive for me. Two florists came to my rescue and took me to a third. Although its concrete floors and badly painted walls were not particularly welcoming, the hotel was very quiet and very cheap, as the owner gave me a reduction both for being a friend of the florists and for being a cyclist.

Two hours later I was wallowing in a hot bath reading the latest editions of *World Soccer*, *International Herald Tribune* and a number of American current affairs magazines. This was not some fantasy, but the work of the florists who, while I was asleep, had gone to the Tarsus Amerikan Likesi to ask them if they could cope with another cyclist. Every two weeks or so this American school is dropped in on by an English cyclist who invariably finds some member of the beleaguered staff prepared to issue an invitation to stay – either in the guest room or, if that is already occupied, on sofas and cushions. Incredibly, the rest of the staff (and even the pupils, who must get a little bored with it all) then succeed in making the guest feel not just welcome but the best thing to arrive in Tarsus since, since, well, since the last cyclist.

In common with most of my predecessors I discussed the possibilities of going to Cappodocia, possibly taking my bike on the bus. The bus station which handled the route to Goreme, tired by the repetition of such problems, had issued a notice announcing that, whilst bikes could be taken to Goreme, there was no possibility of bikes being brought back – one would have to cycle. It seemed that I wasn't the only person to have reached Tarsus a little disillusioned with the attractions of cycling, and the school staff implored me not to take my bike unless I was definitely going to cycle back, as the hordes of people who ignored the bus station notice, but then tried with methods varying from abuse, logic and humiliation to get their bikes on board were beginning to cause considerable international tension.

One of the disadvantages of following the coastal route around Turkey was that I only saw the fertile coastal plains or spectacular sea cliffs, when everyone knows that the chief feature of Turkey is supposed to be mournful Anatolian steppes. Gertrude Bell wrote: 'It is Asia, with all its vastness, with all its brutal disregard for life and comfort and the amenities of existence; it is the ancient East, returned after so many millenniums of human endeavour, to its natural desolation.'

Sitting in a succession of Greek theatres and council chambers, and exploring ancient stadia and agoras, it was hard to think of Turkey in such bleak terms. While the Turks in general did appear to be naturally depressive people, they were also extremely friendly, some were exceptionally generous and, perhaps a little paradoxically, they seemed to quite enjoy being gloomy.

Looking out of the bus window as we drove across the bleak, cold plateau towards Cappodocia, I saw how different the coastal belt was from the interior and, superficially at least, how much nicer life was by the sea – for some people a truism, though possibly not for the Turks.

Although partly covered by snow, most of the plateau was a dark, infertile place, similar to the most barren and exposed parts of the Pennines, but of much greater extent. Cappodocia was covered with tufa – a soft volcanic stone of solidified mud, ash and lava which, though varied, was predominantly a pale pink and yellow colour. The houses on the plateau were spartan, clumsy buildings obviously made from the few materials immediately at hand – some wood, mud-bricks and a few concrete slabs. In Cappodocia, the locals had again used the materials available so lived in extraordinary tufa sculptures that the erosion of rivers and wind had created from the soft stone, hollowing out the cones and hills in places like Urgup, and digging underground cities about twelve storeys deep at Kaymakli. There is some debate about whether Kaymakli or any of the other dozen or so underground cities were used for temporary emergencies or permanent accommodation, and when they were last lived in. The owner of a souvenir shop at Kaymakli insisted that his family had, until the beginning of this century, lived underground, but a guide book I looked at in his shop claimed that no one had ever lived in the underground cities permanently, and that they were last used to hide from the invading Egyptian army led by Ibrahim Pasha in 1839.

In Nevsehir, where I was staying, I met a French-speaking Turk who said that Armenians had hidden in the cities to escape the Turkish persecution in the early 1900s, and completely dismissed the shop-owner's alleged family residence. Such a claim was just an attempt to get me to buy some of the rotten stock sold in the souvenir shops, he said, and he knew that, as a man of distinction, I could only possibly want to buy carpets. The level at which we both spoke French was so poor that this relatively straightforward statement took us about five minutes to achieve. At the end of our feeble efforts towards understanding I found that I had somehow been manoeuvred into the 'best carpet shop in Nevsehir', a surprisingly modest claim as it seemed to be the only carpet shop.

As in Kusadasi, the method of the carpet-salesman was to ply me with glasses of tea, and act in the disconsolate manner of someone having his family heirlooms seized by the bailiffs. As each carpet was dramatically unfurled, the owner of the shop – an elderly man with an enormous white moustache – let out an anguished moan and sadly shook his head, unable to express his grief at the prospect of being parted from his carpets. The French-speaker, who sat paternally beside me, occasionally gripped my thigh in support of my position as bailiff – each grip or pat implying that what I was doing was right.

I tried to reassure the carpet-dealer that I had no intention of buying any of his carpets, however nice they were, because I was cycling to China. The first time I made this great pronouncement there was a respectable hush before they anxiously asked if my bike was safe. I assured them it was as I'd left it with friends.

'In Nevsehir?'

'No. In Tarsus.'

They looked disappointed, and I was asked to confirm that I hadn't cycled from Tarsus. Where had I cycled from?

'England.'

'Did you like Istanbul?'

'I didn't go through Istanbul.'

They looked even more disappointed, particularly after I'd shown them the map of my route sketched on to the world map at the back of my diary. Ferries from Italy to Greece, ferries from Greece to Turkey, flight over Iran and Pakistan ... it was quite obvious that they didn't believe that I had a bike at all. Their discovery that I had not just misled them, but lied, plunged them into still deeper depths of gloom and despondency as they realised that the carpet wasn't even going to a good home.

'So which carpet are you going to take?' said the old man, his voice heavy with sadness.

'I'm not buying a carpet. I can't carry it on my bicycle.'

They gave hollow laughs, and looked contemptuously at me as I persisted with this dreadful invention. Suddenly it occurred to me that there was no reason why I should stand these attacks on my integrity, I owed no loyalty to these people, had no cause to suffer in silence. I stood up and angrily announced my departure.

Such haughty pride justifiably ended with a speedy and rather humiliating retraction as, on my way out, I noticed a carpet hanging on a wall which earlier, as I sat beside the caressing French-speaker, had been out of my sight. My dilemma was that, having wasted several hours looking at carpets and assuming that I would never buy one, I now found that I appreciated the appeal of the rich, natural-dye colours, the deep blues, golds and burgundies, liked the feel of the thick, double-knotted wool and entirely accepted that it would be a very sad thing if I left Turkey without one.

As for my feeble objection that I couldn't carry carpets on a bike – I could leave the carpets in Tarsus, cycle into Syria and then go back to pick up the carpets and take them to Athens by bus and ferry. My sister, who had already announced her intention to come out to Athens to see me, could then pick them up. Nothing could be simpler so, with no attempt to apologise for my earlier rudeness, I bought the carpet and took a bus back to Tarsus to find a suitable store for it while I went to Syria.

There was probably no need to go on to buy four more carpets once I'd worked out how to get them home, but I felt that such excesses could safely be put down to my illness and (in the case of two of them, bought in Kus Kalis) to sympathy for the carpet-salesman's first wife, who periodically appeared clutching the babies of the younger and considerably more attractive second wife. This pleasantly Eastern arrangement, further confirmation that I had at last managed to cycle into Asia, took place in an unprepossessing shack overlooking the Armenian Maiden's Castle. This castle was built by the King of Korykos to protect his daughter from her prophesied death by snake bite, a catastrophe he attempted to avert by keeping her a prisoner on the small island. The King was unsuccessful in his attempts, as a snake was accidentally (though the carpet-dealer refused to accept that it was not deliberate) taken across the seventy odd yards from shore to castle hidden in a basket of vegetables and, unluckily, the princess was killed.

This story was told to me by one of the Tarsus Amerikan Likesi lecturers, who had accompanied me to the shop. She translated the carpet-dealer's views on the King's arrangements for me. It was clear that, for various reasons, he regretted his inability to follow the King's example and lock up not just his daughter but all women. Apart from the fundamental inferiority of women, which he considered self-evident, he was highly suspicious of their behaviour and convinced of their basic infidelity, impurity and overwhelming urge to corrupt and pollute the unprotected Turkish male. His ability to live with two women, both of whom he publicly treated with contempt, was apparently not inconsistent with his views on women in general – views, indeed, which were fairly commonly held in Turkey. It helped explain the absence of women in public places, and re-emphasised the incongruity of the smart dress shops in Antalya.

After hearing more gruesome details of the subordination of women, and temporarily satisfied with the number of carpets I had, I left Tarsus for Syria. Heading east I crossed the Cilician Plain, perhaps the richest agricultural area in Turkey. Xenophon described it as large and beautiful, 'well-watered and full of trees of all sorts and vines', nourishing 'an abundance of sesame, millet, panic, wheat and barley'; Ibrahim Pasha added sugar and date-palms. Today it has been significantly developed as an industrial centre, with just a few orange trees and cotton plants surviving the apparently unfettered pollution.

Equally depressing, after I had grown accustomed to the virtual absence of vehicles on the roads, was joining the main Trans-European Highway from western Europe to the Middle-East – a title which might suggest a large road, a dual-carriageway at the least. Such a suggestion would be misleading, however, as the road was single-lane in both directions, and both lanes were filled with huge lorries fighting for space amongst the cars and carts that chugged along.

It was strange being amongst the Mercedes and Porsches (and even an Aston Martin) after the comparatively simple vehicles of southern Turkey. Unfortunately, I remained obsessed by the standard of hotel I was prepared to stay in, and in Ceyhan, Iskenderun and Antakya those standards were as lamentable as any I had yet encountered. It was hard to believe, as I was buffeted by the drag from the lorries or barged aggressively off the road by a Mercedes anxious to get home to the wealthy Middle-East, that I was crossing the field of the Battle of Issus, where Alexander defeated the Persians, or that Iskenderun was Alexander's city – Alexandria ad Issum, Alexandretta, Iskenderun. A few Crusader castles, of which the most impressive was used as a hoarding for nearby restaurants, were the only signs of any earlier existence than the dreary, unimaginative present.

Antakya, the classical Antioch, for two centuries the capital of the Seleucid Empire and for three centuries the capital of the Roman province of Syria, was now reduced to a shabby provincial town with a small museum and the remains of the pleasure gardens of Daphne. I spent a day in the town, waiting to watch the Turkey–England soccer match, shown live from Istanbul. The Turks in the café I was sitting in were, at least to begin with, delighted to have an Englishman watching with them, offering me tea and cigarettes and, with some bravado, predicting the scale of the Turkish victory. They reacted with what was considerably more grace than some English soccer fans would show in their place as England went on to win 8–0, and indeed at the end six people shook my hand in congratulation.

There had been nothing in my six weeks' stay in Turkey to give me any cause to imagine that the reaction to a humiliating defeat would be in any way aggressive. It was a remarkable contrast to the suspicion, even fear, with which I had entered the country from Samos, and made the behaviour of the Turkish soldiers at the Turkish–Syrian frontier even more mystifying than it would otherwise have been.

At the particular point where I crossed, the Turkish customs were at one end of a valley about five and a half miles long, with the Syrian customs at the other end, thus creating a no-man's-land between the two countries – a legacy presumably from some long-distant political dispute. For no reason other than the officials' wish to be obstructive, it took me an hour and a half to get through customs as they emptied my bags, shook my bike, smelt the saddle and generally conducted a thorough search – though, curiously, not bothering to see what I had in my pockets.

I cycled off, infuriated by the delay which meant that I would arrive in Aleppo after dark. A mile into no-man's-land two men standing on top of the northern side of the valley began to wave and shout. Throughout Turkey people had stood on hills and furiously waved and shouted at me. I had sometimes waved back, sometimes shouted back, sometimes both, and very occasionally done nothing other than curse the inanity of the entire Turkish race. I had never stopped, which was what I realised that these particular men wanted me to do when a bullet kicked up the earth about five yards in front of me.

I looked up at the men, perhaps a hundred yards away, and tried without success to identify them. One was looking at me through binoculars and the other was looking at me through the sights of his gun, which looked alarmingly as if it was pointed straight at me. Although I am sure that there is never a convenient moment to die, and that everyone feels there are one or two things they had hoped they would be able to do in life, I was particularly conscious that I didn't want to die then and that I didn't want to lie rotting in the middle of no-man's-land, possibly the subject of a minor dispute between Syria and Turkey as to who was going to cart my remains away. Most important of all, I wasn't sure that the people in Tarsus who were looking after my carpets knew what my surname was.

Later that day, I was shocked at how banal these thoughts were, having assumed that at such critical moments the meaning of life would suddenly become clear, the heavens would part and I would be greeted by angels – or at least that there would be some sign that death wasn't just two men on a hill with a corpse at the bottom.

At the time I simply concentrated on how to get out of the situation alive. If *Casablanca* had ruined my great farewell, dozens of Westerns came to my help now, and I put my hands up, uncertain whether I should supplement this by smiling at the man holding the binoculars – the danger being that he might misinterpret this as unseemly amusement rather than a brave demeanour in the face of adversity.

'Binoculars' decided the matter for me by lowering his glasses, picking up another gun and, while the original gunman continued to keep his gun aimed at me, beginning to run down the hill. When he reached me he showed a rather unnecessary amount of aggression by shoving his gun first against my chin and then up to a nostril. He was wearing a soldier's uniform with a red and blue pip on his shoulder, and was probably no more than nineteen or twenty. Nothing about his conduct suggested that he would show any sense in his dealings with me, or that the slightest mistake would not be severely punished. Finding it all rather alarming, I thought of my carpets for comfort.

The first gunman then appeared and began to punch me, which in a strange way seemed so pathetic that I stopped feeling at all worried, confident that the two boys had absolutely no idea what they were going to do with me. They carried on punching me for a while, then emptied my bags all over the boggy ground beside the road, kicked a few things around, unreeled some films and stared greedily at my camera, the $100 note I had to get me into Syria and the wad of sterling traveller's cheques.

At last they told me, with further needless aggression, to get out of Turkey.

4

Cold kidneys in Syria

The time-consuming business of crossing the Turkish frontier made it impossible for me to reach Aleppo before dark. Apart from not having any lights (I had sent them back with my sister in Athens as I never used them and they were bulky and heavy), the generally destabilising effect of being shot at meant that if I had to cycle anywhere, I was only happy if it was in daylight in the company of a dozen extremely tough and preferably armed guards.

Unfortunately, I was still alone, unarmed except for my steel bicycle lock and a corkscrew, and cycling into a country about which I knew almost nothing other than that the capital, Damascus, was supposed to be a rather ugly place; that there were at least two sites worth visiting, Palmyra and a famous Crusader castle; that there was the Hotel Baron in Aleppo, and, finally that I had to change $100 cash at the border, at a deliberately poor rate of exchange.

When I'd been told about this tiresome requirement I had resolved to do everything within my power to resist the government responsible, to spend as little as possible in the country and to try and confine what little I spent to the black market. But when I found myself stuck between two countries – one determined to exploit my imagined wealth, and the other including at least two soldiers who found happiness in taking pot shots at me and sticking guns in my face – this resolution smacked of a very foolish and false bravado. There was, however, not much choice about continuing into Syria as I suspected that the two Turkish soldiers would take a rather dim view if I so quickly and flagrantly disregarded their orders to leave the country.

At the small collection of huts which constituted the Syrian border post I was approached by six seedy-looking yobs who asked if I wanted to change any money. At first, I wasn't sure if they were black-marketeers or representatives of the Syrian government trying to extract their $100, but their fingering of my other possessions and their

unpleasant enquiries about the price suggested that I might find someone more official in one of the huts.

The whole situation was rather depressing. Even after finding the
bank, getting my passport stamped and being told, with surprising
charm, that I was welcome in Syria, I was still faced with about two
hours' cycling in the dark. It was bitterly cold and the country I had to
cycle across was barren, practically deserted and wholly unwelcoming,
though it might in more auspicious circumstances have possessed a
certain biblical beauty.

Indeed, after a few miles of cycling in the moonlight and feeling a
growing confidence that I wasn't going to get shot at again, I began to
quite enjoy it, relishing the exotic sandstone igloos, the Arabic headwear
and the great 'foreignness' of the written Arabic on signs and shopfronts.
There were only two nervous moments: the first when I passed a stone
quarry and, still rather jumpy, mistook the explosions for gunfire, and the
second when I experienced on the outskirts of Aleppo the more familiar
problem of cycling without lights on a busy dual carriageway.

Before leaving Tarsus, I had carefully prepared for the moment when
I entered Aleppo, and had copied out, in Arabic, the squiggles meaning
'Do you know the way to the hotel?' I shoved this under various
people's noses, and carefully and clearly insisted on the 'Hotel Baron'.

The problem with asking a question in Arabic was that most people
understandably assumed that I would be able to understand their Arabic
replies. That assumption was of course wrong, which created a difficult
situation made considerably worse by a peculiar Arabic reluctance to
point. After the tenth person had stood apologetically before me,
unable to give me directions, I was just about to abandon the Hotel
Baron and stay at the first hotel I came to, when a couple of men asked
me if I spoke German. I replied, quite untruthfully, that I did, on the
basis that I was more likely to understand directions in German than in
Arabic. The drawback was, however, that the German–speaker was at
that moment somewhere else, and I would have to accompany the two
men to wherever he was.

Having already been shot at that day, it seemed beyond the call of
duty to allow myself to get kidnapped, and particularly to cooperate
with my kidnappers in walking to such an unlikely rendezvous. The
sensible thing would have been to refuse to go with them, or to demand
that if there was a German–speaker, then he could come to me. Unfortunately, both these possibilities would have appeared so rude, even
offensive, that I decided to go and ask for 'ein karte' in the hope that it
would produce a map.

We walked along, one of the men pushing my bike, until we reached a remarkably expensive-looking block of flats, took the lift to the sixth floor and entered a large flat, totally unfurnished except for dozens of Persian carpets and, in one room, a long row of four beds. Three other men joined us, all in their mid to late twenties, and all equally solicitous and courteous towards me. Leaving my bike in one of the other rooms, we sat in a line on one of the beds, and grinned at each other.

'Konnen sie die Hotel Baron?' I asked.

'Ja . . . (gabble, gabble in German) . . . essen.'

'Ich wohlern fahren auf Hotel Baron. Woe ist das Hotel?'

Further gabbling in German, none of which I understood, except the repetition of the word 'essen'.

'Haben zie ein karte die Hotel Baron?'

It was obvious that they were a little bored by my one-track mind, and one of them stuck his head around the bedroom door and yelled something at someone. There was a scurry of feet, a muttered apology from an unseen woman, and the man came back into the room carrying a plate piled with unpleasant browny-green blobs dipped in flour. They turned out to be cold spiced kidneys, and I was supposed to eat them.

Although I knew I wasn't being kidnapped, it was quite clear that I couldn't just get up and walk out, so I began ploughing my way through the kidneys until, finally, a nervous knock at the door preceded the arrival of coffee. Throughout the eating of the kidneys, which by the end of the plate I was beginning to enjoy, the six of us had done almost nothing but stare contentedly at each other. After coffee, I continued with my pathetic attempts at formulating questions in German until they tired of me and announced that we were going.

Two taxis were hailed, and after an unsuccessful attempt at putting my bike in the boot we travelled in convoy for about a mile, with taxis in front of me and behind, until with some ceremony we arrived at last at the Hotel Baron. Using the receptionist as a translator, the five declared that they would come to the hotel at ten-thirty the next morning to take me on a tour of the city, and with these comforting words they piled back into the taxis and went back to whatever activities they had interrupted for the hour our meeting had taken.

The receptionist then announced that I would have to pay my hotel bills in foreign currency, so I was forced to try and find someone to change the useless Syrian pounds I'd bought at the border back into dollars – a fairly simple task in Aleppo, but one which added to my disillusionment with the events of the day. Nothing else, I felt, could

possibly go wrong, as I slumped back into my armchair, a gin fizz by
my side, and read a fairly recent copy of the *Daily Telegraph*. I was
wrong. The sports pages included a column giving the rearranged dates
of the English cricket tour of India, following the assassination of Mrs
Gandhi. For the last two months, ever since leaving Athens, I had been
looking forward to the second Test match in Bombay and had planned
dozens of excursions around the original dates; now I found that the
date had been changed, and I would arrive in Bombay on the morning
of the fifth and last day. I groaned, so loudly and so pitifully that the
person in the chair next to mine asked whether I was all right. I explained the full extent of the disaster, to which he responded by offering
to take me out for a commiserative dinner, about which I can remember absolutely nothing. Back at the hotel, I had a pleasant chat
with the owner and his wife and daughter before drifting off to bed,
totally exhausted.

The prospect of touring the sights of Aleppo with four kidney-
lovers and a German-speaking guide next morning was not something
I looked forward to with any enthusiasm. Rather cravenly, therefore, I
decided to leave a note at reception announcing that I had gone for a
bike ride, and that I hoped to see them some other time. My plan was
to bicycle around the town for about an hour, before going off to the
museum and the Omaayud mosque, but when I went to get my bike I
found that it had disappeared.

I returned to the receptionist and told him my bike had been stolen,
the obvious inference when one finds a padlocked bike has disappeared.
The receptionist arranged for the police to come and get a description,
but announced gloomily that it would already be on its way to the
Damascus black market.

I was delighted. Just one Arabian night had solved two problems.
The theft had provided the perfect excuse for not going on a tour of
the city, and had made my return to Athens, laden down with the
Turkish carpets, infinitely easier. As for the future, I assumed that a
quick phone call or telegram would end in the shipping-out of a new
bike to India; and if it didn't, I concluded, I might have to continue by
train and bus, paid for out of the vast sum I would get from my
insurance company. The theft really was excellent news, and I went off
in search of the *Telegraph* to write down the new cricket dates.

By the time the kidney-lovers appeared I was in such a state of
elation that I agreed to meet them the following night for dinner.
They trooped off and I waited for the police to arrive. It was of course
inevitable that the good news would prove unfounded. Flicking

idly through a copy of *Soviet Armenian*, I was interrupted by the owner of the hotel, desperately apologetic at having put my bike in a safe place without telling me. Coffee was called for, and we chatted about life in Soviet Armenia, though my contribution to the conversation rarely went beyond appreciative exclamations of either joy or surprise.

This was further interrupted by the arrival of the Soviet consul, who had recently returned from the Soviet Union and had promised to bring the hotel-owner back a bottle of Armenian brandy – supposedly the best in the world but absurdly difficult to find. The consul had himself clearly failed to find any, but had brought with him a bottle of 'Ancient Kiev' vodka as a conciliatory gift. The three of us admired the bottle of vodka, the harmony of its lines, the beauty of the label – a vivid red splintered with silver dashes – and commented on the clever design of the screw top. Such time-wasting proved successful, as the moment the chimes signalling eleven o'clock began, a great bellow for glasses went up and the barman arrived with a tray of peanuts, ice-cubes and three glasses. The ice-cubes were sent away by the consul, who found their presence distasteful, and we proceeded to work our way through the bottle until the barman came and announced that lunch was being served.

The information that it was lunchtime reminded the consul of some diplomatic business he had to attend to, which unfortunately prevented him from joining us for lunch, so he disappeared off to his meeting and the owner of the hotel and I were decanted into the dining-room. Throughout the time we had been vodka-tasting the conversation had been an interesting discussion on the state of Armenia, the history of Armenia and the difficulties facing Armenians. This was interposed with the occasional appreciative analysis of the texture or the colour of the vodka, but in general it was remarkable how little effect the vodka had had on me, and certainly on the other two.

Lunch was different, however, and I found it increasingly difficult to prevent my nose dipping into the bowls of soup and various Arabic sauces that were put in front of me. The hotel-owner, on the other hand, looked as fresh and urbane as it is humanly possible to be, and showed absolutely no sign of the vodka he'd been drinking. Feeling embarrassed about how uncontrolled and dishevelled I was in comparison, I tried to concentrate on the rather glamorous woman I was sitting next to.

Still thinking of the vodka and the Russian consul, I turned to her and drunkenly demanded:

'So are you a diplomat as well, then?'

'Yeears,' she drawled.

'Russian?'

'Libyan actually.'

Gosh, I thought. Students, people's bureaus, St James's Square, WPC Fletcher.

'Were you in London when a Libyan diplomat shot the British policewoman?'

'I was in London when the woman was shot, but the shot didn't come from our bureau, and I don't want to say anything more about it.'

'Several people saw a gun pointing out of a window of the bureau.'

'I am not going to discuss it further.'

'You can't kill people and refuse to discuss it.'

'If you don't stop, I shall leave.'

'Well, I'm not going to stop until you tell me . . .'

She turned away from me, and announced that with regret she had to go as she wasn't feeling very well. Everyone else muttered sympathetically and she swept out of the dining-room, while I felt desperately embarrassed about my lack of tact, although I could see no possible reason why I should try and be pleasant to a Libyan who admitted being in the building when the shooting occurred.

It was another extraordinary day, a bewildering series of bizarre encounters compressed into an amazingly short time: a little disturbing in a peculiar way, so I decided to stay in my room that evening and read one of the novels I'd borrowed from the Tarsus library. The next day I trudged round the town, at last visiting the covered bazaar, the museum, the mosque and the citadel. The incessant rain acted as a rather satisfying depressant, reminding me of the normality that existed outside the hotel.

I had forgotten about the kidney-lovers in describing non-hotel life as normal, and indeed would have forgotten all about our engagement that evening if I hadn't been hailed loudly as I went back to the hotel, hoping for a rather late tea but finding instead two of the five waiting to take me off to the arranged supper party.

We drove by taxi past the university to what seemed like the farthest corner of Aleppo, where another large and under-furnished flat contained the remaining three members of the original five, plus two friends. Our 'conversation' continued in German as we confirmed that the chairs which lined three walls of the room were otherwise known as 'der shtool' and that the water we had to drink was called 'vasser'. We limped along like this for what seemed like hours, before the father of one of the men asked us to go into a bedroom. Once there I began to play chess until, after an absolute eternity, some food was brought in.

The bedroom contained one large double bed, a wardrobe and a vinyl-covered card table beside which one folding chair leant against the wall. Inevitably, I was asked to sit in this throne, first to play chess and then to pick at the lukewarm fried eggs, yoghurt and fruitcake which were carried in. The other seven sat pressed together on the side of the closest bed, selecting cassettes and smoking an endless number of cigarettes.

At about midnight one of them produced a Boney M cassette and began to dance. The song came to an end, and the next in line danced to the second song. Finally, on song number eight everyone demanded that I dance my turn. I stood up and began self-consciously to twitch my leg unrhythmically and shake my wrist. It was utter torment, which seemed to last for hours before the song finally ground to a halt. The nightmare didn't end there, however – the dancing continued until half past two in the morning, by which time I had stopped caring what I did or how long it went on for.

Away from the flat, as I waited for a taxi to take me back to the hotel, I suddenly saw Syria as an endless succession of cold kidneys, fried eggs and dancing competitions. Impulsively, I decided that the next day I'd cycle back to Antakya and Tarsus, preferring to face the risk of the valley of the shooting Turks than the slow torture of Syrian nights.

Throughout the autumn and winter a Western conveyor-belt churns out at two- or three-week intervals a series of British cyclists, usually on their way to India but occasionally going through Africa or even just to the Middle-East. Most seem to turn up at the ever-welcoming Tarsus Amerikan Likesi to regale the staff and students with tales of their adventures, and by the time I arrived back from my Syrian jaunt the next two were already in residence and occupying, to my dismay, the school's guest room. Even though I knew it was all my fault that there were so many of us there, I still felt a slight feeling of indignation as I curled up on a sofa.

The next morning, armed with my five carpets, I began the long trek back to Athens, forced to use my bike as a trolley between buses and ferries as I zig-zagged across central Turkey and the Aegean to wait in my friend's flat in Athens for my sister to lug the great mound of carpets back to London, and for my cheap flight to Bombay.

5

Bombay

There have been people writing 'Indian travel books' for about three thousand years, an activity begun by the Phoenicians, who wanted 'ivory apes and peacocks' to use as decorations for the palaces and temples of King Solomon, and thought it would be of interest to record their search. The first Englishman alleged to have visited India was Sighelmus, around AD 883. If he did in fact do so he was probably the last person from Britain who decided that their thoughts weren't worth recording. Everyone else, whether explorer, missionary or sub-librarian based in Poona, has succeeded in finding some publisher to knock up a few copies for distribution amongst friends and relatives.

Most write in acknowledgement of an ancient civilisation with one or two modern blemishes easily ignored if one properly explores the Indian culture. A smaller group concentrate on the blemishes and write lengthy analyses of the evil within Hinduism, the corruption, the violence, the evil within Hinduism and the poverty. Both sorts of books might be said to have a vested interest in somewhat exaggerating the exotic or the terrible.

My first impressions of India were rather marred by the fact that I was reading the results of a Dacca schools cricket tournament when we flew over the coast, and my first sight of the country followed the air hostess's request that I should fasten my seat belt. For a few minutes I bitterly regretted not having a window seat, until finally the plane banked and I was able to see the ground. I was sure there had been a mistake. I couldn't see one temple or palace. There were no policemen beating people up, I could see no money changing hands to smooth the way for some illicit deal and I couldn't see anyone who wasn't walking on two legs and swinging two arms. A few rather unattractive concrete buildings seemed to be accepting deliveries from brightly painted lorries. No one had ever said that a normal life went on in India. I called the air hostess over.

'Is this India?'

'Yes, sir. We'll be arriving at Bombay International Airport in about five minutes.' Whereupon she checked the tightness of my belt.

I looked outside again. I even saw a car, in fact I could see quite a few cars.

'Are you sure? I mean this is really Bombay . . .'

She obviously couldn't see the cause of my confusion and went off to look after one of the numerous babies obviously trained by its Bangladeshi parents to scream as loudly as possible at any Indian encounter. In due course an announcement asked all passengers disembarking at Bombay to move towards the exits. For a moment I thought we were being asked to jump out, and was about to demand that they took extra care with my bike when I noticed that amidst the crescendo of bawling babies we had landed. I leapt to my feet, anticipating a mighty scrum, and was a little disconcerted to find that I was the only person standing up. The air hostess approached me.

'It is Bombay you are flying to?'

I nodded.

'Please go towards the exits.'

Eventually about twenty-five slightly dishevelled people stumbled anxiously up the aisle to discover, almost unbelievingly, that the door was open and a band of red-shirted porters were emptying our luggage from the hold. There was no justification whatsoever for our confusion and trepidation, but for my own part such rational considerations were unable to dispel these emotions as we trudged through to customs and passport control. For most people flying to India from Europe this moment is the first encounter with the legendary Indian bureaucracy, and delays of two or three hours are considered lucky as huge jet after jet dumps hundreds of passengers at between two and three in the morning to face the delightfully courteous, but interminably slow, passport officer. Fortunately, Bangladesh Biman had delayed my flight for slightly over eighty hours, in which time passengers of less considerate airlines had at last shuffled their way through passport control and into the baggage collection department.

Less than ten minutes after leaving the plane, I was standing with my three panniers, a litre of Scotch and a small map of Bombay waiting for my bike. After about fifteen minutes I saw two men dragging it through some plastic swing doors, desperately trying to emphasise the sheer enormity of their task and bring out the otherwise hidden complications. Despite months of persuading myself that I should behave at all times with a grovelling humility – to compensate in some

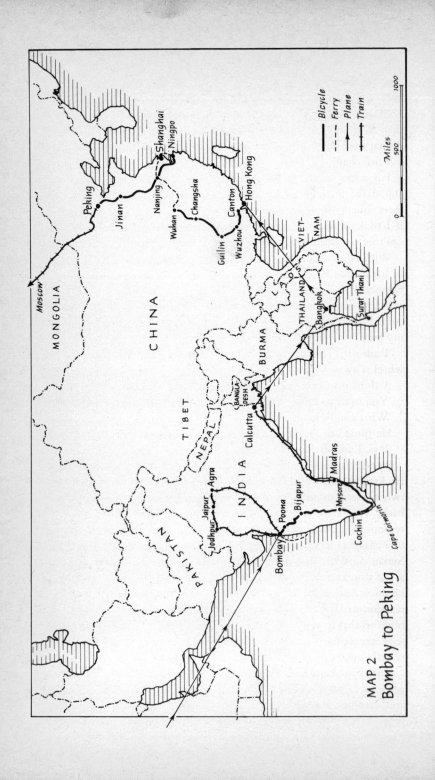

MAP 2
Bombay to Peking

way for the strident attitudes of the Raj – I immediately adopted the very worst of those old mannerisms.

'Right, that'll do. Thank you,' I barked, and briskly presented the men with my ticket label. With an extravagant demonstration of military bearing I thrust my bike pump under my armpit and puffed out my chest.

For a few moments the porters concentrated on chewing their pan and stared intensely at the floor, no doubt trying to remember how their fathers had dealt with such behaviour. One smiled as if to say that if I took it all back we could start being friends again. Although I can't be certain, I might have bristled.

With a weary shrug, possibly a little upset that I had started my time in India with this display, both men stuck out hands and demanded baksheesh. I was conscious that I really ought to pay. It suddenly occurred to me, however, that it wasn't me who had begun this silly comedy, but these two men with their exaggerated efforts in moving my bike.

'Push off,' I said, and took the crossbar of my bike, intending to wheel it away.

A third man came up and leant against the crossbar.

'You must pay extra for this extremely difficult and heavy luggage.'

'What's so difficult? It's not heavy.'

He turned to the two men and had a brief conversation.

'It is, I am afraid, very heavy.'

'Look!' I cried jubilantly, and lifted the bike up with two fingers. He looked suitably stunned. A moment later he turned angrily on the two porters, shouting at them and even beginning to pummel their backs with his palms. With a slight feeling of embarrassment that I was responsible for this scene and, perhaps worse, had so distressingly failed to behave as I would normally, I rather ineptly thrust a packet of Syrian cigarettes into the fray and guiltily, conscious of how feeble my act of atonement was, asked if that was a suitable reward for the porters' kindness and help. It was quite obvious from their contemptuous reaction as they briefly stopped assaulting each other to inspect the offering that it was very far from suitable. Despite this, I decided to seize the opportunity of escape while the violence had temporarily ceased, and stormed off.

The customs officers, who I assume must have noticed this incident, possibly decided that I was bound to cause trouble and, despite the very obvious bottle of Scotch clinking against the front wheel, didn't prevent me from barging through the terminus and into the great outdoors. Apart from the sensation of walking into a rather smelly sauna I was particularly struck by the somnolent atmosphere. Half a dozen trolleys blocked the exit, and it was with some surprise that I realised they weren't being used as beds. Across the road a row of taxis stood around, seemingly quite uninterested in whether any potential fares were coming off the plane. A handful of porters squatted in the shade, deep in discussion and obviously much too hot to bother with the assorted rucksacks that formed the major part of Biman passengers' luggage.

The prospect of cycling off into the heat haze was rather alarming; as far as I could see I would be the only person expending any energy. Dismissing these reservations as both cowardly and contemptible, however, I plunged out into the damp air.

For perhaps a mile all was well; airport approach roads are, even in India, not the most popular places to live. Unfortunately, however, the smooth tarmac and light traffic soon came to an end and I joined some more typical Indian roads. A peeling sign beneath which a couple of men were squatting, presumably to benefit from its shade, showed a curving arrow pointing to 'the City'. But regrettably some earlier accident had smashed the sign and the arrow pointed straight up into the sky. I examined it at length to try and calculate its original position and, having arrived at what seemed to me the most reasonable conclusion, pushed my bike off – narrowly escaping the wagging head of a passing bullock. The driver of the cart, who might have noticed the impending accident, made no attempt to warn me but lazily flicked the bit of string which served as reins to maintain his hazardous passage. Above and around him towered an extraordinary number of kitchen taps.

Fifty yards on, there was a small shanty town, its pavements covered with loose bits of cardboard and corrugated iron. Two women were cleaning metal cooking pots with what appeared to be gravel from the gutter. A group of men stood disconsolately around a burst water pipe taking it in turns to scrub themselves furiously under the resulting shower, and far away some small children and little black pigs were playing in a pond formed by the escaping water. Above this distressing scene an advertisement, possibly for a film, featured an almost indecently overweight man surrounded by several plump and pouting women. All were significantly pinker, as well as immeasurably fatter and more heavily laden with jewels, than any of the real people I could see.

Almost as incongruous as this advertisement, the shanty town was built up around a crossroads controlled by traffic-lights, which introduced an element of sophistication wholly at odds with the surroundings. I pressed on and found myself going deeper and deeper into the crowded depths of a market, attracting a growing crowd of boys who ran along beside me, occasionally hitting my panniers and maintaining a chorus of 'Lo, lo, lo!'

I was somewhat uncertain what to expect, but this scene did seem slightly too off-beat to be the main road from the airport to India's largest commercial city. The street, which had become narrower and narrower, was lined with what appeared to be fairground stalls. Multicoloured fascias, unencumbered by windows or doors, revealed a sort of stage at about chest height on which people were involved in various activities, some demonstrating the ridiculous over-specialisation I'd seen in Turkey: a sewing machinist, a typist, a puncture-repairer and others occupied in, to Western eyes, more lucrative employment, suppliers of grain, rolls of cloth and, incredibly, insurance policies.

Still slightly bemused by what I was seeing, I decided feebly that the insurance broker would probably prove the most reliable source of information. Presumably guessing that I was not interested in buying insurance, the broker – a Sikh sitting behind an attaché case with the most cynically complacent expression I had, at that stage, seen – did not respond when I came to a halt in front of his stall accompanied by the gang of boys.

'Hello. Do you speak English?' I began.

'Of course.'

'I want the city centre.'

'Then you have found it.'

'Hmm.'

He closed his eyes and seemed a little distressed to discover on reopening them that I was still there. I had, however, given further thought to the problem, and was prepared to enlarge on my original question.

'I want to go to Fort.'

'I don't know.'

Anyone who has ever contemplated cycling in India can imagine how encouraging this was. I tried again.

'Where is the Gateway of India?'

'Not here.'

'Where is it?'

'Bombay.'

'How do I get to Bombay?'

'Go straight on and turn right a little and then straight on before turning left. You are going by bicycle?'

'Yes.'

'It is a very long way. It will take you eight to ten hours.'

Quite unexpectedly, a shape which I had assumed was a bizarre stack of papers suddenly turned and began to speak with a most unusual conviction, almost anger.

'It is not eight to ten hours. I myself have often cycled to Bombay. You will be there at . . .' He stared almost disbelievingly at his watch, as if amazed that it was so late. 'You will be there at five o'clock this afternoon.'

That left me five and a half hours, which, although better than the Sikh's estimate, was quite absurd if my guidebook was right in its claim that the centre was about ten miles from the airport.

I plodded off, deeply regretting not having taken a bus or even woken up one of the taxi-drivers sprawled across the front seats of their cabs outside the terminus exit. Worse, I discovered about fifteen minutes later that I was back at the advertisement of the fat man and his tubby floosies. Despairingly, I asked a rickshaw driver how to get to Bombay and with a distinctly fatalistic approach set off again, following his instructions.

The map that I'd held so confidently in the airport unfortunately didn't have any indication of where I might be likely to enter Bombay, so I cycled blindly on until I found a recognisable feature. In fact the first place I came to was Mahim Creek, possibly the most dismal place on earth. I think that it's fairly widely known that Bombay used to consist of seven islands, separated at high tide by the sea, which at low tide left a wilderness of malarious mud-flats where 'two monsoons are the life of a man'. The area around Mahim Creek was the only place I saw which made this unpleasant past vividly clear. Sadly, modern Mahim is probably an even more repulsive place as a huge slum has settled around the bridge, railway line and sewage pipes which are the demarcation lines of the area. The cardboard and scrap-metal houses I'd seen near the airport looked as if they were slowly sinking into the foul-smelling mud, like some satanic version of Venice. I thought morbidly of stopping and exploring this macabre place, but knew that it was much too early in my Indian holiday to contemplate such a task.

Selfishly, I cheered up as I cycled away with an impossibly mundane feeling of satisfaction that at least now I knew where I was. It was a deservedly short-lived pleasure, because I soon found out that my map gave the old British street names of the city, and the address of the hotel that had been booked for me was given in its post-Independence version, apparently used exclusively by bureaucrats and certainly unheard-of amongst the cross-section of Bombay society that I questioned.

At last I found it and, leaving my bike in the custody of an elderly man who had offered his services for a couple of rupees, climbed the three floors to reception. Unfortunately, however, there wasn't any reception. All I found was a young man in a white shirt and baggy blue shorts pushing dust around the floor in what might have been a religious exercise in its devotional nature and complete pointlessness. Without stopping his twitching and shuffling of the wicker brush he announced that the hotel was full.

'I have a reservation.'

'You have a receipt?'

I had to admit that I hadn't, and tried to explain that the reservation had been made for me by friends living in Bombay. He had clearly lost count of the number of times he'd heard that one before. Contemptuously he told me that the hotel was full, adding for effect an angry smacking of his pile of dust.

'Please can I speak to the manager? Will you at least tell him that I'm here,' I said, giving him my name and, a little unnecessarily, my passport. Sighing, he picked up an antique phone and began to explain languidly the undoubtedly fraudulent claims I was making.

I flopped down into one of the wicker chairs and gloomily stared at an old copy of *The Times of India*, which I found on a little table by the chair. Nothing that had happened that day gave me any cause for optimism that a reservation had in fact been made for me or that, if amazingly one had, some deeply regrettable mistake wouldn't mean there was now no room for me.

Some time later – maybe five minutes, maybe several hours – a man came bounding into the room.

'Hello. You have a reservation. Why are you not in your room?'

I was so confused that I began to accept responsibility for this obviously illogical position. 'I wasn't sure if you had received my booking and the telegram that I would be late.'

'Oh yes. Would you like some tea? I'm afraid you've lost the Test match.'

The acknowledgement that it was an interesting subject delighted me more than the actual information upset me. To the man's great surprise, I replied, 'Oh, good. I am pleased. I'd love some tea.'

Days later he challenged me about my reply, wanting to know what terrible matter of principle had been offended to warrant such disloyalty. During that time I realised with some amazement how traumatic my first few hours had been, but I gradually became accustomed to the peculiar Victorian Gothic architecture which made central Bombay look like a series of Yorkshire town halls and imposing Prudential buildings. However, within a week I was looking forward to getting out of the city and away from this curiously mean-spirited architecture into a more flamboyant and exotic India.

Such a highbrow aim was banished after a late-night meeting at the hotel, following my somewhat ritualistic walk back through central Bombay from my friends in Colaba to the hotel behind the Prince of Wales Museum (sadly closed by a strike). A little romantically I tried on these walks, when the dilapidation of the buildings was slightly less obvious and the skyline of steeples, chimneys, arches and turrets could be admired without the jostling that inevitably followed daydreaming on the crowded streets of business hours, to find some link with the old British days and to try and reconcile the starched collars and heavy woollen suits of those times with the inescapably Indian elements – the indescribable smells, the close heat, the nature of the moonlight and the several hundred people who slept on the pavement around the museum.

Such exercises, invariably undertaken in a state of inebriation, were never likely to succeed in view of the unanalytical emotional and sensual state in which they were conducted. Their main effect was that I allowed myself to roll around Bombay until, in the early hours of the morning, I would pull open the long-closed hotel shutters and climb over the various sweepers and clerks who had to sleep on the stairs and in the corridors, and stumble into bed. On one of these uncoordinated rambles I ended what had already been an unsatisfactory evening by barging into the wrong bedroom, an event which at that time of night would normally pass unnoticed.

Unfortunately, however, the occupants were both awake – sitting opposite each other wearing long white cotton shirts. One, who turned out to be a banker based in Tokyo, sat cross-legged with the soles of his feet pressed together, legs splayed apart and his fingers lightly touching his upturned knees. The other was in a similar position except that his fingers were pressed against the sides of his forehead. Had I not slightly delayed making a hasty departure to take in this unusual sight, I might have managed to close the door and escape before they opened their eyes to stare dreamily at this impertinent intrusion.

'I'm sorry,' I said, and started to close the door.

'Forgiveness is a human emotion.'

I felt it appropriate to thank the speaker – Fingers-to-forehead.

'Gratitude is a human emotion.'

'But being is the truth,' stated Fingers-to-knees in what might have been agreement, but was more probably a statement that represented a great chasm between the two believers.

Fingers-to-forehead glared at Fingers-to-knees and, possibly to remind him of the correct lines, observed, 'Being is the universal absolute.'

What could I say? I racked my brain and tried to remember some faded slogan from the sixties, to remind myself of the lyrics of half-heard psychedelic rock bands. At last I thought of Dr Trelawney.

'The essence of the all is the godhead of the true.'

Fingers-to-forehead looked intently at me, obviously having recognised this phrase but uncertain where such a momentous truth originated. Finally he said, 'The vision of visions . . . oh damn, the vision of visions does something to the blind . . . hang on, the blindness of sight . . . cures? Heals . . .?'

'Heals,' I confirmed.

'Are you going to the ashram?'

'Which ashram?'

'*The* ashram.'

'I'll think about it. I'm going to bed now. Good night.'

One thing was clear – after this incident I was going to do all I could to avoid it, or anything like it, happening again. For some this represented my blinkered, if not completely closed, mind, and they would earnestly analyse me in order to discover what it was I was afraid of. In fact, such analysis usually ended up as a form of inquisition which made me even happier that I'd resolved basically to steer clear of the India of 'self-exploration'.

In any case, I was soon faced with the boringly practical issue of how to replace my spare inner tubes, which had mysteriously disappeared between Athens and Bombay. It seems a little fanciful to say that they were stolen, although realistically that must have happened. Whoever carried them off must soon have discovered that they were a completely different design from Indian tubes and therefore presumably worthless (unless they had some rarity value as unusual Western goods). The problem I faced was not greatly helped by my discovery that this fact also meant that it was impossible to buy replacements. I briefly thought about continuing with just the tubes I was using, but became immoderately depressed at the prospect of repairing punctures at the roadside instead of just bunging in a new tube. Indeed I couldn't imagine that anyone would think such a journey, so fraught with dangers and frustration, worth pursuing.

These two incidents convinced me that wherever I went for my week away from Bombay (previously earmarked for the Test match) should be a long way from any ashram, particularly if patronised by Western bankers, and should be sufficiently pleasant for me to stay in the same place throughout. At the time I felt that Goa was the only possible place, and relished the idea of a hut on the fringes of a beach on the Arabian Sea. Further justification, if needed, was that all my advisers were agreed that the steamer from Bombay to Panjim is one of the many Great Indian Experiences.

The peculiar feature of these experiences is that they are only to be had if the most stringent conditions are complied with. Thus, I had to go 'upper deck', to eat the fish curry for lunch and a vegetarian *thali* for dinner. I should have at least one game of 'housey-housey', which I should lose, and I should avoid at all costs playing gin rummy with any tourist who invited me to do so, even at the risk of causing offence. The only thing I didn't know was the correct response to an Indian request to play; though after a great deal of private debate I decided that this should be accepted on the basis that it would in general be a 'good thing' for me to play rummy with the locals.

I need not have worried. 'Upper deck' was occupied exclusively by Western tourists who, having succeeded in fighting their way on board, now loafed around with the air of weary resignation and deep inner torment affected by so many of these self-styled 'travellers'. After tossing and turning for a while, desperately trying to convince my bottom that it was comfortable on the tarred deck boards, I opted out of the fashionable life of assumed hardship and poverty and hired a mattress before beginning *The Master and Margarita*.

The hero had hardly begun to sip his apricot juice at the café in Patriarch's Ponds before my reading was interrupted by a Dutch waif dressed in pitifully thin cotton rags and dragging behind his bare feet a moth-eaten sleeping bag. 'Hello,' he said. 'Do you have any shit?'

I wasn't quite sure how this extraordinary question fitted into my Great Experience or how I was supposed to reply. I was fairly sure that he wanted marijuana, however, and knew that if I told the truth I would, amongst the upper deck occupants, be admitting to an awful social inadequacy. Fortunately, I remembered a conversation I had overheard in a restaurant.

'Sorry, mate. Bombay shit's no bloody good. I'm only into Keralan black.'

It was a triumph. Murmurs of agreement came from all sides. A number of people questioned the entire ethical basis of western India in terms of the dealers behind the Taj Mahal hotel.

'No wonder this country's in such a mess,' concluded one.

'Yeah.'

'Right,' we agreed, deeply satisfied with ourselves.

So the day wore on. I abandoned any hope of finding companions for an amusing game of 'housey-housey', and struggled through quite a reasonable fish curry – though the outraged remarks of militant vegetarians prevented any real enjoyment.

My stay in Goa was pessimistically dismissed by my fellow travellers as a waste of time. Nothing in India could be hurried, I was told by people with voices full of authority and conviction. Staying there for any period of less than three months was just not worth it; I wouldn't be able to get a beach hut, wouldn't have time to make friends and would certainly fail to adjust to the Indian way of life. Saddened by these observations, I unhappily peered at the Portuguese architecture of Panjim, knowing that the baroque churches, villas, squares and alleys would remain unknown to me. Convinced that I would have a puncture at any minute, I cycled slowly towards Colva Beach and pondered on the unseemly haste of my journey.

I was roused from this rather maudlin behaviour by a passing van proudly carrying an enormous hand. At the centre of this a large 'I' for Indira showed it was canvassing for Gandhi's Congress Party. The serious national papers had covered the election in a fairly idiosyncratic way, demonstrating a bias towards Rajiv Gandhi which must have seriously depressed the factious opposition. In any case, all were agreed that Rajiv was the only politician truly sincere in campaigning for a clean-up of politics and who might try and do something about corruption and violence. The press seemed to hold these views primarily on the grounds that his previous lack of involvement, even interest, in politics meant that its corrupting influence hadn't affected him.

Such cynicism was not the attitude of the supporters on the Goanese van, however. Huge photographs of Indira Gandhi lined the sides and a tinny microphone blared out the unexpected slogan:

> Show Indira you love her,
> Show Indira you need her,
> Please vote for Congress I,
> Our love for her will never die.

For the next week dozens of such vans maintained an hourly rendition of the Ricky Vallance song, although canvassing appeared to be limited to the sing-along enthusiasts. The local papers refused to discuss wider issues, possibly reluctant to attribute policies to parties who found them unnecessary. Several featured self-congratulatory articles on the abiding strength of Indian democracy, despite the acknowledged problems of a largely illiterate electorate, intimidation of one's opponents' supporters, lost ballot boxes, rigged registers, uncritical obedience to religious leaders, and the manipulation of the Untouchables' votes. Considerable satisfaction was expressed in comparing this, admittedly flawed, system with the dictatorship of Pakistan and the misery of Bangladesh. More detailed analysis was left for local stories – for example, an enterprising stall-holder who claimed to have solved two of India's most pressing problems, over-population and a shortage of small change, by handing out condoms – or slightly pompous complaints about the propriety of painting party symbols on roads, thus encouraging a disrespectful attitude towards both the election and the politicians.

Sadly, the only speech I saw advertised gave the wrong date, and just as I was about to set off to Panjim to hear Rajiv Gandhi I read in the paper a vigorous leading article complaining that his speech, given the day before, had been made in Hindi, which was considered a particularly disgraceful act of Northern/Delhi arrogance. This lack of political distraction meant that I spent the major part of my time going from my hotel to the beach, from the beach to the secondhand bookshop, and from there to one of the many restaurants that had been put together with bits of driftwood, coconut husks and the other flotsam and jetsam that collects on an Arabian Sea beach.

These restaurants, each of which attracted a highly partisan group of Western tourists, served food immeasurably better than their surroundings would lead one to expect. Their supporters usually based their favouritism on factors other than the quality of food, however, such as how long the food actually took to be served, the extent to which the food provided coincided with the food ordered, the collection of cassettes and the reliability of the cassette-recorder. For many, this was their only topic of conversation, and the cocktail hour was usually wasted with anguished debates about where to have dinner. Everyone would put forward their favourite candidate, to be met with horrified cries from others who had suffered some abomination at the suggested place. The result, as compromise was clearly impossible, was almost invariably to walk miles up the beach to an untried restaurant which nobody except the lazy could justifiably boycott.

In the course of one of these journeys up the beach, to a restaurant

which had a highly recommended bouillabaisse, I was savagely mauled
by one of the many stray dogs that lurked around the undergrowth. It
is in the nature of such unexpected and undeserved violence that subsequent analysis fails to produce any motive for it. One minute I was
wandering along, happily admiring the combination of a particularly
colourful sunset, the crashing of the waves and the outlines of dozens
of palm trees, and the next I had a dog gnawing at my ankle.

Just a few days before, it will be remembered, a pair of Turkish
soldiers had whiled away a boring patrol by firing a bullet at me and
sticking a gun in my face. Few could disagree that my calm consideration of what would happen to my carpets if, as briefly seemed likely,
the soldiers went on to kill me demonstrated a remarkable equanimity
likely to see me through most foreseeable crises. Absolutely nobody,
however, could dissent from the proposition that little is more unpleasant than dying from rabies. I vividly and clearly saw myself
writhing on the floor, foaming at the mouth and dementedly trying to
bite people.

'Aaah,' I squeaked, before holding up my hands in the desperate
hope that I might find something I could use to haul myself out of the
situation. The dog contemptuously barked, before resuming its assault.
Eventually I remembered that I had two feet, and that so far the dog
had confined its attentions to my right. Years of playing football had
confirmed my suspicion that my left leg was really only useful for
standing on, an impression briefly dispelled as I kicked the dog in what
I hoped were its kidneys, simultaneously letting out a wild and in-
coherent scream. This combination briefly caused the dog to let go,
perhaps the decisive moment in determining the result of the fight, and
I was then able to use my right foot to establish an undoubtedly Pyrrhic
victory.

Both the dog and I crept miserably away, the dog no doubt to
reflect on the disadvantages of attacking someone bigger than itself,
and me to examine the seriousness of the damage. After perhaps ten
minutes gloomily studying my ankle, I thought that if I was going to
go mad it might as well be after the recommended bouillabaisse.
Arming myself with a stick, I resumed my walk along the beach and
regretted not having thoroughly researched the timetable of rabies-
induced madness and death. Naturally, my first question on arriving at
the restaurant was what, if anything, people knew about rabies.

'The bite must have broken the skin,' said one.

Optimistically I shoved my foot on the table and demanded their
opinion.

'Of course the skin's broken.'

'Ugh. You know you must have fourteen injections.'

'And they're in the stomach.'

'Gosh. Imagine having them in India.'

'How long before you start frothing at the mouth?'

'Do you think he'll start biting us?'

It was obvious they knew no more than I did. Angrily I told them to shut up and stop being so alarmist, as I reconciled myself to enjoying my last few hours.

The next morning I carefully examined my pillow for signs of nocturnal frothing. There were none. I peered intently into a mirror for early evidence of crazy facial contortions. There were none. A little heartened by this apparent normality, I cycled off to Margao, where I was assured I would find the best rabies doctor in Goa. She was situated on the third floor of the building to my left as I walked away from the covered market towards the station, I was told – instructions which, despite my complete lack of confidence in them, proved exceptionally accurate.

Unfortunately, in carrying them out I had to walk through the covered market, part of which was occupied by ear-cleaners and street dentists. The ear-cleaners, who often touted their unpleasant practices on the Colva beach, relied exclusively upon bicycle spokes and dirty cottonwool, while the dentists displayed a wider collection of tools, none of which looked remotely like anything seen in a Western surgery nor, more particularly, anything I wanted anywhere near my mouth. For a few minutes I wallowed in dreadful images of the rabies specialist's methods and the horrors that were about to overwhelm me. Finally I trudged up the staircase, lugging my bike past the offices of lawyers, accountants and insurance brokers.

A cruelly jovial woman wearing a spotless white coat bellowed at me that she didn't do bikes.

'I've been bitten by a dog,' I wailed.

'What? On your bike? That's unlucky.'

'No, no, no. On the beach. I was going to a restaurant . . .'

'Which beach?' she interrupted.

'Colva.'

'Was it a black dog?'

'I don't know. It was dark.'

'Oh well, let me see the wound.'

We peered at my ankle, which when seen under the cold medical eye suddenly seemed remarkably undamaged. Shuffling a little, I mumbled something about being in Margao anyway and, well, though I wasn't really worried about it I thought it might be worth checking up on. After all, I rambled on, one hears about dogs with rabies.

'Did your dog have rabies?'

'I don't know. How could I tell?'

'I think you'd know. There is a black dog with rabies in Colva . . . Mmm . . . I don't think you have it. Do you want the injections anyway?'

I gulped. 'Is it fourteen injections?'

'Well, it is unless you had the preventive injections before you were bitten.'

'And then?' I whispered, happily realising that I had.

'You only need one injection and then you have complete immunity for six months.'

I yelped and did a little jig before crying 'Whoopee!'

'Please, please. Now you can go back to your bicycle.'

'It's great!' I trilled. 'I'm cycling from England to China.'

'How fascinating. How did you like Pakistan?'

'Er, well, I flew over Pakistan.'

'Why?'

'The Iranians wouldn't give me a visa,' I feebly replied.

'So you didn't go to Iran?' she asked incredulously.

'Mm, not really. I meant to. Well, you see they wouldn't give me a visa quickly enough.'

'Well, have a good ride to China,' she sneered. 'And now, please roll up your sleeve.'

Feeling decidedly shamefaced, I cycled back to Colva determined to do something about establishing my credibility as a long-distance cyclist. The immediate prospects were discouraging. In a few days my girlfriend was flying out to see me before we left for a luxurious tour of the various palace hotels of Rajasthan and, apart from sending a telegram to supplement an earlier letter requesting replacement inner tubes, nothing very tangible emerged from this guilty feeling that I was being a fraud. A couple of days later I cycled up to Panjim to catch the steamer back to Bombay. I had in the twelve days since landing in India cycled no more than about seventy miles, a total which hardly seemed adequate. Resolutely I plotted routes as I relived the Great Indian Experience, to which was added the bonus of sailing into Bombay. Something, I knew, had to be done.

6

Christmas in Rajasthan

The steamer docked in Bombay at eight o'clock in the morning. In my new determined mood I barged my way through the crowds, frantically trying to be the first to disembark. My bike, resplendent with awkward handlebars and pedals, proved an excellent weapon to help me get through. Grimly I pedalled off, anxious to make progress with my plans to cycle the route carefully worked out on the passage up from Goa. Less than two hours later, after depositing my bags at the hotel, I marched into the offices of the Western Indian Automobile Association to buy some detailed maps and to ask their advice on road surfaces, accommodation and other practical matters.

According to my *Shorter Oxford Dictionary* the word 'automobile' was first used in America in 1886, and whoever designed the Bombay offices of the WIAA had clearly been a member of the etymological school of architecture. The interior resembled nothing so much as an out-of-the-way telegraph office somewhere in the mid-West – somnolent, even bored, but shortly to be visited by a notorious bunch of hoodlums. This atmosphere was conveyed not just by the antiquated furniture and filing system, and the clerks sitting in waistcoats with their shirt-sleeves held up by elastics, but also by the gloomy bunch of people who huddled morosely together in the wholly inadequate waiting area.

Only one voice disturbed the tense, silent atmosphere, and this belonged appropriately to a fat and obviously prosperous businessman who was loudly castigating one of the identikit clerks for not providing the right information on importing a foreign car, a mistake which had apparently led to the car being held indefinitely at the docks. The clerk sat transfixed, as if the news of his inefficiency had resulted in an utterly immobilising seizure. His white knuckles gripped an invoice which presumably related to the imported car and his eyes, startled and numb, were fixed upon it.

Beside these two, another clerk was shuffling some papers before a large woman who looked remarkably like one of the pouting women I had seen on the film hoarding near the airport. Other funereal scenes stretched away into the dark corners of the office, each desk reinforcing the impression that nothing of any use had ever been achieved here. Despondently, I joined the collection of people gathered haphazardly around the entrance.

Some ten minutes later I was longing to sit down if I was going to continue my hopeless vigil. The only free chair was beside the pouting woman, who was still patiently waiting for the clerk to find whatever document he was hunting for. Almost on tip-toe I inched towards the chair, gently tapped the back and, murmuring, asked if I could borrow it. The woman glared at me, angry for some unfathomable reason, and the clerk merely raised his sad eyes to try and confirm that I really had made such an outrageous request.

'What is it you want?' he eventually asked, obviously reluctant to believe this revolutionary proposition.

For a moment I debated whether to repeat my simple request to borrow the chair, or whether to state boldly the real reason for my presence in the building. Glancing round, I saw that there was still a complete absence of activity or achievement, and pessimistically concluded that this might be the only interest shown in me for several days. So I opted for the real reason and asked if I was at the right place to buy maps and make one or two enquiries about cycling in India.

The pouting woman grabbed a handkerchief from somewhere in the nether regions of her voluminous sari and began to mop her brow furiously. The clerk looked puzzled, and with considerable confusion turned to the other clerk, who was still being harangued by the fat car-importer.

'Is he a member of the WIAA?' queried the catatonic clerk, in what was the first sign that the seizure hadn't bereft him of speech or action. 'He must be a member of the WIAA.'

'I'm not a member,' I said, anticipating the question about to come as the shuffling clerk turned expectantly back towards me. 'But all I really want are some detailed maps, which I think won't take long.'

There was a long silence. Clearly this situation had never faced him before. Eventually he asked in a bewildered voice, 'What do you want maps of? What do you want maps for?'

'I want to cycle from here to Cape Cormorin and then up to Madras. I only have a large map bought in England which isn't detailed enough. Do you have any maps of each state on a large scale?'

'You are cycling! This will take a very long time. There are many dangers and difficulties. You must put your request in writing. I think so much work must go into this task.'

'Can I buy the maps now?' I pleaded.

'Please put your route in writing and ask all the questions you have when you give us the information.'

It was obvious that, although I had been successful in queue-barging, such behaviour would never succeed in speeding up the workings of the WIAA. Thanking both clerks, I asked if they would consider a written application from me, even though I was not a member, and upon their assurances that they would I left this scene from the late nineteenth-century mid-West to return to the familiar Victorian architecture that surrounded their office. It was an inauspicious start to my new determined approach to get things going, particularly as the next task I had set myself was another Great Indian Experience (grade two) in terms of the level of bureaucratic obstruction I was likely to face. Pessimistically, I pedalled up towards the station to book train tickets to Agra for Laura and myself.

As with the Goan steamer, which had to be enjoyed under the most stringent conditions, I had been given detailed instructions as to which class I should travel in, how to ensure I would get a ticket by pretending to be a VIP, the enormous problems I would face when I was first confronted by one of the seat reservation forms and exactly how long I should allow for queueing for tickets. The general consensus of opinion was that unless I travelled in a reserved second-class mail or express train with a two-tier sleeper at right angles to the window I would suffer the most unspeakably awful deprivations. I took comfort from the fact that, as I had left my booking to just two days before the chosen date of departure, these experiences would remain undiscovered as I would never succeed in getting a seat, let alone two reserved berths. I had rather dismissed these unhappy prophecies, but as I cycled away from the WIAA they seemed remarkably optimistic assessments of what was likely to happen.

The scene at the station lacked the somnolent atmosphere of the WIAA offices, the gloomy people waiting to be seen and the general air of depression. The only similar features were the slow and method-ical clerks who here presided over the tempestuous anarchy of the station. Hundreds of people achieved the impossible by charging in twenty different directions at once, or staggered beneath huge loads of trunks, suitcases, cooking equipment and mysterious embroidered sacks. Some, more sanguine, sat silently around a steaming pot waiting for the eventual result, seemingly oblivious to the chaos around them.

Nothing in this labyrinthine ferment gave me any feeling of confidence that I would succeed even in establishing that all tickets had been sold, let alone emerging with a couple of tickets for a train leaving two days later direct to Agra, as in fact happened. This remarkable feat was achieved by the straightforward expedient of asking the man at the enquiry counter if he could help me buy the tickets. Incredibly, in all the frenzied activity nobody else seemed to find the services of this man useful so, rather than send me off to Counter 12 or whatever, he completed the reservation form for me – asking me my name, age, sex and date of departure – and disappeared with the form and some money to return a couple of minutes later with the tickets. Seen in terms of outmanoeuvring the system, this was by far my most successful day in India. With some jubilation I cycled back to the hotel, and in possibly my most over-excited and over-optimistic mood yet I solemnly sat down to try and complete my statement of intent for the WIAA.

My euphoria was short-lived. The train reservation had been made to allow Laura, who was flying out to see me, thirty-six hours to recover from the effects of the flight from London. But unfortunately, fog in Damascus meant that while I was waiting at the airport Laura was languishing in Cyprus. I had expected *some* delay of course. My friends in Bombay, who had wasted endless hours waiting for the various cheap airlines to deign to land, had eventually decided on a six-hour compromise so that in my situation, for example, if Syrian Airways announced an arrival time of six-fifteen in the morning I could drift gently up to meet the plane slightly after midday. Foolishly I ignored their advice, which was in fact hopelessly optimistic as the plane eventually made it at 3 a.m. the next day, in the middle of the great rush hour of long-haul flights. The baggage-handlers, who presumably had stopped fighting each other over the difficulties with my bike, had decided, I suppose quite reasonably, that people flying on a reputable airline which showed some concern for the advertised times of departure and arrival would provide a more profitable tip than the impoverished masses who were dumped by the more cavalier air companies. I watched the labels despondently as the baggage slowly arrived until finally, an hour and a half after landing, Laura staggered through the customs section and, as they say, into my arms.

I was very conscious that in about twelve hours we would set off on a thirty-six-hour train journey, sleeping on wooden planks and eating the few pickings offered on station platforms. Upon checking with the hotel, I had discovered that we would be expected to leave the premises by midday, which emphasised the near cruelty that I was imposing.

We climbed into a taxi, and while I half-heartedly rambled on about Turkey and the depressing state of my stomach we watched with considerable fascination the rows of people crouched determinedly on their haunches, *dhotis* gathered up, and raptly defecating. Back at the hotel, we climbed over the bodies of people sleeping in the street and avoided those carefully washing beneath a water pump, pulled open the shutters and climbed wearily up to an early breakfast.

For the next few hours we drifted rather aimlessly around some of the more indispensable sights of Bombay, missing the Prince of Wales Museum, still closed by an unexplained strike, and the Towers of Silence, considered too remote and, in any case, a little too ghoulish for Laura's first few hours. Finally, after a slightly pointless division of our luggage between items to take and those which could remain behind, we thought about heading off to the station, an event preceded by a last check on essentials. In the course of this, and possibly one hour before the train departed, I discovered that somewhere on our distracted and weary excursions I had succeeded in losing the tickets. Only one outcome seemed possible, that we would be prevented from boarding the now fully booked train and have to stay for an eternity in Bombay. Incredibly, however, the requirement that I provided names, ages and addresses – which I had thought so absurd at the time – meant that the enquiry man, still ignored by the other passengers yet still marvellously helpful to me, was able to arrange a certificate from the police reporting the loss, and for a small fee the replacement of our lost tickets.

Clutching these securely, we found the appropriate platform, climbed aboard an ochre cattle truck and sat morosely on the wooden boards we were to spend the next two nights on. The other people in the compartment had already laid out mattresses and quilts and changed into pyjamas, and were sitting there with what seemed an absurdly exaggerated serenity.

Interrupting their reflections, I asked if this was the right train for Agra. Only one of the five considered that it was, an encouraging result in one sense because he too was going to Agra, so wherever we ended up at least three of us could point to the confusion at the station to justify our mistake. The other four insisted that the train was variously going to Delhi, Dehra Dun or Kanpur. The fifth was the Dehra Dun man's wife, who watched over the proceedings with a quiet satisfaction and never spoke for the twenty-four hours or so we shared the compartment, except very softly as she handed food to her husband.

We made the decision to stay on board with almost no debate or anxiety at all, having begun to adopt a slightly fatalistic approach towards train rides to Agra, and not in the least unhappy at the prospect of arriving at any of the alternative destinations. Any discussion about this dilemma was quickly silenced by the final occupant's arrival, a young Sikh wearing rather incongruous dark glasses. He was obviously conscious of the sudden hush, even animosity, caused by his arrival and huddled against the window staring at the platform. A couple of minutes later the train heaved its way out towards wherever it was.

The next morning I noticed that the Sikh had left the compartment, presumably of his own volition. We had been woken early by the Dehra Dun man, who offered us a tin, lined with thick cotton and filled with steaming samosas. Neither Laura nor I could imagine how they had arrived, or if they had been brought on to the train how they had been kept warm, but left that issue unresolved as we gratefully took two for breakfast. Anxious to direct my thanks to the real provider, I smiled at Mrs Dehra Dun, who turned bashfully away though she continued to offer food throughout the day. Her husband, who had rather annoyed me by his unpleasant behaviour towards his wife, made considerable amends by talking enthusiastically about the English cricket tour. A little sycophantically, we both praised beyond all conceivable merit the various talents of the other side, something made easier by the squaring of the series in Delhi just two days before, following England's defeat in the Bombay Test.

The discussion became increasingly difficult because, as the train slowly steamed north, the compartment was opened to unreserved passengers during the day, and they succeeded in cramming more people on to the benches than I would have thought possible. Sitting with elbows digging into my ribs and someone's foot about six inches from my face, I realised that I might quite enjoy cycling when I eventually started, although, peering out across the dusty plains of northern India, I could imagine one or two difficulties. The slow speed of the train provided quite a good opportunity to examine the surrounding countryside, particularly as the train frequently and mysteriously ground to a halt and remained stationary for periods of up to forty-five minutes. It looked as though we were passing through an uninhabited and uninhabitable desert until we saw, at the first unexplained stop, that the bushes and trees were full of people laden down with baskets of bananas, tangerines and, sometimes, nuts. Once the train had demonstrated an intention to stop, these people would start sprinting towards it, jump on and usually manage to sell their wares.

Assuming that there was no collusion between these sellers and the engine driver, which in any case could not have been based on anything other than sympathy as they could not have afforded any financial inducement, their presence – based on a faint hope that a train would happen to stop by whichever tree or bush they had settled under – emphasised how marginal their existence was. I gloomily began to reflect on the misery of their lives and the implications of cycling through their villages and eating what I assumed would be a disproportionate amount of food, when I was interrupted by one of the sellers who, having sold all his goods, then provided a sort of cabaret act occasionally assisted by a small monkey. Surprisingly, it was a performance which continued for slightly more than four hours, divided between the ten or so compartments in our carriage but never out of earshot.

The conjurer left the train at our last big stop before the second night on the boards began. Foolishly, we hadn't considered the drop in temperature that would occur as we moved hundreds of miles north and both spent a rather miserable night suffering from freezing cold and impossibly sharp bones quite incompatible with the boards. At ten the next morning we were put out of our misery by the train's arrival at Agra Fort. The other passenger who had come up from Bombay with us insisted on negotiating with the rickshaw drivers on our behalf, explaining that they were widely considered a disgrace to their country. Too tired to bother with trying to win a good deal for ourselves, we accepted, to find that he managed to obtain the highly satisfactory outcome of a scooter for the day for just ten rupees.

We had been given a recommendation for one of the hotels in the Indian part of the city, and we tried to persuade the driver to take us there – completely without success as the hotel concerned wouldn't give him a commission. He agreed, however, to take us to the *area* of the hotel, and we plunged into a chaotic mass of houses, clumsily leaning against each other, filthy living quarters and bazaars stretching out along an irregular central street beyond the open tunnels of the drains.

To the south of this area lay the old British cantonment, rows of peeling bungalows standing in large, overgrown gardens beside wide, straight streets laid out on an obvious grid pattern and methodically signposted. The few buildings not in danger of imminent collapse were generally used as hotels, and we set off on an unwanted tour of the more expensive of these as the driver searched for his commission. In due course we tired of this pointless waste of time and demanded a cheaper place than those costing 200 rupees a night, which the driver promised was the going rate in Agra. Assuming an authoritative bellow, I informed him that we should pay no more than 75 rupees, and if he didn't know such a place we'd find another driver who did.

With an alarming screech of the tiny tyres we thereupon roared up a gravel drive to a particularly dilapidated building surrounded by terraced lawns, one of which had a few tables and chairs scattered haphazardly around. At one of these tables a group of three men were sprawled, looking like a scene from the final moments of a debauched party. The rickshaw driver yelled towards this unpromising group, one of whom burped out some answer which the driver – no doubt generously – translated as a request that we sit down and have a cup of coffee while we waited for the manager, who was regrettably busy in his office.

A few minutes later, during which time no effort was visibly made to convey the coffee order to anyone able to meet it, a fat man wearing a white, baggy shirt and an orange tea-towel draped around his waist shuffled towards us looking as if he had just got out of bed, an impression enhanced by the small candle he carried in his right hand. The sensation of fresh air and daylight was obviously too traumatic for him, as a minute later he abandoned his slow promenade of the garden and drifted back to the small extension, which I then noticed had a sign dangling from one of the pieces of washboard proclaiming 'Reception'.

His return to 'Reception' possibly reminded him that he had shortly before abandoned his task to receive two tourists who might still be around. With evident bewilderment he peered around the tables, saw us and came halfway towards us before declaring that he had a room for 70 rupees which we could have as long as we stayed less than three nights.

My request to see the room caused him such pain that, wincing slightly, he turned and went back to the extension. The driver looked simultaneously pleased at our discomfort and nervous about his own position, which remained a little uncertain. We sat around for a bit longer, waiting for the coffee and considering the peremptory offer of a room. It was a deadlock the driver instinctively knew was unlikely to be resolved, but as he had some interest in the eventual outcome, he determined to make the decision for us. He raced off to the group of sleeping men, kicked one of their splayed-out hands and demanded some information. Satisfied with the answer, which was a vague wave towards the gloomy bungalow and some more burping, he inspected two rooms and came back to us with the information that the room at the slightly higher rate of 75 rupees was better value. Despite our annoyance at his earlier insistence that we should spend as much money as possible, we both nodded and gurgled some agreement to his proposal, before returning to our vacant, semi-conscious states. The driver reminded us that we had hired him for the day and went off to join the three sleepers, curling himself up under the shade of the table.

Perhaps thirty minutes later a boy nervously tapped my shoulder to announce the arrival of our coffee, an occurrence which seemed almost miraculous in the great swampy lethargy that had descended on the gardens. To his disappointment we used the opportunity of being awake to shuffle into one of the rooms we'd seen the driver inspect, and collapsed wearily on to the beds – which were marginally more comfortable than the train boards.

We eventually woke, almost feeling refreshed, and found our rickshaw driver to let him know that after a coffee we wanted to be taken to the tomb of Itimad-ud-daula, the Chini-ka-ruaza and the Taj Mahal at sunset. Even if I had wanted to, it would have been impossible to forget the presence of the Taj; in Bombay it appeared on tea-towels, posters and postcards, had been modelled in every size and in every conceivable type of material and could be found adorning lampshades, cushions and bedspreads. This overkill in some ways encouraged a certain cynicism. Throughout my stay in Goa I heard people explaining how the Taj was just an exploited landmark which should be left to the tour parties. There was much amused sympathy for those who considered that a monument built by an occupying force – who thought the 'real' Hindu architecture of India repulsive, grey and vulgar and who proceeded to destroy every temple they could find in northern India – could be perceived as the quintessentially Indian building.

Its extraordinary beauty is in some ways a little out of place in modern India. To walk away from the extravagance of the semi-precious stones inlaid in marble and then be carted off by some chap on ten rupees a day, to compare the poise and elegance of the white marble tomb set in its spacious grounds with the turmoil of the Indian section of the city inevitably causes one temporarily to question the justification for such a building. But for such an emotional reaction to become one's permanent view of the Taj seems strange.

The travellers' demands for contemporary relevance did not, for some reason, apply to Fatepur Sikri, the deserted city some twenty miles from Agra, abandoned after about twenty years because the water was polluted. Built to celebrate the birth of Akbar's son Salim, it was effectively an Emperor's playground: a marble mosque yellowing through age in a vast courtyard paved with red tiles, with a decorated marble basin in the middle and a large abundant tree. All around there were little palaces, built in soft red standstone, the dominant colour of the town. From courtyard to courtyard one passed from the palace of the King to the palace of the women to the palace of meetings and the palace of the 'Divan'.

The modern town of Fatepur Sikri lies perhaps fifty yards from the great Bulad Darwaza, the gateway to the ancient city built to com- memorate Akbar's conquest of Gujerat. Standing at the gates, one looks down at the crowded roofs of the modern town and hears a great cacophony of noise coming from the unseen inhabitants: hammers bashing, sewing machines, bicycle bells and the strange sound of hun- dreds of people talking to each other. The design looked like the construction for a revolutionary barricade, the shops the familiar temporary-looking stalls huddled together, selling what seemed an absurdly narrow range of products. Why, I wondered, hadn't the local population simply moved into the palace when the Emperor left? I knew that now the international tourist circuit had reached the place there would be an international outcry if it happened today, but I imagined the palace remaining empty and unrecognised for centuries while, below, people lived in hovels. (When I later saw people living in the old Dravidian buildings of Vijayanagar, now called Hampi, I wanted to go back to Fatepur to point out that it had been done.)

A little callously, I abandoned such concern for their living accom- modation when watching two people – each with, at most, a quarter of an inch of toe placed on the platform – attempting to squeeze on to a bus. Three people, including the conductor, were pushing them in with a succession of terrifying whoops and screams until, at last, and quite incredibly, the passengers already aboard somehow moulded themselves even closer together to allow the two on. As another bus was already waiting to take that bus's place I couldn't understand why the two didn't just wait another five minutes for the next one. Re- signedly I concluded that perhaps Indians were so used to crowds, discomfort and struggle that it formed an essential feature of their lives, not to be discarded just because an empty bus, or an empty Emperor's playground happened to come along.

A snake-charmer then shuffled into the bus station to confirm my rather disappointing conclusion that I didn't understand India, and was unlikely to do so. Two sad, downcast snake-eyes peered out of a rather jowly head which desperately tried to sway in time to the thin music played by an equally down-at-heel charmer. The main achievement of this bedraggled pair was probably that they were still able to inspire each other to do just a little more than remain stationary before slowly and unhappily collapsing.

Wearily shaking my head at how incomprehensible it all was, I suddenly realised that the bus-driver had just climbed into his seat and blasted the horn – presumably to announce the bus's imminent departure. At least forty other people had come to the same conclusion and a huge scrum had developed around the doors, so dense that no one was actually succeeding in getting on to the bus. I took advantage of the congestion by following the example of three or four others who were climbing through the open windows and thus grabbing hold of one of the few available seats. I hauled Laura up after me, and we sat feeling tremendously pleased with ourselves and rather ostentatiously began to read books, occasionally leaning out of the window to ask the crowd to calm down a little.

Such behaviour was, unfortunately, rather premature. Once the crowd managed to unravel itself the bus quickly filled up and soon resembled the earlier bus which we had so disdainfully thought we would never bother to travel upon. Someone dumped a large basket of bananas on Laura's lap, while, before I had a chance to complain, two people plonked themselves on me. Leaning hard against the two on my lap, a crowd of eight more stood in a space comfortable for, at most, two – more were pressing down upon us, preventing us from squeezing off the bus to catch a taxi. From outside I could hear anguished cries as people were pushed millimetre by millimetre aboard. Eventually, at a stage when I had to breathe in unison with the half dozen people pressed against my chest or risk suffocation, the bus, triumphantly blowing its horn, lurched out of the car park and began the twenty-mile journey back to Agra.

It was inconceivable that we would ever get there as the bus swayed helplessly along the narrow roads. If we weren't crushed to death I was sure that we would crash into a ditch or river and that none of us would be able to move or even wriggle a finger to signal our dismay. I began to appreciate the importance of religion and was about to undergo some major devotional changes when the conductor somehow presented himself in front of us and demanded the fare. There was no plausible explanation as to how he had done so, or how, after he had taken the money, he managed to move through the crowd to those further down the bus. It was either magic or a miracle. Too frightened to speculate further, I abandoned these supernatural explorations and concentrated on the successful coordination of my breathing.

Back at the bus station the rickshaw driver, who had offered to stay with us throughout our time in Agra, complained bitterly about the length of time we'd been at Fatepur, on the unlikely grounds that the bus station was an unpleasant place full of nasty characters. We had already negotiated a deal with him whereby he was paid ten rupees a day by us, which he supplemented with visits to two shops where he would be given a small amount for taking tourists, regardless of whether they actually bought anything. The amount varied but was always between two and five rupees, the difference depending on how genuinely interested the shop-owner considered the tourists to be. Five-rupee shops demanded such extraordinary interest to be shown, and such lengthy examination of their collections of ivory, jewellery and carpets, that in general we stayed within the meaner, less prosaic worlds of the two-rupee shops, and very occasionally sank to the almost bestial level of one-rupee dives.

This arrangement appeared to be pretty foolproof, allowing us the satisfaction of having our rickshaw driver at a subsidised rate (and helping to salve our consciences at paying so little), and presumably giving some satisfaction to the driver, who cleverly increased the original rate negotiated for us at the station. There was, in fact, a loophole. Few people, if any, can tour these souvenir/antique shops without eventually seeing something that they want to buy. By the end of the second day of this scheme we had bargained fiercely for marble elephants, plates, earrings and, inevitably, carpets.

I had had a lot of letters from home, and even amongst those who supported the mass purchasing of oriental carpets there was a move towards believing that I had bought enough. Some based this on the pleasure to be gained in collecting them over a period of several years, each one representing the nice holiday we had in Islamabad, or successfully completing the tour of Hittite ruins. For such people, to have bought five on one holiday was quite indecent. Others, more practically, warned against buying so many without a sound knowledge of the history, designs and methods of handmade carpets and the range available in London, which any number of people assured me were often at prices 'cheaper than source', a statement which seemed to reduce the Middle and Far East to the status of a cut-price warehouse called Source.

Many more people raved against the monstrous working conditions that my purchases perpetuated, that I was encouraging slavery, child labour, blindness, rotting fingers and the maintenance of all evil. A few sarcastically queried how I had carried five carpets from Turkey to

India on a bicycle, apparently taking seriously my claim that I was cycling from England to China.

These criticisms became the vicious ramblings of mean-minded morons when I stood shaking with excitement in front of the staggering Persian designs I saw in Agra. Such banal trivia as the number of knots, the age, the use of vegetable or chemical dye seemed pathetically philistine – like asking the capacity of the Taj, or how many visitors it had on an annual basis. Unlike the Taj, though, these could be mine.

Fortunately, the hotel insisted that we left after the three nights we had originally agreed would be the maximum length of our stay, otherwise I think it inevitable that I would now be languishing in some debtors' gaol, having bought countless more than the two which I happily, almost deliriously, arranged to have shipped back to England. In any case, the rickshaw driver was thoroughly fed up at having agreed such a marginal daily rate with people who went and bought two enormously expensive carpets. Sulking bitterly as we cycled off to the station, he demanded a letter from me confirming that it was entirely due to the good offices of Mr X the rickshaw driver that we had ever gone to the shop, and that it was only reasonable the shop should give some percentage to the driver.

The important relationship between rickshaw drivers, carpets and commission was treated with equal seriousness in Jaipur. Still suffering from the effects of another hard bench journey, we acquired another driver who wanted to earn extra money by taking us to some of his tame shops. His initial indignation when I began to negotiate a similar deal to the one we had in Agra changed to utter dismay when I went on to tell him that from now on he could only take us to places which paid for appearances in shops, not commission on actual sales, as I had bought two carpets and couldn't afford anything else.

'You must not buy anything in Agra. The rickshaw drivers are so dishonest in Agra. The shops are so dishonest in Agra. The carpets are no good in Agra. The whole city is for tourists, it is not for you. You must buy in Jaipur. If an Indian wants to buy a carpet he comes to Jaipur. If an Indian wants to sell a carpet he goes to Agra . . .'

'Then they'd be right to do so, because I'd buy a carpet in Agra and nowhere else,' I indignantly replied, a little annoyed by this howling about an irreversible purchase.

For some inexplicable reason the result of this conversation was an agreement to visit a carpet factory the next day, where the error of my ways would be forcefully brought home to me. This rather masochistic decision on my part was primarily based on the worthy aim of seeing how the carpets I'd bought, now seven in total, were made.

It was a visit which brought further distress, though not because I found superior carpets there, as I had feared. Inside a dingy den a rotund Sikh was presiding over a collection of manifest rubbish, the whole atmosphere polluted by the awful rotten-egg smell of cheap cigars being smoked by a seedy-looking Englishman slumped in an armchair in one of the darkest corners of this unpleasant place. His grubby desert boots tapped angrily as the claims for the inherent qualities of these carpets grew more and more extravagant, until finally he could stand no more.

'Tell 'em about the tax they'll have to pay when they get home,' he blustered, accompanying the words with a great waft of cigar smoke. The customers, who I think were Dutch, peered sympathetically in his direction and, in a quiet, confident tone said they didn't think there was any duty.

'There is in England,' he snorted, obviously refusing to accept that any country could deviate from English patterns of behaviour.

'There isn't,' I chipped in, suddenly acutely conscious of my seven carpets about to arrive into the greedy clutches of the Customs and Excise men.

He spat out another puff of smoke, and studied the soggy stub.

'Last time my brother went back, he had to pay . . .', he chewed away at his stub, 'he had to pay thirty-eight per cent.'

'Eahg, aar, og, og, og,' I observed. Laura remained silent.

'Thirty-eight per cent,' he mused. 'That's what they charged him . . . the buggers.'

'They couldn't have done,' I succeeded in gasping.

'Thirty-eight per cent,' he reiterated, and stared bleakly at the floor as if asking it for confirmation of this dreadful pronouncement.

The rotund Sikh wisely decided that this conversation was unlikely to encourage me to buy any of his mouldy offerings, and grandly announced that the tour of the workshop would begin. We trailed off to watch the time-consuming activities necessary to complete a handmade carpet – the weaving, the cutting, the singeing of excess wool, the washing and the drying – distressingly justifying the high prices charged, soon to be so cruelly increased by HMG.

Worse, the information soured the subsequent tours of the various palaces of Jaipur and nearby Amber, as we stared at the disintegrating carpets made centuries before for the local maharajahs. If even theirs didn't last, we illogically concluded, we faced irreversible penury for a transient pleasure, impossible to justify to whichever bankruptcy court bothered to hear the sad tale. Slowly I succumbed to the ever-present nagging of my Turkish tummy problems and flopped into bed, where I discovered the Christmas stocking so carefully concealed from me, and now opened in such unhappy circumstances.

Wallowing in self-pity, I dedicated myself to the relentless consumption of the various bottles that made up the bulk of the presents, occasionally finding sufficient reserves of optimism to continue my reading of *Anna Karenina*, which I'd found on one of the secondhand bookstalls in Bombay. From time to time, when the savage convulsions were at their lowest and least traumatic, I would go out and, clutching at Laura's arm, stand at a street corner to try and imagine what it would be like to cycle.

The pot-holes, I concluded, could be avoided. The lorries, though driven in an insanely selfish manner, were obviously fitted with horns which blared permanently, so I should be able to avoid a collision with them. The rickshaw drivers, scooter drivers, camel-cart drivers and the car drivers at least drove in the centre of the road, and usually broadcast any intention to change course. The problem was that no such logic applied to the pedestrians, cyclists and cows who all possessed one characteristic: a tendency to walk out into the road – without the slightest concern, attention or observation – and stop, if the mood took them at any point of the road, for a chat, a rest or simply to watch the world go by. Among 700 million pedestrians, of whom perhaps half were also cyclists, and 176 million cows, it was inconceivable that I would remain unscathed. I began to have nightmares about the results of the collisions to come, and faintly remembered stories of the hacking to pieces of those involved in accidents by friends of the victim. Would anyone take my part when I crashed into someone crossing the road, or would everyone relish the opportunity of stabbing a machete into me?

Laura, who was by then both bored and alarmed by my continual nightmares, declared that for the remainder of the time we spent together we would abandon cheap hotels and restaurants and move into the luxury of the Rajasthani palace hotels, eating in the more expensive Chinese restaurants. In Jodhpur we listened to the well-rehearsed stories told by a maharajah of his ancestors' battles against Alexander the Great, and fell asleep in the hotel he ran to the distant sounds of tigers growling, crocodiles snapping and parrots squawking which came, appropriately, in our newly sanitised and distanced world, from the nearby zoo. Suddenly, it was rather like being on a film set, and everyone began to cooperate in this new India: walking up the hill to Jodhpur Fort we would seemingly electrify small groups of people who would suddenly shake themselves out of their stupor and frenziedly dance and

Mouldering ruins, the theatre at Perge

Bilingual antiquity

Asian minors

Goblins for Ataturk, Anamur

Chinese fishing-nets, Cochin

'Great Indian Experiences' – the backwater trip

High Street, Madurai

Stopping for a coconut

Car- and cow-wash, Tamil Nadu

Street-dwellers, Calcutta

Spring in southern China

Follow the Highway Code – or else

More Asian minors

A Cantonese packed-lunch

Tiananmen Square, Peking

Red Square, Moscow

wail some remote version of an Indian folk song. The strange shaking and howling would continue for a minute at most before they demanded money, our names or a pen.

Even museums and galleries maintained this air of unreality. The museum at Jodhpur had the air of a building maintained by ghosts: stuffed birds had either fallen to the ground or, more ludicrously, were suspended upside down – ghastly moth-eaten corpses hanging by a slowly disintegrating piece of cotton. In Udaipur, the City Palace had a series of hunting prints in which half a dozen grandees pointed rifles at elephants inches from the ends of their gun-barrels. Had hunting ever been so easy? If so, no wonder the Indian tiger population declined from 30–40,000 at the beginning of the century to just 1827 in 1972.

However, the anaesthetised environment of the Lake Palace Hotel appeared just too remote from whatever the 'real' India was. One knew that it didn't include glasses in sealed plastic bags 'sanitised for our personal protection', or tissue-wrapped lavatory seats. Despite the enormous pleasures of being able to sit on a balcony with a drink and a book, watching the sun set over the lake, or bathe in the undoubtedly sanitised swimming pool, it was about time to re-enter the world of hard benches on the train back to Bombay, of unpleasant food and – eventually – the rigours of cycling. We left the Lake Palace, where the room cost 400 rupees a night, haggled over the rickshaw fare to the station and clambered aboard another of the second-class cattle trucks to wake up, early the next morning, to the heart-warming sight of row upon row of defecating Bombay slum-dwellers.

7

Deccan plateau

Once Laura had been despatched, with great sadness, back to England, I knew that I would have to make a start on cycling down to Cape Cormorin. The deserted, flat plains of Rajasthan had not helped ease my fears about the availability of accommodation, so I went back to the WIAA to see if they had done anything about preparing a list of hotels and a description of the road surface.

It would not have surprised me unduly if the same clerks had still been dealing with the prosperous businessman and the fat lady of my earlier visit, so strong was my impression of their permanent bureaucratic inertia. I was wrong. Not only were the people in the waiting area different, but two new clerks occupied the desks, though they retained the pathologically slow methods of their predecessors. On the grounds that I merely had to pick up an envelope already prepared for me, I went directly to one of the clerks and asked if he knew where I could pick it up. It was a question which clearly profoundly shook his perception of the sense of reality of Western tourists; indeed, it was with sadness rather than anger that he told me that even if my request had been deposited three weeks ago nothing would have been done and would I like to go back in about a month.

It was quite obvious that I was not going to be able to speed things up, so after a couple of days spent reminding myself that I hadn't needed such information before, and that if I did have it, it was as likely to prove an obstacle to enjoyable cycling as a benefit – forcing me to follow set plans rather than whims and removing the thrill of staying in unexpected, even unsuitable places – I optimistically decided that I could manage to survive in India without anyone's help.

To do so, I first had to get out of Bombay. My plan had been to follow the eastern docks, and keep along the coast until I came to the Panvel bridge, after which I should be on the road to Poona. Although fine in principle, this plan failed to allow for the fundamental chaos of

Indian suburbs. Just half a mile from the relative tranquillity of Fort (the town centre) there were hundreds of garishly painted and dangerously overloaded lorries stuck in what could have been a permanent traffic jam. Several drivers appeared to be asleep, and those who weren't sat with their foot or elbow resting on the lorry's horn. Nobody paid any attention to their protests, and rightly so, because there was absolutely nothing that anybody could do to get the traffic moving.

The few gaps between the lorries were filled with auto-rickshaws, bullock-drawn carts, the odd Ambassador saloon car, hand-drawn carts and motorbikes and sidecars. Hundreds of cyclists and pedestrians were trying to squeeze through, underneath or over the jam, which necessarily had to be done through the epicentre as the 'pavements' were used as building sites for cardboard and scrap-metal shacks, whose owners would squat in the gutter staring contentedly at a lorry's hubcap.

It was obviously impossible to actually pedal through this traffic, and I slowly walked my bike along the road, hoping that I was heading in vaguely the right direction and wondering whether I should go back to central Bombay and buy a compass. There was of course no shortage of people to ask, but most, with charming Indian courtesy, preferred to agree with me rather than tell me either that I was going in the wrong direction or that they didn't know. It was fairly easy to test whether this was happening by asking a series of three questions, pointing in completely different directions, and asking if that was the way to Panvel. If the person replied 'yes' after each question I knew not to take his advice. I hoped that the solution would be to ask a question which didn't allow the answer to be yes, but this too failed.

'How do I get to Panvel?'

'You must go by train.'

'No. I want to go to Panvel by bicycle, and I want to go across the Panvel bridge.'

'Panvel is not a good place. You don't want to go to Panvel.'

'I do. Please will you tell me where the Panvel bridge is.'

'There is no Panvel bridge.'

Another person whose advice I could ignore. Finally, and incredibly, I found a policeman standing at a crossroads, surveying with some satisfaction the four columns of traffic that had congealed about his little watch-tower. He told me that I should, 'Go straight down the road and then turn right', at which point he waved his baton to the left. 'Go straight on a little, and turn right and then left', and again he waved his baton in the opposite direction.

'When you point to the left, do you mean I should go left or right?'

'You go down the road, and turn right.'

'But you're pointing to the left.'

'I am not pointing', he said, pointing his baton. 'I will say it very slowly . . .' and he trailed through his bewildering directions again, leaving me too depressed to ask for more specific details of exactly when I should turn left or right.

Just before I left the hotel, the owner had told me that it would take about three-quarters of an hour to get to the bridge. It took me nearly two and a half hours, during which time I had built up a fantasy of some high-technology arch gracefully soaring across an impressive and beautiful bay. Instead, I found an antiquated series of struts embedded in the swamp with, in the far distance, a few birds sitting on the puddles of the muddy creek.

A gang of about fifty men were wading in the mud either side of the bridge, building up small islands on which, once the mud had dried, other men built mud shacks, supplementing the mud with pieces of cardboard, metal and wood. It was inconceivable that such structures could survive the monsoon, and hard to accept that such an existence could possibly be an improvement on life in rural India.

Although there might have been forces I couldn't see – such as unemployment, intimidation or caste discrimination – driving these people on to the mud islands, the superficial impression I had on crossing the creek and starting to cycle through the farm land around Panvel towards Poona was that the mud people, however desperate, were mistaken.

These thoughts were interrupted by a cyclist tapping me on the arm.

'What is your name?'

'What is your native place?'

'Where are you going to?'

'Where are you coming from?'

By the end of the day about thirty-five to forty people had asked me these questions, either simply demonstrating a curiosity about the outside world, trying to establish my place and status in the world or just being a damned nuisance. At first I chorused my replies like a liturgical response, until, exhausted by their repetition, I withdrew into an invented and exclusive world.

'Niet Eengleesch. Niet Eengleesch. I Russkiye. I Russkiye in India to spy for Russkiye invasion. Yah. Russkiye good. Eengleesch niet good.'

It is perhaps too much to hope that anyone believed this story, but it was an effective method of getting rid of the over-curious questioners, and allowed me to concentrate on avoiding the lorries and buses lumbering along the Bombay–Poona highway. Although there was plenty of room, particularly on the section from Panvel bridge to the Western Ghat foothills, almost every lorry that passed felt obliged to try and run me off the road, usually with success. By acting as though the whole thing was a joke, and raising my wide-brimmed cricket hat or sticking my tongue out at the driver, I succeeded only in further wounding their pride, and they drove wildly at me blasting their horn.

To begin with I thought this was some sort of reaction against three centuries of British rule, possibly taking revenge for an insult against the driver's father or grandfather in the pre-1947 days, but then I noticed with alarm that Indian cyclists immediately pulled off the road whenever a lorry appeared. The prospect of trying to cycle about 2000 miles in such conditions, constantly at risk from homicidal lorry-drivers, was appalling, and it was only the assurance I had been given that the Bombay–Poona road was the busiest in India that encouraged me to go on. Once on to smaller roads I was fairly confident that I could, if necessary, just get off my bike whenever the odd lorry came along, as I had done in Turkey.

The problem was that until I reached the smaller roads I had to keep dodging off the tarmac, which, with Indian road-building methods being what they were, guaranteed a high number of punctures as the tarmac was at least six inches above the stony ground, which was covered in thorns.

The combination of the chaos in Bombay and my constant halts to change inner tubes made it impossible to cycle the 110 miles to Poona that day, as I had hoped to do, though it would have meant breaking my rule that I wouldn't try and cycle more than about fifty miles a day. The reason for attempting this was that I wasn't sure that there would be any accommodation between the top of the Ghats and Poona – an absurd fear when I arrived to find a great mass of hotels catering for rich Bombayites trying to escape the heat of the coastal plains in summer. As it was December, several of the hotels were closed and, of those open, most were alarmingly expensive. In the end I took the advice of the receptionist in one of the expensive hotels, and went off the main road to a holiday camp, which I'd been told was cheap.

This was simply an old hospital thrown up, undoubtedly by the British, using cheap Nissen huts and clearly based on the Aldershot school of architecture whereby economy and gloom prevail over aesthetics and durability. The conversion had been achieved with the minimum of effort and a complete lack of imagination – indeed it probably entailed no more than painting over the sign at the entrance. These structural disadvantages were compounded by the fact that the whole area was out of season, thus creating an atmosphere appropriate for a hospital for the terminally ill, but unwelcome in a hotel.

There was no sign of life other than a man sweeping, with unexpected vigour, the road that curved like an English suburban crescent through the compound of huts. He assured me that the establishment was open, but the manager was, at that moment, asleep. The best thing for me to do was to find the most habitable 'cottage', and register when the manager woke up. Groping in his pocket, he pulled out two candles and presented them to me with the dismal prediction that I would need them.

Each cottage consisted of three uniformly damp rooms with metal beds drooping on sagging springs, heavy with the weight of the sodden linen and blankets. At the back of these rooms a door led on to a private courtyard with two small sheds in a corner, one containing a bucket and the other a hole in the ground. The only good news was that, at least to begin with, the electric light worked, although after I had registered the electricity was cut off and I had to use the candles to try and read Albee's *The Monkey Wrench Gang*, chosen deliberately because its story of a gang pledged to destroy industrial and tech-nological intrusions into the American countryside was delightfully incongruous when read in my present dismal surroundings.

The next day, I was further plagued by cyclists asking inane ques-tions, and this time they refused to believe that I was a Russian spy. Somehow I found the experience exhausting, always trying to get rid of someone, constantly having to dodge out of the way of lorries, and repairing frequent punctures under the lazy scrutiny of other cyclists, cart-drivers and passers-by.

After what seemed an eternity I finally reached Poona, reminiscent of Agra in its division between the old British cantonment and the Indian city – the cantonment neatly laid out with wide roads, lawns and spacious bungalows; the Indian part a confusion of houses pressing in on each other and jumbled around chaotic roads. Under British rule, soldiers were forbidden to enter the Indian part of the city, and significant sections of the British 'way of life' were closed to Indians. Although not alone in this unpleasant arrangement, Poona became the great butt of music-hall jokes about imperialist blimpery – the town of clubs, racecourses and bridge parties preserved in splendid isolation from the awful natives.

I found a poignant reminder of this old reputation in the words of a song which I found on a flowery print hanging on my bedroom wall. The card had aged to a light shade of brown, with dark patches almost obscuring the old coloured flowers which surrounded the words, still largely legible:

> The Ladies of Mahableshwar,
> Have strawberries for tea,
> And as for cream and sugar
> They add them lavishly;
> But Poona! oh, in Poona,
> Their hearts are like to break,
> For while the butter's melting
> The flies eat up the cake.
>
> The Ladies of Mahableshwar
> In wraps and furs delight,
> And often get pneumonia
> 'Neath blankets two at night;
> But Poona! oh, in Poona,
> The gauziest wisps appal,
> And ladies sleep (they tell me)
> With nothing on at all.
>
> The Ladies of Mahableshwar
> In such sweet charms abound
> That doctors say their livers
> Are marvellously sound;
> But Poona! oh, in Poona,
> They scold and nag all day,
> And contradict their husbands
> Until they fade away.

A wretchedly frail old man, wearing an old blue uniform held loosely together by three buttons, all of different design, shuffled around the rooms asking if anyone wanted any tea. He was an ideal image for a morbid contemplation of the decaying remains of the British Raj. Naturally, away from the hotel, and in the 'Indian' part of the city, a completely different atmosphere prevailed – full of noise, energy and, unfortunately, hundreds of little boys wanting to know my name.

Despite the unrepresentative view of modern India derived from looking at the remains of past empires, my route south was fixed with two immediate aims – to see the great Muslim buildings of Bijapur, and the ancient imperial capital of Vijaynagar. Apart from the temples at Badami, I was assured that the whole of the Deccan plateau would prove dreary cycling, a matter of plodding relentlessly across dry, infertile plains with no trees to protect me from the sun. With such an encouraging prospect, it would have been strange if I hadn't found the attractions of the ancient capitals worth making substantial detours for.

Cycling south of Poona to Miraj, I was surprised at how green – even abundant – the landscape was, watered by the great network of irrigation canals supplied, according to notices every few miles, by the World Bank. These canals had a significant social function beyond the benefits of greater fertility. Numerous people used them to wash themselves, either fully submerged or, wrapped in their *dhotis*, scrubbing with a rag of cotton while standing on the convenient steps which led from the bank to water level. There were two aspects of this washing which remained constant: it was done with the utmost gravity, almost reverence, and with total disregard for time; and, secondly, I never saw a woman with the groups of squatting men, who after washing would quietly sit by the canal and smoke a cigarette and watch the water go by.

Women were always nearby, ferociously bashing clothes against the concrete canal banks as they stood up to their knees in water. Homer chose a similar setting, the epitome of drudgery and endless hard work when seen in World Bank irrigation canals, as the setting for Odysseus's meeting with Nausicaa, though his was a more lavish version, manipulated by the gods and resplendent with music, anointing of oil, bathing and ball games. In Maharashtra such leisurely activities were far removed from the continual smashing of clothes on to concrete, the slapping sound of which was one of the few characteristics I found all over India.

Another 'All India' characteristic was the complete absence of women doing anything other than work or trail behind their husbands in a secondary and subordinate fashion. It was difficult not to feel outraged at the pious and lengthy sponging indulged in by the men, and the way they would wearily squat down to discuss the enormity of their exertions while, yards away, women were relentlessly bashing away. The overwhelming impression I had (though possibly unfair) was that, however ghastly an Indian man's life was his wife's was worse.

In the early nineteenth century, J. W. Massie observed that it was difficult to imagine a state of dependence more strict, contemptuous and humiliating than that ordained for Hindu women:

. . . and to consummate the stigma, to fill up the cup of bitter waters assigned to woman, as if she deserved to be excluded from immortality as well as from justice, from hope as well as from enjoyment, it is ruled that a female has no business with the texts of the Veda. . . . To them the fountain of wisdom is sealed, the streams of knowledge are dried up; the springs of individual consolation, as promised in their religion, are guarded and barred against women.

Little appears to have changed. And, unfortunately, their subservient role meant that I was unable to ask questions, as any approach on my part was swiftly rebuffed to avoid what I supposed would be some dreadful and undeserved recrimination.

Whenever I was able to do so, I asked Indian men about these obvious inequalities, and without exception encountered complete incomprehension that I was seriously suggesting that women should be treated equally. Opportunities for such discussions were surprisingly frequent in southern Maharashtra, as the restaurants there adopted the strange practice of providing curtained-off cubicles in which to eat and drink. These appeared to be occupied by a disproportionate number of people claiming to be Brahmins, who were able to eat, and more importantly drink, without discovery. In retrospect, my discussions with Brahmins on equality, and particularly female equality, were singularly pointless; it is hard to think of a subject on which there could be less common ground, and unfortunately logic tended to be rather ignored in the interchange of our increasingly dogmatic ideas.

The other peculiar aspect about these private cubicles, compared with the widespread public defecation, was the complete reversal of English attitudes to these two activities. In Bijapur, I watched with – possibly naive – fascination as three boys squatted together in a triangle and, when they had finished, took it in turns to pour water from an old bucket over each other's bottoms while waiting for the pigs to come along and clear up. I noticed this scene because I wanted to take a photograph of the Ibrahim Rauza, two tombs just outside the city walls, and suddenly realised what the three boys in the foreground were doing. Behind the boys, the minarets, arcades and exquisite verandahs, with ceilings carved with verses from the Koran interspersed with groups of flowers, provided an inspiring and beautiful contrast to the simple activities in their shadow.

There were other less vivid challenges to my perception of what was 'normal'. Until I'd started cycling I had succeeded in avoiding the full horrors of a rural restaurant, with its unappetising choice between heavily spiced scraps of either lamb or chicken. In Goa I had feasted on delicate seafood curries prepared for Western tastes; in Rajasthan I had survived in predominantly Chinese restaurants with a very occasional foray into grand and very expensive Indian establishments. I had twice broken this rule, and both times had suffered from violent recurrences of my Turkish stomach problems.

Unfortunately, I couldn't find a route through India which would allow me to eat in a non-Indian restaurant at least twice a day, so I was forced either to cycle on an empty stomach or to try and eat the awful over-spiced objects sold in the villages. In the Deccan plateau the restaurants were normally made of large mud walls, one side of which would have a curtain hanging down as an entrance. Inside, a few pieces of wood would be balanced on old oil cans or something similar, and a table of some sort suspended in front of this bench. A pan rather like a Chinese wok was frequently the only cooking implement, and it would be placed on a fire on the ground after being scoured out with grit from the earth floor. The choice of food was easy as the restaurant normally only had one dish, so one either accepted what was offered or went on in search of another place. In any case, I didn't know how to ask for anything else in the local language.

The absence of choice extended to highly specialised outlets: throughout the country there are stalls allegedly selling only soft drinks. I stopped at one such stall in Koppal and asked, perhaps optimistically, for a mango juice. He didn't have any. I asked for the least revolting fizzy drink, Limca. He didn't have any. Thumbs Up? He didn't have any. In fact he didn't have one single bottle of any drink, and had to get a cup of tea from the next-door restaurant, a cup which cost me 25 paise – worth at the then rate of exchange a sixth of a penny.

Koppal, and the area around it as far north as Miraj and Bijapur and south to the Tunghabhadra Hydro Project near Hospet, was full of examples of such hopeless commerce – fruit stalls with two or three bananas; four men squatting around a pile of young coconuts which cost, away from the towns, about one rupee each; restaurants with just one small pot of foul meat, heavily spiced to disguise how awful it was, and a large container of rice. Few other activities were available, as the land was not irrigated by any World Bank canals but by earthern pots carried, inevitably by women, from a well to the patchy plots of cultivated land. There was a peculiar hush about much of the country – a dry, predominantly yellow landscape without trees, bushes or more than this hand-watered agriculture, and without any sign of birds, animals or anyone apart from despondent groups squatting in the shade of a rock, or behind a wall of one of the dried mud huts.

Cycling through this exhausted poverty wasn't pleasant, with the sad realisation that my temporary physical discomfort was the permanent condition of the local population, suffering the inevitable consequences of protein, vitamin and mineral deficiency, and the increased exposure to disease that such malnourishment brings.

The only evidence of any government support was in the jeeps outside the 'Sub-Engineer's District Office', the 'Roads and Highways DO' and numerous other arcane departments, whose splendid offices and cars bore no relationship to the amount of work performed. The 'Roads and Highways DO' had, in a remarkably token gesture, repainted all the road signs with signs written exclusively in Kannada, but, pathetically, using paint so thin that the old signs, written in both English and Kannada, could still be read without great difficulty. Nothing was being done to tarmac the fifty or so miles that were just gravel and sand, or to repair the potholed and uneven sections that *were* covered in tarmac.

While pushing my bike along one of these sandy roads I was approached by two men, who were holding sticks with the vaguest of menacing gestures and pointing at my watch. My refusal to hand it over led to a dull drumming against my panniers, perhaps the least frightening threat ever encountered, and I was almost embarrassed at my assailants' obvious lack of intent to do the sensible thing – hit me over the head with their sticks, grab the spoils and make a run for it. I suppose I should have tried to get away, in which endeavour I would almost certainly have been successful, but some curious feeling of inertia gripped me, and the three of us stood gazing without interest at each other, idly wondering how the situation would end, but none of us prepared to precipitate that end.

In due course, the sound of one of the hundreds of official jeeps on patrol for signs of the English language forced us out of our trance, and with a final drum-roll the pair began to meander across the infertile soil, to entertain their fellow villagers with tales of Europeans on bicycles. The jeep eventually appeared and, as usual driving at a ridiculous speed, hurled along the sandy track with its horn blaring until I was forced to leave the road, suffering another puncture and a further blow to my enjoyment of India.

From Koppal I cycled to Hospet, the nearest town to the Old Telugu capital of Vijaynagar, which dominated southern India from 1336 to 1565, the date of the battle of Talikota. The battle was particularly disastrous for the future of southern India as it opened the area up to invasions from the Moghuls, the Mahrattas and the British, and thus an end to the political identity of the south.

The great city of Vijaynagar, relying on the profits from its control of the southern spice trade and the south-eastern cotton industry, extended seven miles from north to south, twenty-four miles round, and contained within its seven concentric city walls marble palaces, colossal elephant stables, ladies' pavilions, baths, bazaars, ceremonial gateways and hundreds of temples. Its population of half a million was the same as that of contemporary Renaissance Rome.

Today, the ruins are occupied by a few stall-holders selling tea and *lassis* to the tourists and another colony of the weary travellers, in residence at one of their few inland 'hangouts', and taking great delight at sleeping in the baths of the old King's Palace and their ability to order a *chai* in one of the southern Dravidian languages. Their presence only slightly spoiled for me the abandoned beauty of the ruins, spread over the hard rock and the banks of the Tungabhadra river. It was a stimulating and timely restorative after the depressing and uninspiring Deccan plateau, though, alarmingly, the energy and imagination I saw was 400 years old and bore little relation to the contemporary lassitude; the incredible architecture of Vijaynagar had no influence on the boring functionalism of nearby Hospet, a typically dusty town with bullock carts, bicycles, battered buses, restaurants with just one, possibly two, items available on the menu, and dozens of over-specialised shops.

8

Currying favour

After Rajasthan and the hot and dusty Deccan plateau, I had more or less abandoned any hope of a change in the monotonous landscape, not really believing in the rumours of lush, sub-tropical Kerala. I had become almost conditioned by the prevalent sense of timeless struggling against the constant heat and dust, so frequently seen in the heart-breaking toil of the ancient farming techniques, and even began fondly to imagine some empathy between my cycling and the farmers chipping away with a hoe at the stony ground.

South of Hospet, however, the scenery did begin to change and, incredibly, more and more trees appeared – as well as natural water supplies. The change came just in time, as I was about to abandon the long journey south to Cape Cormorin and take a more direct route across to Madras, which from Hospet was no more than 350 miles away. At last I could see that India wasn't all the same, and that there might be some point in embarking on my 800-mile detour.

Equally encouragingly, I was no longer so intimidated by Indian driving behaviour and not so irritated by the never-ending questions and continual staring. The staring had never been a great nuisance, as privacy was obviously an unattainable state, and once I had realised this I found it relatively easy to eat with a crowd studying every jaw movement and to write without being unduly distressed by my pen being periodically pulled from my hand for a communal inspection. The renewed success of my claim to be a non-English-speaking Russian spy allowed me to talk when I wanted and to banish potential inter-rogators when exhaustion, misery or just dislike of the person meant that I didn't want to recite my responses.

Until I reached Hospet, though, I had constantly been in a state of nervous shock at the dangers I was in from the lorry drivers who, for whatever reason, showed a most depressing disregard for my life. From London to the outskirts of Athens I had experienced the more familiar concern that, even though the driver and I had no knowledge of each other, I could be confident that he or she would go to considerable lengths to avoid injuring me. In Athens, the drivers might have been psychopathic monsters, but they did acknowledge the bravery of anyone cycling in their midst, and so long as I maintained an aggressive and macho bravado towards cars, they always resisted the opportunity of knocking me over. In Turkey there had been so few cars, lorries and buses that I was able to get off my bike virtually every time I heard an engine approaching and just sit and wait for it to go past. This didn't lose me a great deal of time, and guaranteed that the lunatic element on Turkish roads was frustrated.

India posed different problems. Everybody showed a complete disregard for any other road user and relied solely on the principle that might would be right. Unfortunately, this coincided with a fatalistic approach which meant that nobody bothered to check whether might was actually on their side. For the lorry drivers to behave in such a way was, if selfish, at least understandable as they could be reasonably confident that they were as large as anything else on the road. For everyone else it was just stupid, quite insane, to barge out across a road without bothering to check whether it was clear, yet pedestrians, cyclists, bullock-cart drivers, donkey-handlers and motorcyclists all steadfastly refused to follow even the most basic of 'Green Cross Codes'.

So long as I observed the standards of observation and consideration found on English roads, cycling in this anarchic chaos was a nightmare. On countless occasions I watched lorries roar towards a crowd of un-concerned people, who totally ignored the horn which was permanently pressed down. Finally, by some miracle, as no one ever bothered to look up, the lorry would race through the tiniest of gaps, and the bat-like pedestrians (relying on instinct rather than sight) would pass on, apparently unaware of how closely they were dicing with death. India's appalling traffic statistics show that I was just lucky, and the pedestrians even luckier, to have avoided some terrible carnage. (This possibility was always made worse by the dozen or so people who clung to the already hopelessly overloaded lorry, and who would be added to the numbers of dead.)

Equally traumatic, despite my advantage in 'might', were the people who walked out in front of me. Foolishly, I would either desperately try to spin out of the way or launch into a hysterical tirade against the person concerned, who, having behaved in that manner all his life, understandably found my yelling and howling a little mystifying. The whole situation was made even more hopeless by the habit of all those who lived by a road to treat it as a personal convenience – a useful surface for the women to spread the drying grain, for the men to doze by, as a venue for family celebrations and as a convenient counter for the local pedlars to set out their selection of needles, cotton reels, brooches and combs.

I tried the responses which had been so successful in other countries. They all failed. If I stopped to allow the larger vehicles time to pass, I succeeded only in attracting another crowd of curious villagers who merrily amused themselves by fiddling with my bike – feeling the pressure in my front tyre, realigning my gear levers and examining the contents of my water bottle. If I reacted with Athenian aggression, I knew I was bound to end up being killed, as it was behaviour guaranteed to annoy the proud and possessive lorry-drivers. The only option left to me was to adopt the Indian approach, to abandon all sense and caution and charge relentlessly on, ignoring the anguished horn-blowing of on-coming lorries and showing a complete disregard for any injury I might cause an unobservant pedestrian.

That I managed to accept uncaringly the fatalism implicit in this method was another manifestation of my growing acceptance of things as I found them, and the change in my expectations and standards, although such adjustments were probably essential to prevent myself going mad. It seemed perfectly acceptable to join the crouching Indians in the outdoor lavatories; to pick one's way through the scattered faeces and dodge the loathsome little black pigs and the comparatively acceptable rats; to ignore the visibly unhygienic surroundings of the roadside cafés and chew unthinkingly at whatever I was presented with; to ignore the condition of the bedrooms, so sadly lacking in my accustomed comforts; and, above all, to accept the continual intrusion of the people I met, whether through passive staring or through the physical mauling of my bike, the snatching of books or pens and the examination of my belongings as they lay scattered around my bedroom. This lack of privacy was an inevitable consequence of cycling around India. Had I stuck to the much more comfortable existence of the expensive palace hotels, I would certainly not have encountered the same problems. I was, however, forced to stay in whatever accommodation I could find, which in the more remote villages and towns was rarely either exclusive or comfortable.

In Chiknayakanhalli, a small town two days' cycling south of Hampi, I was told I could stay at the Travellers' Bungalow, usually very good news as they were the cheapest pleasant places I found in India. The town itself was the familiar collection of half-finished buildings constructed from either mud or the small, powdery, fragile bricks used throughout the Deccan plateau, giving the strong impression of built-in dilapidation. These buildings huddled round a minor road junction which provided the pedlars with a fairly stable source of custom. Perhaps fifty yards from the unsignposted junction, but in the direction of Chitradurga, a slightly wider stretch of untarmacked road provided parking space for four and a half buses, the half being used as a source of spare parts in the event of some mechanical or structural problem.

About sixty people squatted intently around one of the more complete buses, patiently waiting for a new mudguard taken from the half bus to be screwed on to the chassis. Two dozen salesmen buzzed around the sedentary passengers attempting to sell their coconuts, bananas and peanuts. One of these coconut-sellers agreed to tell me the way to the Travellers' Bungalow if I had one of his coconuts, a bargain which I was perfectly happy to enter. Young coconuts were, without question, the most enjoyable food I had throughout Maharashtra and Karnataka.

The directions told me to turn right, go out of the town and then stop, because the bungalow was just outside the town. I went on to the junction, where the other fruit-sellers and pedlars were marginally in favour of my turning right – three saying right, two saying left and six saying not just left and right, but back the way I had come from. Turning right, I soon came upon a collection of virtually identical buildings, which suggested an old British cantonment, in varying states of repair and performing a variety of functions. What they did was announced on a blackboard, the 'Sub-Inspector, Dams and Waterways', the 'Junior Engineer, Chiknayakanhalli District' and, to my great relief, the 'Travellers' Bungalow'.

I turned into the drive and began to cycle towards the house, when a wild-looking gardener jumped out of the overgrown rhododendrons and began aggressively to wave a hoe at me. Not surprisingly, this peculiar reception caused great excitement amongst the crowd of children who had followed me from the 'bus station', and they cheered and whooped as I tried to explain that I wanted a bed. This information was evidently so unexpected that the gardener temporarily suspended his hoe-waving and thrust it up towards the sky. We stood facing each other in this impasse until I resolved to take matters on a bit, and began to move slowly towards the bungalow. Immediately, the hoe was pointed menacingly at me, though more helpfully the gardener went on to point at a small hut almost hidden amongst the bushes in a corner of the garden.

Inside the hut four rather seedy men were loafing around a table beneath a creaking electric fan. The hoe-carrier began to outline the extent of my misdemeanour until I was impatiently asked what it was I wanted. Meanwhile the hoe-carrier was despatched to disperse the children who were on the point of entering the room. With a furious bellow he began a series of charges, reminiscent of the scuttling of an injured crab, and succeeded in getting the children away from the hut. The loafers and I watched as the children responded with a vigorous volley of stones, which achieved a temporary abatement of the crabbish darts.

'You were going to the Travellers' Bungalow?' asked one of the loafers.

I agreed that I was, and that the reason was that I wanted a room. A terrible hush descended until all that could be heard was the grating sound of the electric ceiling fan. After a minute's heavy contemplation they resumed the interrogation.

'Do you have a reservation?' asked one loafer, sitting on a bench.

'Do you have an introduction?' asked his fellow bench-mate.

I shook my head.

'This is a "Travellers' Bungalow",' said the most visibly distressed loafer, his voice heavy with the poignancy and gravity of his words.

'You must have a reservation.'

'You must have an introduction,' chorused the two loafers sitting on the bench.

'All I want is a room for one night,' I wailed.

'A room?'

'Well, a bed then,' I compromised.

The fourth of the group, sitting in the most senior chair behind the desk, took matters in hand.

'For a small fee, heh hem, it might be possible to arrange a letter of introduction, and then we should be able to find you a bed.'

'How much is the fee?'

'You must understand, there isn't an official fee. You should pay an amount suitable for the work necessary to get you a letter. If you had written two months ago, there would be no fee, but to arrive the day you want to stay, well . . . well, there must be some fee.'

'Would five rupees be enough?'

There was a strangled gargling sound before the senior loafer, amidst much wheezing and gasping, pompously reminded me that this was a Travellers' Bungalow.

'Ten rupees?' This amount was obviously satisfactory.

'What is it you want?'

'A bed, please.'

'Have you written to the district officer asking for permission to stay?'

'No.'

'Will you please write a letter to the District Officer asking for permission to stay here.'

I scrawled out a request on a piece of old paper the senior loafer handed to me, which he'd found lying in one of the ill-fitting drawers of the table. He examined my effort and asked for my passport number to be added to the otherwise bald statement that I wanted a room or bed for that night.

'Thank you. And the fee please.'

I handed over the ten rupees, whereupon he savagely bawled for the hoe-carrier to come and escort me to the bungalow. The carrier arrived, obviously in some distress after the deluge of stones and mud thrown at him by the children. We plodded gloomily towards the bungalow, the hoe-carrier occasionally darting off into the rhododendrons to root out some child, and in due course we arrived at the door, which the carrier thumped three times with his hoe.

A timid head poked round the door and asked me to come in. Three men in suits were in the room – the one who let me in and two others who sat behind an impressive attaché case carefully, almost ceremoniously, placed on the table. A double bed and two single beds made up the rest of the furniture.

'Where's my room?' I demanded, turning towards the hoe-carrier, but he was already back in battle, the air thick with missiles and excited yelps.

'What are you doing in my room?' I asked the door-opener, who stood ingratiatingly by the double bed, slowly rubbing his hands together.

'We are also sleeping in this room. We run a business selling life insurance in the evenings.'

'But this is the Travellers' Bungalow. You can't work here.'

'We have an arrangement with the authorities.'

'Where do you sleep?'

The two other men leant away from the attaché case and patted the two single beds. The door-opener smiled weakly at the double bed.

'Do you know if there's another hotel in Chiknayakanhalli?'

'This is the nicest place. You must not go into Chiknayakanhalli now. It is a very bad town, and it is getting dark.'

'Well, I'm going, and I hope I'll find another place to stay.'

'You must be careful of the spirits in the trees. They are very bad spirits.'

I stomped out and went back to the fruit-sellers at the junction, buying two more coconuts, some bananas and a papaya. Everyone I asked confirmed the insurance salesmen's claim that there was nowhere else to stay, and eventually I stopped worrying about the prospect of sharing a bed with the sycophantic door-opener and walked back to the bungalow. The hoe-carrier, skulking in the bushes, glared angrily at me as I filed past his hiding place, but allowed me to pass un-challenged. The children were out of sight, though in the half light I might have missed them.

Inside the room the three men remained in their morose seclusion, clearly having failed to receive a single enquiry about life insurance. Had they thought of persuading the hoe-carrier to allow people through to the bungalow, I asked, which threw them into a deep gloom. Later they told me that their 'arrangement' had proved un-satisfactory and someone, they would not say who, had ordered the carrier to challenge all new arrivals. Even if he wasn't outside, they suspected that it wouldn't have made much difference as they had come to the conclusion that life insurance was not a popular commodity in Chiknayakanhalli. Still full of good ideas, I asked them why they didn't go and sell it by the departing buses, as anyone who saw the condition of the vehicles would be bound to consider the possibility of a fatal accident, particularly in Indian traffic conditions. The policy did not include road or rail accidents, they informed me. 'Policy?' They confirmed that their impressive attaché case contained just one policy, which excluded cover for the most obvious dangers. I joined them in a silent lament, as we gathered before the attaché case and pondered on the smashed expectations it had caused.

By midnight, two had removed their suits and were plodding about the room in the more familiar *dhotis*. The other stared intently at the door until finally, by about half past twelve, he clicked the attaché case shut, shoved it under one of the single bed mattresses and, meta-phorically, put up the 'Closed' sign. The three of them had failed to make any money that day, although they took the view that just two new policies a week would generate enough commission to make it worthwhile.

Happily, while I had been exploring the town for an alternative hotel they had agreed that I could have one of the single beds and share their papaya for breakfast, as all agreed that the one I had bought was inedible. They woke me at seven, the papaya neatly cut into four slices and occupying the space normally reserved for the attaché case. A group of children, possibly the same as the missile-hurling brutes of the night before, took advantage of the hoe-carrier's absence to crowd into our bedroom and stand transfixed as I dressed, which I suppose might have been of some interest to a child who had never seen a white bottom, and watch me eat my papaya, which must have been unbearably dull. All eyes focused on me, as the insurance salesmen insisted on my occupying the best position, sitting on the edge of the bed and facing directly towards the table. Incredibly, the hoe-carrier then appeared with a thermos flask of hot water, donated by the cronies in the hut 'to wish me good luck on my bicycle'.

This was the sort of incident which made me feel absurdly happy, and conjured up very woolly ideas of fundamental human kindness and the unity of mankind. Moved almost to tears, I cycled away from the bungalow, dramatically and poignantly waving goodbye to my 'friends'. In this kind of mood, I could see advances from other cyclists wanting to know my name, native place, destination and place of departure not as a dreadful irritation but as a perfectly reasonable curiosity about strangers, and an attempt to make them feel welcome. Slowly, this mood would disappear until I resorted to my new technique of staring blindly ahead until they went away, which was my own version of Indian behaviour in such circumstances, based on the stony faces of pedestrians. Even in my irritated state, however, I still felt guilty about my failure to be more friendly, and was concerned about whether my behaviour was inexcusably rude, or whether I was 'normal' in reacting so violently against certain individuals, despite my general enthusiasm for India and the Indians. Cycling alone, I found it difficult to compare my reaction with others, as when I did meet other tourists a discussion of the various irritations peculiar to India seemed a little unnecessary, a foolish concentration on quickly forgotten petty incidents.

In the seventh century the third caliph, Osman (644–56), had ordered a detailed report on the affairs of 'Hind and Sind'. Among the succinct comments on the country and its people were these: 'Its water is dark and dirty. Its fruit is bitter and poisonous. Its land is stony and its earth is salt. A small army will soon be annihilated there, and a large one will soon die of hunger . . . [The people] are treacherous and deceitful.'

I read this unpleasant little description in the library of the house in

Shirangapatnam which I reached the day I left Chiknayakanhalli. In a rather contrived fashion I used it to float my own tenuous ideas on 'the Indians', which denied that they were treacherous and deceitful, but admitted that occasionally some of them were a damned nuisance. Such trimming was considered, by someone who had lived in India for nearly twenty-five years, little more than romantic codswallop. For twenty of those years my hostess had run, and privately funded, a clinic attempting to educate village women in the importance of basic hygiene, diet requirements and the value of the old maxim that 'prevention is better than the cure', particularly in a country where the cure was often unavailable.

For the next two days I heard a damning tirade against the corruption, inequalities and violence of daily Indian life. This description was not a great surprise, because, as the report to Osman indicates, Indians have consistently won both enemies and detractors. Strangely, in my experience, the dishonesty and savage violence which did undoubtedly take place was always directed against fellow Indians or, as in the case of my Shirangapatnam hostess, against long-term residents.

The reason for her inclusion in the catalogue of victims was the fact that she had successfully restored her beautiful house, misleadingly called 'Scott's Bungalow'. It was built in 1800 for Wellesley's second-in-command following the defeat of Tipu Sultan, and stands on the banks of the river Cauvery between huge oak and chestnut trees. The balconies and verandahs which divide the thick sandstone walls give the building a slightly Palladian appearance, although the interior is less grand, having an almost rustic, southern Mediterranean simplicity. This was appropriate as the owner had fled from the fascism of Franco's Spain, to end up buying the ruins of this house while out walking along the river.

The restoration had had two effects. The local 'corrupt classes' assumed that she must have huge reserves of money which they could redistribute amongst themselves, and they therefore demanded numerous payments to discourage burglaries, arson and the unfortunate accidents which so easily took place in rural India. (The police chief's reaction on hearing of this dreadful situation was to announce that he would be sending his man down to pick up some of the fruit that grew in the garden.) Unfortunately, the overlap between the corrupt and the violent classes was not complete, and there were other powerful elements who considered that such a fine house could, by a mixture of intimidation, thefts and violence, become their property.

Similarly unattractive behaviour was used against the villagers, whose meagre property represented an affront to these greedy sharks. They stole what little land there was, burnt down the houses and variously murdered, raped or assaulted the people, knowing that in general their victims were denied access to legal and medical advice or to higher education which might help their miserable situation, for the awful reason that the scale of corruption placed these remedies out of their reach.

I left Shirangapatnam in a state of some shock. The temptation was to allow my increasing capacity to ignore unsavoury and irritating aspects of life to prevail, and continue happily chirruping on about how much I was enjoying myself, but such unruffled composure was beyond me as I cycled the short distance to Mysore, angrily determined to find out more of the harsh world that had been described to me in the tranquil surroundings of 'Scott's Bungalow'. Predictably, I was disappointed. The other tourists I spoke to described with affection the corrupt nature of Indian society, seeing it not as an evil which should be removed, but as the inevitable consequence of the caste system, which had produced from its rigid hierarchies and obligations a network of vested interests whose dealings with each other were carefully controlled for protection, profit and the maintenance of the social system. There was some unspecified Hindu 'nobility' in doing one's duty to one's family and friends. Thus, nepotism was elevated into a virtue, and my suggestion that this system was nothing but corruption was rudely dismissed as revealing a profound misunderstanding of India.

Desperately I quizzed any Indian prepared to speak to me about their views on the forthcoming election and the likely efficacy of the proposed policies with regard to removing corruption and providing for greater equality of opportunity. With just two exceptions I heard endless recitals of how Rajiv was going to 'clean up' politics, although no one furthered any details of how this was to be done. The exceptions were two young university students, who told me that my questions assumed an un-Indian approach to problems, relying on logic and analysis and not on an emotional reaction to the leading figures, which was the Indian way.

I toured the streets of Mysore searching for bookshops stocking radical texts on the need for the restructuring of society, but there was nothing. Just endless accounts of the superlative steel production figures achieved in the last decade, collected interviews with Keralan co-operative workers congratulating themselves on the increased production of coir mats, and learned texts on why the Nehrus and Gandhis didn't constitute a dynasty. Other shelves had the latest books from

Progress Publishers, Moscow, who, as if frightened of the possible consequences of sending books which might be useful, had off-loaded hundreds of copies of scientific textbooks on such irrelevant and over-specialised subjects as *Orthopaedic stomatology* by V. Karlyondsky, *Complex thermo-dynamic systems* by V. Y. Sycker and *Fundamentals of the theory of plasticity* by L. M. Kachanov.

My current mood of disaffection meant that I failed to appreciate the pleasant atmosphere in Mysore, the absence of filth, over-crowding and narrow congested streets. The whole centre, dominated by the enormous Maharajah's Palace which had been built in 1911–12 at a cost of 4.2 million rupees, seemed confirmation of the smug complacency and uncaring acceptance of what should have been unacceptable. I watched with utter dismay as about 2000 schoolchildren rehearsed some future act of sycophancy on the vast parade ground in front of the Palace.

I decided that the best cure for this unhappy condition was to get down to the Keralan beaches as quickly as possible, buy a few R. K. Narayan novels and try and understand through fiction how the Indians lived in the villages and what they thought about, because I was quite sure that I would never understand the country just by cycling through.

Although I did later read half a dozen of the Narayan novels, I read them with rather less serious motives as I had been considerably heartened by the trip from Mysore down to the Keralan coastal plain. I knew that I would have to go down the Western Ghats at some time, but imagined they would be the unpleasant scrubby things I'd seen between Bombay and Poona. I failed to take any account of the complete change in vegetation, moisture and temperature which created a lovely succession of different landscapes as I went lower in altitude – from a fairly dry plateau, through undulating coffee and tea plantations, then the most spectacular steep mountains at the foot of which was a sub-tropical scene of palm trees, rice and dozens of rivers and ponds.

Midway between Mysore and the coast, the road passed through the northern limits of the Bandipur wildlife sanctuary. Staying in Shirangapatnam I had been warned of the only possible danger, rogue elephants, and told of some of the signs to look out for as I cycled through – uprooted trees, smashed undergrowth, signs of deranged and un-coordinated charges and, of course, sounds of angry bellowing. If I came across any of these signs I should turn back, or wait for a lorry or bus to give me a lift. Unfortunately, however, the vegetation in wildlife sanctuaries is normally in a less than manicured condition and I had no idea what was normal, and what was evidence of a rogue elephant. Careful study of my map showed that there was no easy alternative to cycling through the sanctuary, and in any case I was quite keen to see a wild elephant.

About halfway through the sanctuary this decision was put in its proper perspective when a sign announced that a tiger programme was in operation and advised certain procedures if a tiger was encountered. I took out my steel bicycle lock and carried on, trying to remember from old wildlife programmes whether tigers attacked during the day, and whether, like Alsatians, they could sense whether their potential victim was afraid. From then on, every sound was the growl of a hungry tiger and every uprooted tree had a tiger's face peering round it. The sun shining through the branches overhead even made the road look like tiger's stripes. The one lorry that went through refused to stop, though by the time I realised that that wild continuous roar was a lorry's engine and not a tiger I was in such a horrible condition that the driver was probably justified in driving as quickly as possible past me.

Eventually I arrived at a manned checkpoint where two armed soldiers told me that I was very stupid, and one or two other equally predictable epithets. The grotty hotel I booked in to at Sultan's Battery seemed poor reward for the worries of the day, and in fact, until I reached Cochin, the standard of Keralan hotels seemed definitely irreconcilable with the state's reputation as one of the nicest, most civilised areas in India.

The behaviour of the pedestrians continued to rely on fate, and one day, cycling between Calicut and Trichur and concentrating on the beautiful scenery I was going through, I crashed into an old man who stepped out in front of me. Normally, whenever I stopped for a cup of tea or just a rest, I was quickly surrounded by a crowd of inquisitive people who would fiddle with my bike and anything slightly unusual that I happened to be holding or which was half visible in one of my bags. These crowds, occasionally over a hundred strong, were nearly always uninterested in me so, once I stopped worrying about what was happening to my things, I was able to ignore the people around me and get on with whatever I wanted to do.

The crowd that surrounded me after the collision was different, however. These people *were* interested in me, and particularly in how much money I was going to give the old man in compensation. Two opposing emotions gripped me: firstly, that if I were genuinely concerned about the lives of poor Indian villagers, and seriously wanted to help improve their position in some way, I should donate as much as they asked for. On the other hand, it was the old man's fault, and if, as the Indian rules of the road declared, someone crossed the road trusting in fate, then fate could jolly well look after them without any contribution from an entirely innocent cyclist.

A rude shove from one of the crowd convinced me of the superior logic behind the second argument. Of the fifty or so in the crowd, at least five spoke English and used their ability to put all the blame on me and accuse me of crippling the old man. They expressed amazement that he was still alive, and how lucky I was that the amount they were asking for, 200 rupees, didn't include any provision for his family. For about ten minutes I repeated that it wasn't my fault, that he should look before he crossed the road and that I wanted 20 rupees to compensate me for the damage to my front tyre.

Finally, the old man decided that he'd had enough, climbed to his feet and hobbled off. For a short time the crowd continued to press their claim, though the absence of the victim and the clear proof that he wasn't crippled at all had made some of them lose a little of their earlier enthusiasm. My proposal that our two claims should offset each other, and that no money need actually change hands, was accepted, a little grudgingly, after another five minutes of dogmatic debate.

Cycling away from this incident, I felt ashamed at my mean and uncompromising behaviour, angry almost that I hadn't reciprocated the generosity and friendliness of so many of the Indians I had met. This irritation with my own irritation was a new and alarming development, a sign that my ever-present diarrhoea, combined with the exhausting humidity of the coastal plain, was dragging me further and further into a dull and gloomy mire. Apart from the satisfaction of blaming every unpleasant thought or feeling on my stomach, which absolved me from more alarming self-analysis, there was the further advantage that I now knew that the only cure was to find a nice hotel, with a decent restaurant either attached or nearby, and to stay there for as long as it took to start recovering (I had long since given up hoping for a return to full fitness).

This was an elusive combination in India but, fortunately, one to be found in Cochin, undoubtedly the most tranquil town I visited in India. For several days I sat on a bench between the Chinese fishing nets and St Francis's church, under the shade of mature oak and beech trees and surrounded by large and attractive Dutch mansions. It was the ideal spot for reading letters sent to the nearby *poste-restante*, replying, occasionally reading novels, but spending most of my time simply watching the world go by.

My indolence had just one drawback. I had wanted to attend one of the matches being played as part of an international football tournament in Ernakulum, a short ferry ride away, but kept putting it off. Slowly, the tournament proceeded until finally I read in the paper that the Russians had won.

By chance, I happened to have lunch in the same restaurant as the victorious Russian team, their identity obvious from their red shirts with the hammer and sickle emblem and 'CCCP' written in large letters across the chest. It so happened that I was wearing a blue cycling shirt, donated by F. W. Evans, the people who built my bike, and suitably embossed with their name. The idea was that every now and again I was to wear the shirt as some form of advertisement and, if possible, have my photograph taken in shirt plus bike on the Great Wall or some such glamorous location. I decided to try and swap this Evans shirt for one of the Russian soccer shirts – a scheme which, though perhaps a little ungrateful to F. W. Evans, would if succesful provide me with conclusive evidence to support my claim to be a Russian spy and, almost certainly, provoke some interesting incidents if I wore it when cycling around China.

Sadly, however, the deal was blocked by the team manager, just when I was confident that the Russian number six was going to agree to the deal. I drifted back to my bench, where apart from one or two minor excursions I remained until I felt strong enough to continue my journey south.

9

Sacred cows

Between Cochin and Cape Cormorin, two Great Indian Experiences were to be had – the Alleppey to Quilon backwater trip and Kovalam Beach. Even more than usual the conditions for successfully experiencing the conflicting delights of a boat trip and a beach were rigorously laid down, and did not just concentrate on, for example, where to sit and what to see, but specified exactly where to stay, for how long and on what terms. Unlike Rajasthan, where people continually went off on different tours, in Kerala everybody was doing exactly the same thing: from Cochin to Alleppey, to stay at St George's Lodge, the backwater trip to Quilon, a bus to Trivandrum and then a hut on the beach at Kovalam. Suddenly India began to seem a very small place, and ideas of Western individuality a romantic nonsense.

To apportion blame for this absurd sight of hundreds of young Europeans, Australians and Americans is perhaps a little unfair, but it was impossible not to notice that everyone was carrying what many called their bible, *The Lonely Planet Guide*, clutched to their heart. They virtually refused to enter any establishment or undertake any venture not endorsed by their guru, Tony Wheeler.

Like everyone else, I booked into St George's Lodge, looked for and found my Gideon's Bible and sat around in my room, having read in *The Lonely Planet Guide* that a group of medical students had once told the guru that there was nothing to see in Alleppey. I stared for about half an hour at *The Anatomy of Lies* by Samuil Zivs, an exposé of the partiality of Amnesty International towards capitalist states and the inaccuracy of its criticisms of the Soviet Union.

'Is there,' asks Professor Zivs, 'such a thing as an innate disposition to lie? Yes, there is. It is a kind of pathological craving for lying. It is a life-long passion that consumes the liar. It is a grave disease, which becomes utterly corrupting if one's entire career, one's entire existence are based on lies.'

It was an impressive beginning, which strangely I felt no desire to pursue. I tossed the book aside after reading and re-reading Professor Ziv's thoughts on lying. How was I to spend the fifteen hours before the backwater trip began? It was a depressing moment, as for the first time I felt bored, not because I had explored the town and found it boring, but because I had read that others had.

Angrily, I set myself two deeply tedious tasks – washing my clothes and repairing the punctured inner tubes I had been carrying around with me. The first was an unnecessary thing to do, as dhobi-wallahs were constantly trying to find washing, which they managed to get much cleaner than my half-hearted efforts achieved, and were ludicrously cheap. However, it was a good way of working my listlessness off, and I thrashed and splashed about before starting the even more boring task of repairing tubes.

With mounting horror I realised that I couldn't find my bicycle pump, either in my room, in the 'car-park' at the back of the hotel or anywhere inside the hotel. I challenged the desk clerk, who initially didn't know what I was talking about but after my despairing charade on the pump's function told me, sympathetically, to buy a new one.

'Don't you realise I need a special pump, not available in India?' I shrieked.

The clerk confirmed that he hadn't been aware of that fact, and made the observation that I was in some trouble if I didn't find it, before returning to a Lonely Planet disciple.

I rushed out into the street, grabbed more disciples to ask them to keep an eye out for someone carrying a Western bicycle pump, challenged stall-holders to ask if they had seen anything suspicious and scoured the canals to see if some nasty little boy had thrown it into the murky depths. For an hour I roamed the streets hurling accusations and requests for help in an arbitrary fashion, and encountering a virtually unanimous lack of interest or comprehension.

Back at the hotel, I looked at my Murray's guidebook. In 1971 there were apparently 160,000 people living in Alleppey. At the very most one in a thousand would want to steal a bicycle pump, and of those possibly half were doing something else at the time, another quarter only stole Indian pumps and maybe twenty were in prison. On perfectly sound, logical principles, therefore, it meant that there were only twenty people in the whole of Alleppey who might have stolen my pump, and I was quite sure that the police would know who they were. I hailed an auto-rickshaw and demanded to be taken to the police station.

In the rickshaw I suddenly thought that I had been too pessimistic, and that a significantly lower number of crooks would want an object as useless as a pump which didn't fit Indian valves. The true figure must be confined to the number of mad people in Alleppey whose insanity revealed itself in utterly pointless thefts – say, at most, half a dozen whom the chief of police would certainly be able to name.

I arrived at the station just as the prisoners were about to be given their supper. A huge pile of rice and two saucepans of dark stew were dumped on the floor, and the prisoners were let out to squat around the surprisingly appetising meal and shove handfuls of the stuff down their throats. One policeman shuffled around them, anxiously clasping an ancient rifle and staring in a rather bewildered way at the events he was supposedly in charge of.

'Hello,' I said. 'Does anybody speak English?'

The policeman blinked and tightened his grip on the gun. In time-honoured fashion, I repeated the question, a little slower and a lot louder. The policeman blinked again. At last, one of the prisoners admitted that he spoke English.

'Can you tell the policeman that I want to report a theft.'

The prisoner looked absolutely delighted – possibly at the thought that he was clearly innocent of this latest outrage, possibly that the villains of Alleppey were not too depressed by his incarceration for all crime to have stopped. He translated, which caused enormous merriment amongst the prisoners and absolute consternation for the policeman. He stood in a state of shock before suddenly handing me his rifle, muttering a few incomprehensible words and rushing out of the building.

'He has gone to get the chief,' the English-speaking prisoner informed me, and smiled pleasantly. The other prisoners, who had recovered from their hysteria by now, were calmly getting on with their meal and obviously not about to make a break for it, which was on the whole a source of some relief to me.

'What are you in here for?' I asked, trying to make myself agreeable.

'I have been arrested,' he replied, grabbing a great handful of rice.

'What for?'

'I am under suspicion.'

'Of what?'

'Committing a criminal act.'

'Hmm. Is there any truth in the reputation the Indian police have for corruption?'

Sadly, this potentially unique insight into Indian prison conditions was ended by the return of the bewildered policeman, accompanied by an efficient-looking sergeant. In the course of investigating why the prisoner had been locked up, I had left the rifle on the table on the basis that not only was I never going to use it, but I wanted to avoid giving the impression that I was somehow connected with the police in order to encourage the prisoner to talk to me. The sight of the abandoned rifle in the close vicinity of unguarded prisoners had a predictable effect on the sergeant who, naturally enough, blamed the still bemused constable.

In due course, after the constable had been suitably reprimanded, I was asked to follow the sergeant into an establishment he described as the officer's mess. It was a misleading title, suggesting a grandeur that was totally absent in the room I found myself in, reminiscent of the WIAA offices in Bombay in its overwhelming sense of inertia and Victorian decoration. Two benches were leaning against one wall, surprisingly unoccupied by the half-dozen officers who lounged about the place. A large desk, which was easily big enough for all of them to sit around, was in fact the exclusive preserve of an impressively large figure, who sat with a napkin tucked between his second and third shirt buttons, having clearly just finished a meal.

He dabbed the corners of his mouth, let his head subside into the great fatty mass that made up his neck and boomed:

'So you have had your camera stolen?'

'No.'

'You must have had your camera stolen. Every tourist has their camera stolen.'

'I've lost my bicycle pump.'

He rolled his lips and stared at me for a few seconds. Then, leaning across the table, he waved a finger at me and warned:

'I am a very busy man.'

'And I am cycling to China, and if I have lost my pump I will have to either go to Singapore to buy a replacement or wait for one to be sent from London.'

'We have bicycle pumps in India.'

'Not for my valves.'

'Well, what do you want me to do?'

'Alleppey is a small town. Do you know who would take a bicycle pump?'

'Alleppey is a large town, but an honest town. If you wish to report your bicycle pump as missing, we shall investigate.'

As he spoke he found a piece of paper and pushed it across the desk, inviting – almost daring – me to file the report. I had no qualms about doing so, and refused to feel any embarrassment when he asked for a clear indication of the value of the pump – about £3.

The chief read the report and scratched each of his chins in turn. Eventually he announced that he would find my pump, and that in the interval I should go back to my hotel with three of his men. Greatly heartened by his words, I climbed into a jeep and was driven at high speed back to the hotel, which at that time of night was teeming with Lonely Planet disciples. A few recognised me from my earlier approaches and laughingly asked if I had found my pump. The re-tracing of my earlier movements in the presence of the policeman and the hotel-owner (who was reluctant to have policemen wandering around his hotel unobserved) added to the serious manner in which the investigation was being carried out at that stage.

'. . . and then I put my luggage into my room,' I announced as I unlocked the padlock and threw open the door.

We walked in and immediately two of the policemen began to cough. They tapped the arm of the third and pointed to a bicycle pump that was being used as a prop to hold my washing away from the wall. Suddenly, I began to suffer from the same coughing fit.

'Huh, huh . . . I'm very, huh, huh sorry. Um, huh, huh, shall we, er go back to the chief?'

They glared at me, confirming that they did indeed want me to go back to the police station, where, judging from their angry expressions, they hoped I would be kept for a long time. We drove back, if anything even faster than on the first journey.

The chief heard their account with impressive good humour.

'The thieves have returned your bicycle pump,' he solemnly pronounced. 'Perhaps they heard that I was investigating the case.'

'It wasn't taken,' I mumbled. 'It was a mistake. It was never stolen.'

The chief pushed a collection box across the desk, and observed:

'My police force have fully investigated the reported theft of your property – property which you have told us was of great value to you.' He shook the collection box. 'We have succeeded in finding your stolen property. As I said, Alleppey is an honest town.'

I thrust some money into his box, and thanked him for the efficiency of his investigation. No jeep was provided for the trip back to the hotel, and I trudged back, chastened by this encounter with the Indian police. To console myself, I stopped at an expensive Chinese restaurant and lavishly spent some of the money I had saved by no longer having to fly to Singapore to get a replacement pump.

The next morning, my inner tubes remaining punctured, I joined the mass exodus of tourists from St George's to the ferry terminal. I arrived about ten minutes before departure time, to find the barge-like ferry absolutely packed with Lonely Planetites. There were no Indians aboard, yet dozens of white faces sat contentedly relishing this Great Indian Experience. Suffering a crisis of confidence, I sat down and re-read the 'bible' to convince myself that the trip was genuinely a GIE. The crisis was soon over. The trip was going to be 'one of the highlights of a visit to Kerala and one you will remember fondly for a long time'. I hauled my bike up and began to shuffle down the plank to get aboard, an activity promptly suspended when my keys fell out of my front pannier into the filthy water. Possibly, in a more sanguine mood, I might have cheerfully recalled that I hadn't locked my bike since leaving Greece, that I had a spare key for my padlock and that I was unlikely to need my London flat keys in the immediate future. I was, however, not in a sanguine mood, and the loss of my keys was something I considered as disastrous as the 'loss' of my pump.

Fortunately, one of the sudden fits of despondency to which I was increasingly finding myself subject was prevented by four men offering to dive into the filthy water and retrieve my keys. They bargained between themselves, reducing the asking price from twenty to fifteen to ten rupees, payment to be made only if the keys were successfully retrieved. My acceptance of what seemed an absolute bargain caused a great furore amongst the other hagglers, who suddenly saw the opportunity of what might be easy money pass them by. The price went still lower, but looking at the water and instinctively shuddering at the thought of the foul germs which would infest whichever body plunged into the water, I refused to renege on my ten-rupee agreement. The delighted diver stripped off and found my keys in, at most, ten seconds – a feat which appalled even more those who had either been too greedy, not greedy enough or just uninterested in diving in, because the ten rupees I handed over was more than an agricultural labourer or a scaffolder earned in a day. Obviously none of them shared my distress at the idea of even dipping a toe into the water. I didn't know how long the acrimonious bickering would have continued at my minor assault on traditional Indian wage levels, but the ferry captain, who had watched the key incident to its end, decided that the departure had been delayed long enough and gave two blasts on his hooter, sending two of his men to help with my bike.

For the first few moments after boarding I couldn't identify the strange atmosphere that suffused the ferry. Indeed, I might never have done so had there not been a sudden rush of Indian passengers who had been lolling about the platform showing not only no inclination to get on board, but not even the slightest sign that they hoped to travel with us. Their arrival restored the more usual Indian atmosphere of anarchic chaos, as the Western tourists, who had been sitting in orderly fashion and strictly preserving their right to limit occupation of a three-person bench to three people. What's more, a neat pile of rucksacks and the odd suitcase had been built up in order to allow them space to wave their feet around and walk between the benches without undertaking an obstacle course.

These careful arrangements were contemptuously dismissed by the new Indian arrivals, who, laden down with huge piles of saucepans, buckets, watering-cans, yards of cloth and the other items available in Alleppey and not in their own villages, were prepared neither to add their recent acquisitions to the Western pile, nor to stand all the way home just because some tourists wanted to dump their comparatively enormous bottoms on as large a piece of bench as possible. Unlike my own approach to finding somewhere to sit down, which was a sort of ingratiating shuffling-around, mumbling vaguely about whether anyone minded me joining them, the Indian passengers saw spaces where none had appeared to me and barged their way in, using neighbouring Western laps as convenient luggage racks. Once established, the family and friends who had come along on the shopping trip would be called over and somehow squeezed in.

The existing inhabitants of these benches adopted typically Western defences to these manoeuvres, sitting firmly and impassively in a rock-like determination to withstand the attack. It was the wrong method, easily breached by the whirling Indian bottoms which screwed their way into the gaps and then consolidated their position by the effective use of elbows, knees and foul-smelling cigarettes. The final outcome was rather satisfying to me as, having been refused permission to sit with one group of people, I saw them grumpily abandon the whole bench in favour of sitting on the roof where, at least to begin with, there was a little room.

Whilst this unseemly fighting for seats had been going on the ferry had, virtually unnoticed, set off for the eight-and-a-half-hour trip to Quilon. The country was almost exactly the reverse of the Deccan plateau – a large flat area with dozens of small rivers, streams and man-made irrigation canals providing some relief for the parched land. Here the back-waters were divided by narrow spits of land and a few more substantial islands, creating a sort of rustic Venice, an agricultural world in the middle of an enormous lagoon. It seemed to me another highly improbable way of life, to rival the underground cities of Cappodocia in Turkey and the sandstone-igloos of Syria.

Every so often, one of the little shopping parties would get off and disappear amongst a line of palm trees – a strange sight as they trotted along beneath the mound of watering-cans, apparently walking on water. Camera shutters clicked wildly whenever we passed a dugout barge sailing slowly along, powered by a huge sail but sadly very little wind. Canoes in contrast dashed about the place with disconcerting haste. One imagined that life here would be leisurely and timeless, but this impression was repeatedly proved wrong by the processing of coconut shells, the weaving of coir mats and even animal-husbandry – which supplemented the fishing. That material rewards followed all this activity was demonstrated not just by the shopping parties, but by the not infrequent sight of television aerials – though goodness knows what sense was made of television in this unusual world.

My regrets that I wasn't cycling through the area and allowing myself the opportunity of exploring the villages properly were to some extent lessened by studying my map, which showed that from Cochin to Alleppey I had cycled parallel to a similar stretch of water with identical ferries and the same superficially precarious economy. This was confirmed by two Dutch people who had taken the ferry from Cochin to Quilon and hoped, if it was possible, to go all the way from Cochin to Trivandrum by boat. I suddenly realised that there were no roads on most of the islands, and that the inhabitants either walked or travelled by boat. A bicycle would be absolutely useless as a means of exploring the area, and unfortunately I wouldn't have been able to hire a canoe.

The Dutch couple were typical of the ferry passengers in at least one respect, other than having a copy of *Lonely Planet*. Everybody had dismissed Quilon as nothing more than a place to stop overnight between the backwater trip and Kovalam Beach. Indeed, the only variation between the passengers with regard to their plans for next few days' movement was whether they intended to spend any time in Trivandrum, the state capital of Kerala, but tantalisingly close to Kovalam.

I opted to stay in Trivandrum in the faint hope that I would be able to reserve a ferry ticket from Madras to Penang, and because I felt that a couple of days in a Keralan town might be interesting – so far I had spent time only in the Dutch town of Cochin. Quite by chance, the ferry office was in the same building as my hotel and wasn't opening until Monday, so I was committed to at least two days in Trivandrum. Unfortunately, my first meal in the town was two portions of very greasy fried egg and chips, eaten at the normally 'safe' Indian Coffee House – a chain of cheap restaurants in Kerala. Whether it was the sudden reversion to a Western diet or just coincidence, shortly after this meal I suffered a nasty recurrence of my stomach problems and became virtually house-bound.

This was particularly annoying, as I had planned to try and enter a mile race being held in the sports stadium close to the hotel, which for some reason I thought I had a chance of winning. Instead, I was limited to uncomfortable shuffles to the museum, art gallery and a Keralan Book Fair, as well as sitting in some anguish at the sports meeting. Despite this disagreeable situation I liked Trivandrum, which was pleasantly free of some of the more irritating features of less cosmopolitan and affluent towns.

In the end I left Trivandrum without my ferry ticket, principally because I had taken a dislike to the operator's agent, who rolled up at his office at quarter to eleven because he didn't think anyone would be interested in buying tickets until then. I sniffily told him that I had hoped not just to have bought my ticket, but to have cycled down to Kovalam by half past ten, which he claimed to be one of the funniest things he had ever heard.

When I arrived at Kovalam, I began to see why he found my urgency so amusing. Like Goa, Kovalam had collected a fairly large group of long-term neo-residents, most of whom devoted themselves to an examination of the effects of Keralan black, supplies of which were readily available from various beach salesmen, café owners and hoteliers. The most serious travellers, who measured their stay in terms of how many visa renewals they could obtain, had hired beach-huts on an indefinite basis, from which they would emerge to walk slowly up and down the beach, contemplating the vagaries of their existence.

To my surprise, many of the people I had met on the Alleppey– Quilon ferry had emphatically renounced the touristy photographing of dug-out barges, and drifted around the slopes above the beach trying to get hold of a more beach-credible place to stay. Nearly everyone wore a piece of cotton wrapped around their waist as a statement of their close relationship with the Indian way of life and their rejection of constricting Western clothes. A ready market for their discards existed, as most of the hoteliers would accept clothes in exchange for a couple of nights' accommodation or a meal.

A contrast with this assumed asceticism was embarrassingly close, as a quarry between the beach and the village relied upon a large army of women to chip rocks up into pea-size pieces. These women sat beneath their temporary shelters at the side of the road endlessly knocking stones together. They were a sombre sight in the idyllic surroundings – lush forests, with numerous flowers and fruits, and delicious food available to us in the restaurants on the beach. Despite their close proximity, the beach-life and the quarry-life seemed to be irreconcilably apart.

Cape Cormorin was no more than fifty miles from Kovalam, and after three days lolling around doing nothing I decided to get to the southern tip and then begin my journey north towards Peking, a change of direction which had begun to assume great significance for me. It was gratifying to come across a pair of BBC journalists about five miles north of Nagercoil who were prepared to record my thoughts on the first half of my trip. I was particularly pleased, as it had been made clear to me from reading Rose Macaulay's *The Towers of Trebizond* that I hadn't yet experienced one of the great sights of travel – a BBC team trying to persuade the local people to sing and dance for the eventual edification of the Home Counties.

Sadly, the two I met were involved in a far more serious enterprise: recording the various activities of Oxfam and other agencies they encountered on their journey by bike from Kashmir to Cape Cormorin. However, I found the meeting so morale-boosting that when I eventually arrived at the Cape I decided to risk staying at a religious ashram recommended to me by some Australians I'd met at Hampi. The name, scribbled on one of my spare inner tube boxes, was the Vivekananda Memorial, beside which I had written and underlined the word 'cheap'. After my experiences in Kovalam I had decided to keep away from Westerners seeking salvation, but now thought that I should investigate the phenomenon further.

Physically, the ashram looked remarkably similar to the holiday home at Lonavale just outside Bombay – the same regimental rows of Nissen huts, and an atmosphere of woodworm and rising damp. Unlike the holiday camp, however, someone had gone round trying to smarten it up, by adding superficial improvements such as smart signposts directing one to the 'library', 'lecture hall' and 'restaurant'. Small groups of the converted, dominated noticeably by Scandinavians and Americans, huddled together beneath the signs like teenagers at a bus stop, but instead of snogging they radiated what was, even by the standards of most Westerners in India, an exceptionally vacant complacency. Other individuals prowled about with an intense, almost savage menace – possibly in reaction to the smugness of the others.

At reception a particularly bland individual pedantically inspected my passport and my entry in the register, clearly searching for some inconsistency. To his right, an empty board covered in a piece of decaying green felt announced 'today's activities'. Someone had stuffed a personal note in the plastic net next to it, announcing that he or she had gone to Auroville – a project north of Pondicherry which was supposed to be 'an experiment in international living where men and women could live in peace and progressive harmony with each other above all creeds, politics and nationalities'. The receptionist appeared unmoved by these sentiments, and stared despondently at his register. Eventually he called for someone to escort me to a three-bedded room in which the one faint light bulb made it impossible to tell whether I was getting good value or not. The restaurant, which alone amongst the potential activities of the place was actually in operation, served a peculiarly flavourless amalgam of southern Indian food and that of an unadventurous vegetarian restaurant in the West. That evening, as there was nothing else to do, I cycled to the coast.

Apart from its geographical significance as the most southern point in India, Cape Cormorin (which looked remarkably similar to John O'Groats) is dedicated to the goddess Kanya-kumari, an incarnation of Parvati, and attracts hundreds of pilgrims who showed infinitely more enthusiasm than the dismal occupants of the Vivekananda Memorial. However, I still had absolutely no idea why anyone had bothered to make the pilgrimage. All the pilgrims stood facing out either to the Bay of Bengal or the Indian Ocean, and chattered. Suddenly, they all started rushing back to mini-buses or hotels and disappeared, most of the trinket shops closed up, and I was left standing practically by myself overlooking the small temple that stands on one of the small rock-islands.

I asked one of the trinket-sellers what this behaviour represented.

'They have come to see the sunset.'

'But today was cloudy,' I said.

The trinket salesman assumed a serene happiness, indicative perhaps of his closeness to Kanya-kumari, and, in a fine demonstration of the Indian ability to ignore facts, reiterated his claim that the pilgrims had watched the sunset. I found this sort of incident rather frustrating. Was my insistence on there actually being a sunset just tiresome European pedantry? I hoped that someone at the ashram, which was after all a memorial to the man who helped explain Hinduism to the West, would be able to enlighten me. The receptionist just looked irritated, however, and the Scandinavians dismissed the pilgrims as nasty materialists who had sold their faith for the type of plastic models and cardboard hats the trinket salesman sold. I tried to ask about the significance of the sunset, even when the sun was hidden behind clouds, and also why nobody was using the temple.

The only explanation I heard was that unlike Christianity, which was generally dismissed as a religion which only required attendance at church on Sunday, Hinduism was a religion which entered every social activity – including standing on rocks watching an invisible sunset. The most common reaction to my enquiries was to dismiss me as someone seeking logical answers to emotional questions, which, though not very helpful, might have been fair.

Further north, in the series of temples between the Cape and Madras, I became more and more confused about why people behaved in certain ways and what, if anything, their behaviour meant. One great obstacle to understanding was that in most of the temples non-Hindus were not allowed into the inner sanctum, although this did not mean that one never saw any religious activity. In Madurai, in the outer squares of the temple, hundreds of people would take up a variety of devotional positions: kneeling with foreheads touching the ground; sitting in yoga positions with an appearance of great calm; walking round with an impromptu band bashing drums, blowing strange wind instruments and chanting; sitting in groups reciting from books; and earnestly lighting saucers of oil or distributing garlands of flowers in front of particular images.

At the same time, and within an arm's length of these activities, others were selling pots, pans, baskets, sewing equipment and every conceivable religious aid – oil lamps, flowers, fruit, rosaries, statues made of clay or plastic or precious stones, joss sticks and bells and hundreds of gaudy posters and postcards depicting gods and goddesses. Opposite the Hall of a Thousand Pillars three men were offering elephant rides for a fee.

At other temples, nothing happened. At Tanjore, for example, there were just four people in the whole complex, and whereas at Madurai (and in Tiruchchirappalli) one began to sense the way in which social life and religion are one – the temple and religious life mixing freely with the bazaars and the great gaiety of southern Indian life – at Tanjore one looked at an interesting and spectacularly beautiful museum.

More so than anywhere else, cycling in Tamil Nadu was like cycling through a great religious centre. Every few hundred yards small shrines – some with just a crudely carved lump of wood representing the deity, others with an elaborate stone statue – stood beside the road, the most popular causing a road-block as every vehicle pulled up to throw an offering towards the god or goddess and tap the small dot of coloured paint on their forehead. An incredible number of villages had spectacular temple complexes, which often matched the size of the surrounding village. It was like cycling through England and finding that hundreds of villages had cathedrals.

Fortunately, one of these villages, Chidambaram, did allow non-Hindus into the inner sanctum, and I was able to see a Hindu ceremony. Like most of the Dravidian temples of the south, and like all the large temples that I saw, Chidambaram's temple was surrounded by two squares, each side of which had a large *gopuram* in the middle. At Madurai these outer squares were filled with salesmen, but at Chidambaram there was nobody. The second square contained three small shrines, but again was essentially unoccupied. The third square was covered, and at the heart of this central complex was the inner sanctum, partially uncovered.

In the centre of this final square there was a golden-roofed temple, the silver-panelled doors of which were closed when I arrived. When opened these were no more than four feet wide, and a long queue – later to become a scrum – gathered around for the opening. Nothing happened until six o'clock, when two rows of bells began to ring and about a dozen drummers marched towards the temple. After five minutes of growing frenzy the silver doors opened and three small boys were revealed, impassively holding candelabra. Behind these boys stood what looked rather like a crib, covered in garlands and brightly lit with candles.

At the front of the queue five or six Brahmins wearing white *dhotis* entered the shrine and began to wave candelabra at the 'altar'; each of these was shaped differently – a triangle, a circle, a four-spoked wheel and a simple candelabrum. Each time any of these were waved, the people in the queue made a wide variety of responses: some pressed their palms together above their head, some tapped their cheeks, some tapped their forehead and some chanted. Others did nothing. Immediately after each candelabrum had been waved the Brahmins scattered water over their hands and heads. Finally, after about half an hour during which the bells and drums had continued to strike a crazy rhythm, the silver doors half closed and two Brahmins dispensed small dabs of coloured powder on to the foreheads of the congregation.

Apart from this dabbing of colour on to their heads, which was performed with a slightly condescending disapproval, the audience were completely ignored during the performance, and were made to crush together in some discomfort to see what was happening. Despite this lack of interest in them, however, the audience generated the most extraordinary excitement, and their faces were quite enraptured each time the candles were waved at the idol.

Four hours later I heard the bells and drums again, so ran back to find exactly the same performance, except that at the end a procession – preceded by the musicians and with the Brahmins carrying the idol – toured the inner sanctum and the outer covered square, pausing in front of each small shrine to wave candles and light a bowl of oil. The idol was carried in a small gondola-shaped container, covered in flowers and surrounded by candles. The procession, which took nearly two hours to complete its tour, finally ended with the idol and the Brahmins disappearing into yet another inner sanctum exclusively reserved for the Brahmins and gods. I left at that stage, although most of the others in the procession sat or knelt around their own oil lamps, either in prayer, or in conversation with the Brahmins, who at last deigned to speak to the faithful.

I found it strange cycling the next day. The tremendous sense of energetic and lively devotion that I'd seen that evening seemed almost unreal once I was back in the lassitude of everyday India. I knew that of all the temples I had seen Chidambaram was one of the least animated, yet I had left in a state of some shock at the strength of feeling exhibited, so unexpected after the somnolence of normal life. With dismay, I realised that just three days away from Madras and my leaving India I had seen a vitality and excitement which I had completely missed throughout the rest of the country. Perhaps I had totally misunderstood the gloomy occupants of the Automobile Association offices in Bombay, the dozy and inefficient hoteliers in Agra. Suddenly I remembered that the fat man at the hotel had been carrying a candle, obviously having been praying. I groaned at how little I had understood.

There was little relief to come. Before Madras I stayed in Pondicherry and Mahabillipuram, both quite used to tourists, and not very interested in helping me through my education. However, I soon turned my attention to more practical matters. I learned in Pondicherry that my ferry to Malaysia had caught fire, with significant loss of life and the cancellation of the next voyage. Entirely selfishly, I wondered how the tragedy was going to affect me.

Soon after arriving in Madras I discovered that the ferry was permanently out of service, and that the company would almost certainly not consider replacing it as the route had been losing them too much money, so I went to the Harbour Security Office to try and arrange my passage on a cargo ship. It operated from a small hut opposite the vast red-brick post office, another example of British northern industrial architecture.

Inside the Harbour Security Office, an officer with two pips on his shoulder was on the phone trying to explain some mistake he had made. The upshot of the conversation was that his senior officer announced his impending arrival to continue the criticism in person – a lucky moment for me, being guaranteed access to the officer in command. A blackboard listed the boats in dock, the date of departure and their destination, and I could see that in three days a Yugoslavian-registered boat was leaving for Penang. If I couldn't get on that another boat was going to Singapore the day after. Both left me with the opportunity of a pleasant ride up to Bangkok before my flight to Hong Kong.

The senior officer arrived, bristling with authority and purpose.

'What does he want?' he demanded, addressing the two-pip officer and nodding his head towards me.

'He wants to get a boat to Malaysia,' replied Two-pip.

'Or Singapore,' I added.

'Go to the Shipping Corporation of India in Lungi Chetty Street. They have a ferry service.'

'It's stopped.'

'Well, go to Lungi Chetty Street.'

'I have. They're not replacing it with another boat.'

The senior officer sighed. 'Give him a pass. Let him ask the captains.'

'We can't give him a pass. He can't go on to the docks,' said Two-pip.

'Well, get rid of him then.'

I went through the whole thing again with Two-pip, who added that some regulation existed which prevented passengers travelling on cargo ships. The senior officer grew impatient, so I left with the address of Indo-Malaysian Shipping Lines. They informed me that they would take my bike, but not me. For two days I toured round the various shipping lines of Madras, obtaining courteous but consistently negative replies – some relying on the regulation that Two-pip had told me about, others regretting that they didn't have any ships going to South-East Asia.

The experience confirmed the widely reported cosmopolitan, civilised treatment one could expect in Madras. My half-hearted attempts to cajole or buy myself a place were met with distressing politeness, and with every good wish I was eased out of all the offices. The position appeared fairly hopeless. All the aeroplanes were full, a direct result of the cancellation of the ferry service, and the only alternative was to go up to Calcutta, where regular flights to Bangkok were still available. The question then was how to get to Calcutta.

Since the Cape, my health had been steadily deteriorating. The cumulative effect of long-term dysentery, my inability to retain any food, the inadequacy of the village diet and cycling in high temperatures was taking its toll. Since Tanjore I had eaten nothing other than bananas, dry fruit cake and mango juice, which may have been gastronomically unexciting but caused me the least violent disruption. Even so, I had been forced to stay in bed for three days in Madras because of searing headaches and an unbearable and unbeatable lassitude. It was quite clear that I couldn't cycle the 950 miles to Calcutta, although I thought I'd at least start out and get about a third of the way.

The results of my attempted cycling support those who believe that it's all a matter of will-power. I had become quite used to having to vomit and diarrhoea at the side of the road, and had always climbed back on my bike without giving the matter much thought. I hadn't, however, prepared myself for cycling north of Madras, and despite my new feeling that I had misunderstood the Indians, and now had a golden opportunity to explore further the villages of Andhra Pradesh and Orissa, I was suddenly overcome by a complete lack of interest in cycling, Indian villagers and life on the eastern Indian sea-board. In a childish demonstration of this apathy I pointedly read a copy of *Byzantine Style and Civilisation* which I found in the hotel library, a collection of books donated by various guests.

I had given up cycling about ten miles north of Madras when stuck under a tree being sick. There was really no incentive that I could then think of to go on, so I turned despondently back and went to the station to get the first train to Calcutta, which, almost incredibly, left the next day.

10

Cholera and champagne

There must be some recognised medical treatment for those suffering
from their fourth consecutive month of diarrhoea, an experience which
became more and more debilitating – other people knew me only as a
skinny wreck who kept rushing off in the middle of conversations, and
I began to forget what life was like without regularly squatting in a
ditch under the lazy gaze of passing Indian villagers. So long as I could
cycle along, take in the occasional temple and sustain myself with
handfuls of aspirins and the mysterious collection of pills I'd brought
out from London, I had rather ignored the long-term consequences of
cycling in the humid heat of southern India and failing abjectly to
retain any food.

The solution would probably have been simply to find somewhere
comfortable to stay – no problem in Madras – sip gently at boiled milk
and spend most of the time in bed. Almost certainly, unless one sub-
scribed to the 'shock theory', spending twenty-four hours crouched on
a wooden board in an Indian second-class train was unlikely to result
in any marked improvement.

As I shouldn't sensibly have been on the train anyway, it was perhaps
only logical that the two English doctors who found me slumped in a
corner of the carriage should carry the whole thing a stage further and
decide that the best thing for me was a large stiff drink. They
accordingly produced a bottle of gin and, quite unexpectedly, a bottle
of Pimms. However inadvisable, our steady consumption of both
bottles (carefully preserved for several months while the doctors were
acting as locums in a southern Indian hospital) achieved the spectacular
result of simultaneously helping me to forget about my stomach, ignore
the elbows sticking into my ribs and sleep soundly for perhaps the first
night since my illness began.

The only drawback was that I failed to pay any attention to what
was going on around me, either in the compartment or in the country

we were travelling through, except periodically to leap off the train at stations to try and buy a few more bottles of 'mixers'. The bleary, gin-soaked state we found ourselves in prevented any particular enjoyment of our early morning arrival in Calcutta. The bright sun seemed deliberately harsh, and the noise and density of the traffic across the Howrah Bridge and the chaos of Chowringhee Lane apparently calcu-lated to emphasise the practical advantages of avoiding alcohol, par-ticularly when one was suffering from diarrhoea which had responded to either the gin or the Pimms with a vengeance.

It was fairly clear that I should get some medical advice from a doctor not in the process of celebrating the end of an uncomfortable (but apparently rewarding) locum-tenency, and I decided to ask a chemist for advice about where I could find a reliable doctor. The chemist wanted to know what was wrong with me.

'I have a headache, constant diarrhoea, vomiting, spitting blood, loss of appetite and generally feel dreadful.'

'You do not need to see a doctor,' the chemist declared. 'What medical treatment have you had?'

I showed him my certificates demonstrating that I had been in-oculated against cholera, typhoid, tetanus and rabies. He studied them.

'Of course you are not feeling well. They are all out of date. You should have had more injections.'

I began to feel even weaker, and started to grope wildly for my insurance policy which promised to pay for my flight home to allow me to die in the comfort of home. In the background I could faintly hear the carping of the chemist:

'. . . you should have . . . not very expensive . . . prevention is better than the cure . . . better safe than sorry . . .' and on and on with an endless series of platitudes – all apposite, but all far too late.

'What should I do?' I bleated, my mouth dry and tasting of salt, undoubtedly the first sign of some awful disease.

'You must go to Calcutta Municipal Corporation. They will do everything for you.'

'Calcutta Municipal Corporation' – the very name seemed syno-nymous with urban chaos, appalling housing, colossal unemployment, disastrous labour relations, rebellious students, political instability and, almost certainly, lamentable medical facilities. My pessimism was justi-fied – the Corporation's medical section was housed in a small room by the entrance of a large and ugly Victorian red-brick building at one side of the New Market.

The 'immunisation room', as the section grandly called itself, looked like the sorting room of a small-town post office – and indeed might once have been the Corporation's sub-post office. The walls were lined with wooden pigeon holes, two roll-top desks stood beneath the windows overlooking the market's clocktower, and in the centre of the room there was a large oak table with three chairs placed haphazardly around. The only hint that the room had a medical purpose was one white coat hanging on a hook beside the window, a small gas stove on which stood a saucepan filled with boiling water and syringes, and finally, on the table, a plastic box with some small phials of pale-coloured fluids.

One man sat in the room, concentrating almost nervously on some documents he'd found in one of the desks. I asked him if I'd come to the right place for some cholera and typhoid injections.

'Oh yes, sir. The doctor is away now. I am only clerk, grade three.'

'When will the doctor be back?'

'I don't know. The doctor is a very busy man.'

'Shall I wait, or come back later?'

The clerk, grade three, suddenly looked terrified and rushed over to the saucepan which he then threw on to the table.

'I am telling you,' he cried, 'the doctor is a very busy man.'

As he spoke the door opened and a man wearing a rather incongruous tweed jacket walked in.

'He is the vet,' said the clerk with a breathless passion which suggested they were to be his last words.

I asked the vet if he knew when the doctor was coming back.

'I don't know, old boy,' said the vet in a distinctly Indian accent. 'What's it all about?' He flopped behind a desk and lit a foul-smelling *beedi*.

'I think I may have cholera, and want some injections.'

'You haven't got cholera, old boy – and if you had it would be too late for the injections. Don't know where "doc" is, but I can do the jabs.' He picked up one of the needles, dried it on the white coat and scuffled about in the plastic box.

'Right, roll up your sleeve.'

Without really believing in the suggestion – perhaps imagining it all to be part of the disassociated, fantastic world I was increasingly living in – I did as he told me, only to recoil seconds later as what felt like a cricket stump was plunged into my arm and twisted, an act done with the finesse of a man turning soil over with a garden fork.

The needle was hauled out, put back into the saucepan, rinsed out

by quickly squirting some hot water in and out and then re-dried on
the white coat.

'Typhoid . . . typhoid?' the vet murmured as he rummaged through
the plastic box.

'Don't worry,' I said. 'I'm going.'

'Oh well. I'll give you the certificate anyway. Say you've had it.
That's what you really want, isn't it?'

If the certificates were going to help me get into Thailand, Hong
Kong or China then the vet was probably right – they were all I
wanted; but nothing had been done to help me recover from my
problems. I asked for advice in my hotel, but the request was considered
so impertinent, almost offensive, that I decided to wait until I arrived
in Bangkok – just two hours away by air, with a reservation available
in three days.

I didn't do much in Calcutta, feeling too weak and dispirited to
traipse round more than the barest minimum of tourist attractions –
the museum, the cathedral, the Victoria Memorial and the Maidan.
Most of the time I lay on the grass in the Maidan, following amateur
cricket matches and listening to the fuzzy reports of the cricket world
cup being played in Australia.

I arrived in Bangkok in this dilapidated condition and, too weary to
queue up at the airport bank to change money, I began to cycle miserably down the six-lane motorway towards central Bangkok. Cars, all
driven at the absolute limits of the engine's capability, flashed past,
missing me by inches. It was dark, I had no lights on my bike, no
money, no idea where I should try and get to in Bangkok and was
forced to stop every few minutes to be sick.

Some time around midnight I found an area of cheap hotels, most
either closed or closing and none interested in taking a single person
offering a combination of rupees, sterling, Italian lire and a few American dollars in payment for a room. My 'emergency' money – a 100-
dollar note – was the only solution, and I wandered around central
Bangkok, waving the note and stopping the less seedy passers-by to
ask them to change it for me. In due course, at a disgracefully dis-
advantageous rate, a restaurant agreed to sell me some baht, on condition that I ate there and stayed in the hotel run by the restaurant
management. It was, at about half past one in the morning, an offer I
couldn't refuse, though I vowed that I would leave early next morning
in search of a less exploitative hotel.

'Next morning' turned out to be three days later, something I only
discovered when I was presented with a bill for three nights, instead of

the anticipated one. My arguments were defeated when the manager produced a newspaper which proved that I had slept for more than seventy-two hours without any recollection. My whole situation was beginning to get rather alarming; instinctively I felt that either I should have woken up, or that having failed to do so I shouldn't have still felt like death. In what might seem a rather belated move, I caught a taxi and went to hospital.

Two days later, having been pumped full of vitamins and handed great sackfuls of pills of various denomination, I began cycling down towards Ko Samui, a place I was assured was akin to paradise. The experience was a disaster – too ill to do barely more than stand, I struggled along the excellent roads, forced to push my bike up the slightest of slopes and unable to explain to anyone what I was doing or where I was going. After two days I caught a train to Surat Thani and cycled the short distance to the ferry terminal for Ko Samui.

For £1 a night I rented a small bungalow standing on the edge of a sandy beach and shaded by palm trees. My movements were limited to heaving myself out of bed to the chair conveniently situated on the small verandah at the front of the building, and occasionally stumbling to a restaurant for boiled fish and rice, the only food I was able to digest properly. A friendly American gave me two books – *Pride and Prejudice* and *The Mill on the Floss* – which provided my only stimulation as I remained throughout the week on the island only semi-conscious of the natural delights that were available.

In due course I became aware of the peculiar stares I was receiving, and the unfriendly response of the bungalow-owners who, perhaps understandably, disliked my killjoy behaviour and disapproved of the slow vegetation I was going through. If drinking gin and Pimms on an Indian train was an ineffective cure for my malaise, so was sitting around in a comfortable bungalow in southern Thailand. I decided to try and cycle the illness away – to try and generate enough adrenalin to kill whatever bug it was that had caught hold of me. Strangely enough, this proved quite successful and I managed to drag myself up the eastern coast, barely conscious of where I was but encouraged by the map I bought in Surat Thani which showed that so long as I stuck to the coast I would, eventually, end up back in Bangkok. More importantly, the experience of cycling in a country where scarcely anyone spoke English and where the way of life was so different from the West gave me new confidence about cycling in China, the prospect of which was increasingly dominating my thoughts.

The distraction of thinking about China was blinding me to Thailand

and, rather than whizz up to Chiang Mai for a cursory inspection of the hill tribes, I decided to fly off to Hong Kong where I hoped to meet a few friends and, with a combination of red pillar boxes, bitter and television highlights of English football, consolidate the restoration of my health.

Such limited expectations scarcely did justice to Hong Kong – filled as it was with people who were paid far too much, but were prepared to spend some of their enormous piles of loot on pouring champagne down me, inviting me to their parties, offering me cocktails and feeding me in restaurants. Some token discipline was, however, imposed against the dissolute attractions of Hong Kong night-life by the friends with whom I stayed. Even though they never said anything, they managed to make it clear that just because I had been decanted from a taxi at four in the morning there was no justification for not getting up at eight to examine the sports pages of the *South China Morning Post*, loaf around central Hong Kong and show some signs that I was trying to get my Chinese visa.

Although this method had failed on the train to Calcutta, drinking to excess and staying up until the early hours succeeded in restoring my health, and after two days of little sleep but lots of fun I began to feel capable of cycling the 2500 miles to Peking. In the meantime I was determined to enjoy the 'international' food and drink of Hong Kong, as everyone assured me that China was even more spartan than India. First, though, I had to get my Chinese visa, which had proved impossible in London.

Disappointingly, the China Travel Service in Hong Kong also informed me that I couldn't cycle in China, and I told some friends about this at a party that evening. 'Don't worry,' they said. 'China's not half as much fun as here.' But the friends who were putting me up took a more responsible attitude, and, no doubt alarmed at the prospect of my staying indefinitely, encouraged me to try again.

'Don't tell them that you're going to cycle in China,' they advised me. 'Say that you want to take a bike into the country.'

'That's just silly,' I replied. 'It's obvious that no one would take a bike unless they were going to cycle on it.'

'Don't tell them, and don't cycle across the border. Put your bike on the train to Canton and cycle to Peking from there – that way they won't see you cycling across the border.'

I went back to the China Travel Service.

'Hello. I want an individual visa, please.'

'That's no problem. It will cost you HK$110, and we need three photographs, your passport and, unless you want to pay more, two days' notice.'

'How much does luggage cost?'

'What sort of luggage?'

'A bicycle.'

'I think about HK$30, but I'm not sure. You must ask at the station.'

'There's no problem about taking a bike into China?'

'No. You know, lots of Chinese cycle – you will see many bicycles in China.'

'What a funny lot,' I thought as I left the building, to celebrate getting a Chinese visa over yet another bottle of champagne.

I I

Across the bamboo curtain

I wasn't too happy about leaving the comfortable delights of Hong Kong after just a week. I had already been invited over the next few days to two junk parties and a potentially highly amusing trip to Macao, and had been assured that the special deal of 60 per cent off the price of a particular nightclub's champagne would continue for at least another week. But instead of further wallowing in self-indulgence, I found myself, within hours of recovering from Turkish and Indian diarrhoea, standing on Hong Kong station on a cold Sunday morning waiting for the train to Canton.

My irritation wasn't eased by my slight hangover and the fact that I had been told by the China Travel Service to be at the station an hour and a half before the train left. There was nothing for me to do except read about English football matches in the *South China Morning Post* and study the league tables to see if it was really true that Everton were going to win the league and possibly the FA cup as well.

In due course an announcement was made that the 'flight' to Guangzhou was ready for boarding. It seemed to have absolutely nothing to do with me, but everybody else who was carrying China Travel Service coupons suddenly charged off towards something looking exactly like customs control at Dover Eastern docks.

'I want to go to Canton,' I told the guard. 'Do I get on this train?'

'Guangzhou. Canton. Guangzhou. Hurry please.'

I didn't have the faintest idea what he was talking about.

'Where do I catch the train for Canton?' I said, my voice rising.

'Guangzhou, Guangzhou,' the guard insisted.

'Guangzhou to you too.'

'Get on the train, honey,' said an American behind me. 'Canton's called Guangzhou now,' and while I picked up my bags she rattled off something in Chinese.

'Gosh. Do you speak Chinese?' I asked, a little unnecessarily.

'Ah do, 'n shit, honey, if ya don' spik Chahnese ya ain' gonna get no place,' following which she jabbed me in the chest.

'Cher, cher,' I replied, anxious to demonstrate that I knew the words for 'thank you'.

The woman sneered at me, and fired out a horrible high-pitched staccato which sounded rather like a small dog snapping at one's ankles. Instinctively I kicked out, and promptly stubbed my toe. Groaning, I thought longingly of the junk party the next day and how much more fun it would be than Canton, or 'Guangzhou'.

The only real hope was that the Chinese customs officials wouldn't allow me into the country with a bike, and I could flounce back to Hong Kong and the parties and champagne. Such a refusal was at least possible, as the official policy on bicycles was variable, and at best ambivalent. In London I'd asked at the China National Tourist Office near Baker Street and at the Society for Anglo-Chinese Understanding in Camden Town for permission, and had been firmly despatched with a refusal and a pile of literature on organised tours, Chinese philately and a book called *The Green Revolution Now!* In Hong Kong I had been given a ten-week visa with the specific instruction that, although I could take my bicycle into China, I was under no circumstances to cycle outside the open cities. (A visa allows foreign tourists to visit a hundred cities, and 'special permission' a further hundred; the rest of China is designated a closed area.)

All I had to do was to make it clear to anyone who looked as if they were in authority that I had every intention of cycling in as many 'closed areas' as possible, and get either thrown out or refused entry. Two opportunities were immediately available: I was handed a form on the train in which I was asked to describe firstly the purpose of my journey, and secondly any valuables I was taking into China. To the first I replied, in red ink, 'Cycling holiday from Canton to Peking', and to the second added 'Touring bicycle, manfd. F. W. Evans, London', and underlined the word 'touring'.

Just as I was beginning to feel a little more cheerful, even looking forward to the forthcoming confrontation, a savage machine began to emit the most piercing screams. I clutched my head and tried to see where this atrocious noise was coming from. It appeared to emanate from a television set suspended above the door leading to the next carriage, and quite astonishingly turned out to be our guard speaking. I revised my earlier opinion of spoken Chinese – it wasn't as subtle as a dog snapping at one's ankles, but closer to being hit on the head with a mallet.

The occasional breaks between this woman's screams were filled with advertisements for establishments and facilities supposedly available in Canton – fashion shows with disco music and lights, pleasant-looking bars with sycophantic waitresses, and taxi services offering the latest Japanese models, demonstrated by a smiling driver busily polishing the bonnet of an unrecognisable and characterless car.

A man sitting opposite me, wearing for some unfathomable reason a Strathclyde University tie, started to slurp up rice, soup and some slithers of meat. Despite childhood admonitions that it was rude to stare, I couldn't take my eyes off him as he lifted the silver throwaway container to within an inch of his mouth and then sucked as loudly and vividly as possible, simultaneously shovelling the food up off the plate with a pair of chopsticks. Two other men came and sat beside me and began to eat in the same extraordinary way, so that I felt as if I was sitting between three lavatory cisterns. I sat in a state of numbed shock as they chomped, slurped, guzzled and smacked their lips, while the female guard continued to fire out her mechanised screams at us.

The Strathclyde-tie man, conscious of my horrified gaze, smiled at me and between and during mouthfuls said:

'(Chomp, chomp, slurp.) Welcome (slurp) to (long guzzle at soup) welcome to China.'

I winced.

'It is your (slurp) first time in China?'

I nodded.

'We have been outside China for the first time, so we are opposites, yes?'

He began to laugh, obviously very pleased at this tenuous con-nection, and told his other friends about his joke. They nodded eagerly. I decided to laugh, uncertain whether it would be considered in-appropriate. They laughed back at me. I laughed still louder, began to roll around and hold my sides. It was all very worrying – what on earth were we laughing at?

Eventually it subsided.

'Travel is good for broadening the mind,' said one. 'Many students in China like to travel.'

I wasn't sure what to say, but as laughing seemed to be well received, I roared with laughter. The group looked at me with obvious distress.

'Travel is very important. We have been in Scotland organising cultural exchanges. It isn't funny.'

'I'm sorry,' I said, 'I just didn't think any Chinese people were allowed out of the country, and I thought that all the schools and universities had been closed down.'

They looked at me, not just with distress but with anger.

'We are an education delegation from Canton province,' they shouted. 'Education in China is not like the old days. Those are now ended. Now we encourage foreign travel and want individuals to find new things.'

'Coo,' I said, a little perturbed by this description as it was so unlike all that I had heard about Chinese education – the closed society in which students had traditionally undergone a slavish exercise in memorising the 50,000 Chinese characters and the contents of the most important classical works until they could recite them by heart. I had even read somewhere that Mao had closed down all the schools and universities, forcing teachers to go off and dig fields in the country or clean the school lavatories under the supervision of 'revolutionary' pupils.

'Coo,' I said again, really quite shaken by the delegates' description of a pleasant cosmopolitan society where everyone was whizzing around planning their next trip to the sites of ancient Greece. I began to stop thinking about the junk party and became quite excited about China.

I looked out of the window, as the guard launched into another long harangue. The scene outside was similar to a First World War battle-field, all mud, water and ruined houses. A few trees stood on some of the walkways that divided the puddles and provided the only link between the little groups of mudbrick houses that were scattered about the desolate land. Standing bent double in the water were dozens of people, all wearing faded blue cotton suits and up to their calves and elbows in mud. Several others pushed bicycles along the narrow muddy paths, occasionally slipping off into the paddy-fields as the procession of workers trudged back to their villages.

'What about those people?' I asked the delegation.

'Before the revolution they would not have had any education,' they replied, which seemed on later examination rather to dodge the issue. Once again, though, we were interrupted by a series of strange advertisements followed by a burst from the guard, who wore a green jacket adorned with a red star. I asked the delegates what she was saying. Their account was further evidence that China was still not the individualist paradise that they had described, as the guard was apparently suggesting that we go to the lavatory, that we take a taxi from the station to whichever grand hotel we were heading for and that we must remember to take our luggage with us when we left the train.

The odd thing about this advice was that the vast majority of passengers didn't understand a word as the presenters never spoke in anything other than Cantonese – reasonable enough, I suppose, as that was the local language but practically useless when used to instruct a large mass of Western tourists prepared to pay a fortune to cross the border on this swish de-luxe train.

My image of entering China was that we would go through a tin shed, and then have to stand to attention as a band played 'The East is Red', the 'Internationale' and the Chinese national anthem. This would be followed by some political test to make sure that the foreign 'guest' wasn't going to try and corrupt the minds of the young.

For several months prior to entering China I had busied myself learning the more important dates in Karl Marx and Mao Tse-tung's lives, had read a large number of their collected works and had even, on a day which now seemed a long, long time ago, gone up to Highgate cemetery and had a photograph taken of myself staring reverently at The Grave. All of this was designed to prepare me for the inquisition felt sure I was now about to face. But it was clear as we pulled gently into Canton railway station that this wasn't a tin shed, and there wasn't even a band – indeed the whole station was almost completely empty. The only sign of a radical new world was a selection of posters featuring earnest young workers staring wistfully at various montages of factories, coal mines and cranes, usually against a vivid sunset.

Worst of all, there didn't seem the slightest possibility that I was going to be taken into a room and interrogated. What was the point of having learned how the mode of production conditions the general process of social, political and intellectual life, or being able to recognise the fetishism attached to capitalist commodity production, if I wasn't going to be asked any questions about it?

'Hello,' said a friendly customs officer. 'Welcome to China. Do you have anything to declare?'

I thought about claiming a life-long interest in Maoism but the words somehow failed to come out as I stood before this symbol of the repressive Chinese regime. I handed him my form, which he studied for about a minute before wishing me a pleasant stay in China. I looked at the form; over each of my entries the officer had placed a triangle, which meant I had to take the items out again or risk some massive duty being imposed. He had ignored my bike, however. This made me a little nervous as I thought that if I was subsequently stopped it would be helpful to demonstrate that I had declared my bike at the customs. I reminded the officer, who added a triangle and moved on to the next passenger.

Despite my earlier feelings of reluctance about entering China, the train journey, although slightly anaesthetised from the surrounding countryside, had been sufficiently interesting to make me feel quite excited about my first few steps. This feeling didn't last long. As I walked out of the station, I looked across a sea of Volvo, Mercedes and Datsun taxis at the most horrible building I had ever seen – a huge concrete sprawl which seemed to block out the sun and dwarf the whole area, reducing pedestrians and cyclists to little pin-men. On one wall there was a bizarre squiggle which looked a bit like a bird – possibly the logo of the hotel or, alternatively, a sign for low-flying pilots that a grey building lay ahead and not, as it might easily appear, just another large grey cloud.

With alarm, I noticed that the exit I had come out of was different from the entrance to the station, so I had to walk at least a hundred yards with this awful building in view. I decided against it and began to pedal madly away, concentrating solely on getting the building out of sight.

After about ten minutes I stopped to try and work out where I was, because I was fairly sure that there was more to central Canton than the small factories and workshops that lined the muddy track that I was then slithering over. I set off in pursuit of tarmacked roads, but without any success as after another ten minutes I found myself leaving the industrial section and entering a scrubby countryside that contained a number of squalid houses crammed around the odd standpipe. I could either continue cycling and simply stay wherever I could find a hotel, which would have been the really adventurous course of action, or I could creep back to the horrible building opposite the railway station and have another go at finding the town centre.

A number of reasons supported the second option. I hadn't changed any money, and nothing I'd heard or seen suggested that Chinese villages had facilities to change traveller's cheques; I wanted to buy either a dictionary or a phrase book; I wanted to see the various museums, temples, palaces and other ancient monuments that were bound to be in Canton – a southern imperial outpost since the Han dynasty (206 BC–AD 220) and considered one of the great cosmopolitan cities of the world from the time of the T'ang dynasty (AD 618–906) onwards; finally, I wanted to spend a few days in the one town in China always considered more lively, even anarchic, than the northern cities, cut off as they are from the influence of foreign ideas and access to Western individuals.

The problem was that I had to get to it, and my Chinese was still little more than a twinkle in my eye. My vocabulary was limited to 'thank you,' 'hello' and now 'Guangzhou', all useful words but not really incisive enough to enable me to ask the way. I found it quite impossible to find my way back, as the muddy tracks all looked the same and I couldn't see the monstrosity by the station. I spent about half an hour swooping up to pedestrians or some of the hundreds of cyclists and repeating ad infinitum the various permutations available to me, translated into English as: 'Hello, Canton, thank you' ('Nee-how, Guangzhou, cher, cher') or 'Hello, thank you, Canton' ('Nee-how, cher, cher, Guangzhou').

There were only six alternative combinations, and none worked. I decided to try the 'Bombay method' – asking for a major sight which I knew was in the centre of the city. Unlike Bombay, however, where 'the Gateway of India' was immediately recognised even when announced in English, I didn't think that any of the people I was with would understand 'Memorial Park for the Martyrs of the Guangzhou Uprising', or the 'National Institute of the Peasant Movement', unless I asked for them in Cantonese.

The only other place I knew was Shamian Island, built on a sandbank in the Pearl river by the British and Americans in order to defeat the early nineteenth-century ban on foreigners in the city. The sandbank had been enlarged with rocks and sand, covered with warehouses and, eventually, traders' private mansions, and sealed off at night by heavy iron gates to prevent any Chinese from setting foot on the island.

Understandably, the Chinese found this island rather humiliating, and I wasn't sure how they would react if I began to chant the word 'Shamian' at them – there was at least the possibility that they might misinterpret my attempt to ask the way as some sort of unpleasant taunting about a sad period in Chinese history. Such fears assumed that the single word 'Shamian' meant anything at all, and when I did try it nothing in anybody's reaction suggested that they even knew of the existence of the island, let alone its history.

The whole thing was beginning to get very depressing, and made my early plans to cycle about 2500 miles to Peking quite unrealistic. The sooner I was back in Hong Kong, living it up at junk parties, the better. But even getting back to Hong Kong would be impossible unless I either made it back to the station or, quite by chance, cycled in the direction of the border. Why, I groaned, hadn't I brought a compass with me?

Eventually, the solution came to me – I sketched a picture of a railway engine and acted out a charade of searching for something, which, to my enormous relief, was understood. I was given an escort back to the station, only to discover that the station wouldn't sell me a ticket back to Hong Kong; I had to go to something called Luxingshe, whatever and wherever that was. So just one hour after fleeing from the horrors of the hotel opposite the station, I took refuge in its lobby and tried to get a room.

Things became worse: the price of a room ranged from 90–120 yuan – about £27–36 per night, not including breakfast. I began to feel slightly faint.

'There must be something cheaper,' I declared, more in hope than anticipation. The woman behind the desk ignored me and began to write out a list.

'Do you know if there's anywhere cheaper in Canton?'

The woman ignored me again.

'Please help me,' I wailed. 'I can't afford to pay so much. There must be somewhere cheaper.'

The woman ignored me, and continued to do so for the next fifteen minutes. I began to wish I'd concentrated more on wildlife programmes showing how animals use unlikely objects to help them solve a problem – a bird holding a stone to bash away at a particularly hard nut for example, or a snake swallowing a bigger than expected rabbit. Perhaps pandas or some other exotic Chinese animal knew how to deal with such intransigence. Without their help, all I could do was stand transfixed and gaze at this extremely unhelpful woman. This, I discovered quite by chance, was actually the way to deal with Chinese hotel clerks – not to rely on logic, emotion or threats, but just to stand in a suffering silence waiting for them to lower slightly their defences against cooperation.

After what seemed an eternity, she suddenly presented me with a piece of scrap paper on which she'd written 'government workers' hostel, Shamian', and had even added a Chinese translation so that I could show it to people if I was lost.

She brushed away my profuse and sycophantic thanks and went back to her list, while I cycled down Renmin Lu (the People's Road) to the Pearl river and Shamian Island. In dramatic contrast to the muddy roads of the Cantonese suburbs, where cyclists were faced with an unequal struggle against lorries sliding all over the road, cycling down Renmin Lu one was in the cosseted environment of fenced-off cycle lanes filled with workers on old black bikes cruising at an identical pace down unobstructed lanes. There was a slightly unreal, dreamlike quality about the way in which all these people coordinated their actions so harmoniously that one almost suspected they had been rehearsing for several months. Everyone wore the famous cotton suits, nearly always blue but occasionally green, everyone cycled at the same pace and nobody seemed to make any noise or do anything likely to attract attention to themselves. To a certain extent the sight was similar to watching the suited hordes pour across London Bridge to catch their trains home: the same concentration of purpose, the grim and silent determination, the absence of bright colours. The difference, however, was that exactly the same sight existed on the other side of the road in Canton, and between the two rivers of cyclists only the occasional bus reminded one that this was the centre of a busy modern city.

Across the short bridge across to Shamian, the atmosphere changed significantly. Instead of the long lines of boring, functional concrete buildings that stood either side of Renmin Lu, so similar that it was hard to believe that one wasn't just standing still in the midst of hundreds of identical cyclists while someone unrolled a stage backcloth to give the false sensation of movement, were the peeling and dilapidated mansions of nineteenth-century European and American traders. Above all, there were no more flowing columns of cyclists, as just across the bridge a sign indicated that cycling wasn't allowed on Shamian Island.

Without bicycles, cars and buses the Island, filled with the incongruous architecture of mouldering Western mansions, was practically deserted – nobody quite sure what was to be done with the place. Washing was hanging from lines tied across balconies and round arched loggias, most of the stucco had peeled off the walls, and the masonry was stained with mildew. I half hoped that the workers' hostel would be situated in one of these old places, and imagined the crumbling cornices and possibly even a fresco or chandelier. Sadly, though, the hostel was in a modern corner block, already peeling with mildew, but without the faded charm of the Island's other buildings.

The cost of a bed was either six yuan in the small dormitory or four yuan in the large dormitory. In an unusually extravagant gesture I treated myself to the more expensive, and was waved towards a ground-floor room perhaps fifteen feet by eighteen, and filled with one single bed and six bunk beds. Only one was free, all the others being taken up by another colony of Western 'travellers' who lay slumped on the thin mattresses in the familiar, almost comforting, demonstration of gloomy weariness that I'd already seen in Fethiye, Goa and Kovalam.

After a short time the group was suddenly seized with a strange and highly unusual animation as they recounted tales of black-market deals, methods they had used to get the better of hotel managers, where one could pay in renminbi, and the awful physical pain that some of them felt when they had to part with FECs.

It was all incomprehensible, like just about everything I'd seen so far in China, but slowly I began to decipher this peculiar obsession shared by everyone crammed into the small room. It concerned the divided currency used by the Chinese: where the Chinese use renminbi, the foreigners use Foreign Exchange Certificates (though both have the yuan as the unit of currency). Any foreigner who changed money would always be given FECs, with which all hotel, restaurant and transport bills were supposed to be paid. If that were all, there would be no problem, but the Chinese are able to spend the Foreign Exchange Certificates in the Friendship Stores, where Western goods and rare Chinese goods are readily obtainable. Almost inevitably, therefore, the Chinese were willing to pay a premium to exchange the supposedly equal renminbi with FECs at a rate of 1 FEC to 1.85 renminbi.

For foreigners, this meant that if one could persuade the hotels, restuarants and transport authorities to accept renminbi, then the cost of the holiday could be effectively halved. The travellers' indignation that the Chinese authorities were not prepared to acquiesce in this cost-cutting arrangement was compounded by one peculiar aspect of travelling independently in China – the extraordinary range of prices paid by different categories of people for exactly the same commodity. A bed, for example, cost at least eight different amounts depending entirely on the status of the sleeper. The highest of all was for the foreign businessman, followed by the foreign tourist, the foreign student studying in China, the foreign student studying in Taiwan, the foreign expert employed within China, the ordinary Chinese, the Chinese student and, at the bottom, the Chinese official. Within this scheme a series of occasional sub-groups existed, such as the foreign student at an overseas university and, as I discovered, the foreign cyclist.

The result of this absurdly complicated scheme was that an extraordinary amount of time could be wasted arguing over the twin problems of how one was to be classified, and how one was going to pay. The incentive to go on arguing was the potential reduction of the asking price to at least a quarter and, in exceptional circumstances, to as little as a tenth.

Strangely, this tense and impassioned debate on the various methods employed to minimise the price was taking place in perhaps the only hotel in China where nobody had ever heard of anyone's success in either reducing the rate or paying in renminbi. To some extent this was attributable to the cheap asking price – six yuan a night was hardly worth spending an hour or so trying to reduce, though a surprising number considered it not so much a method of economising as a matter of deeply held and highly important principle.

I left the room in a state of high excitement. Although I had already paid for my bed in advance, the future seemed considerably brighter; all I had to do was to go off and change some money before feasting in one of the famous Cantonese restaurants at nearly half price. Clutching a wad of FECs I prowled around the banks of the river Pearl, winking ominously at the more disreputable-looking Chinese and secretly rehearsing my demands for an exchange rate of 1.9, or even the great breakthrough of 2 renminbi for 1 FEC.

An hour later nobody had responded to my advances and I faced the humiliation of having to pay for a meal in FECs because I hadn't been able to buy any renminbi. Eventually, a sympathetic resident of the workers' hostel offered to 'help me out' and exchanged 100 FECs for 1·5 renminbi, which he swore was the going rate. Finally, after an extremely good meal, I was too embarrassed to insist on payment in my newly acquired black-market currency and crept back to the dormitory feeling a decidedly second-rate traveller.

My only redeeming feature within the overcrowded dormitory was my claim that I was going to cycle to Peking. Everybody agreed that it was certainly illegal and would of necessity mean that I was going to stay in closed towns and villages. This meant that I might meet someone who not only took renminbi without an argument, but had possibly never even heard of FECs. Feebly, I felt prevented by their envy from announcing that I was going back to Hong Kong for a stockbroker's junk party, which since we all lived in each other's pockets meant that for the foreseeable future I would have to languish in Canton wallowing in the dormitory's praise.

The other significant effect of living in this colony of travellers was that my earlier desire to see the remains of the T'ang, Sung, Yuan, Ming and Ching dynasties was immediately dismissed as revealing a highly suspicious desire to be a 'tourist'. Their disapproval meant that I had to pretend that my highly clandestine visits to the fifth-century Temple of the Six Banyan Trees, or any of the other pitifully few 'sights' in Canton, were disguised as recces for some street café where one could get a meal for about 10 pence and, of course, pay in renminbi. This combination was considered to provide a dramatic insight into the 'real China'.

Although the only possible conclusion was that China was rather odd, the longer I stayed in Canton the more I wanted to see of the country. It was a feeling that surprised me, as architecturally and even socially Canton was a fairly dreary and slightly irritating place. The dreadful nanny-like loudspeakers were everywhere, barking out commands at every street corner and inside every park and even temple. The buildings were almost surreally ugly – dingy, dilapidated grey blocks designed by the most boring of Soviet municipal town-planners, and given some cheap glamour by fluorescent signs.

At the meeting point of Renmin Lu and the Pearl river, a row of particularly grand modern buildings did to some extent give one the feeling of being in 'the great southern cosmopolitan city', but the effect was spoiled by the austerely functional activities taking place within these buildings. An enormous corner shop, for example, sold just five brands of cigarettes, and a large clothes shop sold the most dismal selection of brightly coloured man-made fabrics used for badly cut shirts and trousers. These were displayed in piles still tied together with string, and dispensed by dispirited members of the staff.

The impression of being continually in a pharmacy, with items available only on prescription, existed throughout the Cantonese shopping areas – a deliberate reminder perhaps that China is a poor and predominantly agricultural country in which pleasant shops and well-made goods are considered undesirable and in a strange way irrelevant to the normal Chinese life. This atmosphere extended to bookshops, where the pitifully few books for sale were displayed under glass cover and access to the shelves was limited to the counter staff. I toured these bookshops in the company of a Chinese-speaking German who was hoping to buy works by Lu Hsun, perhaps the most famous modern Chinese writer (and, with Mao, the only pre-Cultural Revolution twentieth-century writer whose works were published during the ten years of the Cultural Revolution). My German friend was in despair. Munich had a wider selection of books, he wailed, and he went on to lament the decline of the country which had invented encyclopaedias, dictionaries, paper and printing, and was renowned for its peoples' reverence for the written word, into what he saw as semi-literate depths where 'books' were something to be handled with care.

Even if people had succeeded in ignoring the soulless and clinical environment of the bookshops and actually bought one of the books, it was hard to imagine where they would be able to curl up and concentrate on reading. The parks were fed a constant broadcast of music and lectures, and the residential areas had not only the loudspeakers to contend with, but visible overcrowding, which no doubt helped cause the harsh arguments and impatient banging that seemed to dominate the grotty tenements just visible through the washing lines hung between buildings. In some ways they looked like an oriental version of a poor Neapolitan suburb: the same high blocks divided by narrow streets in which men sat in vests while women prepared vegetables and children played with some makeshift toy, their shrieks adding to the clamour that formed the natural background to life; the same appropriation of balconies, windows and drainpipes as places to store furniture and hang food or washing from. There is a difference, though, for while Naples has the Portici Museum, grand squares and elegant buildings, Canton has the National Institute of the Peasant Movement and a succession of ugly streets lined with dreary shops selling mediocre goods; instead of a culinary fame for pizzas and spaghetti, Canton relies on its chefs' ability to make rat, snake and dog taste pleasant.

One clung desperately to the signs that modern Chinese life wasn't as harsh as it seemed – sitting for hours amongst the men with their caged birds, trying to pretend that the loudspeaker above wasn't drowning the birds' twittering and flapping of wings; getting up at dawn to gaze wistfully at the groups of shadow-boxers who exercised so gracefully in the small park beside the workers' hostel; remembering the occasional glimpses of the elegant curves and panels of traditional Chinese architecture and trying to ignore the hideous buildings around me; concentrating on the courtesy and friendliness of the people and not their unbelievable habits of expectorating, spitting and dumping unwanted food on to restaurant floors.

Realistically, these almost inconsequential pleasures were scarcely worth staying in China for, but after three days in Canton I had completely abandoned my earlier plans to get back to Hong Kong as quickly as possible, and indeed the idea of a junk party now seemed pathetically frivolous. Suddenly, I became obsessed by the idea of cycling through the country, if only to see whether a quarter of the world's population could really live in such a miserable place that Canton was considered a cosmopolitan jewel. With great encouragement from the other occupants of my over-crowded dormitory, I cycled off towards Guilin.

12

Pedalling through paddy-fields

I felt a very pleasant sense of adventure as I started cycling out of Canton, a partial restoration of the great excitement I'd felt after making the decision to cycle from London to Peking some fifteen months before. Since then I'd met hundreds of blasé cyclists who'd been round the world several times, gone down the Rockies on penny farthings, or cycled across the Sahara, and who seemed slightly contemptuous of my modest plans. The Italians and Greeks had tended to think the whole thing rather odd, while the poor Turks had suffered such an epidemic of British cyclists on their way to India that they were probably quite justified in not showing more than a vaguely polite interest in the fact that I was going just a bit further into South-East Asia and China. Everyone in India thought that I'd cheated by not going through Iran and Pakistan, and I'd been too ill to identify the Thai reaction.

It was heartening, then, to receive the enthusiastic support of the Western travellers in the workers' hostel. Suddenly I was doing something which I could almost think of as unique – cycling into the interior by myself, staying in closed areas, relying entirely upon the hospitality and complicity of closed villages for food and accommodation, and guided by my instincts rather than the Chinese authorities.

Strangely, my inability to find a map of Canton province in the inadequate bookshops, as well as my virtually complete ignorance of the language, added to this romantic image of a free spirit floating about China. The only problem about cycling with this approach was that it wasn't really compatible with plodding relentlessly on through the rain in order to ensure that I would eventually get to Peking – indeed, it almost required me to think that getting to Peking didn't matter, and that what was important was to try and establish some intangible relationship with the Chinese soil (or something like that).

For some reason I thought that this relationship would be encouraged if I cycled very slowly, with long and frequent stops to smile inanely at trees, paddy-fields and 'the people'. In fact, the only success of this method was to help me ignore the rain and bitter cold, as I spent as much time sitting contentedly in cafés as I did actually struggling along the road. There didn't really seem a great deal of point in changing this policy: I had no real idea where I was going, although I hoped I was on the road to Wuzhou, but I couldn't read the road signs or ask anyone as I didn't understand the replies. In any case, I didn't mind if I never visited Wuzhou (except that it was the most direct route to Guilin) as it had been more or less destroyed during the Cultural Revolution and was supposed to be, even by Chinese standards, a particularly bleak place.

Another reason for sitting in cafés all day was that, despite being in the supposedly tropical south, it rained all day and I had neither the clothes to cope with this nor the patience to repair the dozens of punctures I had from falling into the potholes concealed by puddles.

'Sitting in cafés' might give the wrong impression of life in southern Chinese villages. The cafés were shacks built from pieces of wood and bamboo, usually open on the front side and furnished with some crude wooden tables and benches. They offered a fairly basic diet of spinach, eggs, spring onions, noodles and rice, jazzed up a bit by frying it all in a huge wok together with oil, garlic, ginger and some old pieces of meat. Like India, the meat in China looked, smelt and tasted awful – stringy bits of liver, kidney gristle, chicken necks or pork fat. Unlike India, though, the Chinese solution isn't to disguise how awful it is by bunging in handfuls of overpowering spices, but to use the small quantities of the meat to provide some added flavouring to the rest of the food – and not expect anyone to actually eat the stuff.

The problem is that at the end of a meal one is left with a great pile of inedible meat languishing in the not only edible but absolutely delicious sauce. There are some countries where that would be hard luck, and one would watch disconsolately as the dish was carried off to the kitchen. Such gentility would pass unnoticed in the average Chinese café or restaurant, however, as everybody knows that it's impossible to eat sauce using chopsticks, so one either dips a bit of chicken-neck in the sauce and sucks it noisily from the neck, or one pours some sauce into a bowl of rice and, raising the bowl to within about half an inch of one's mouth, shovels the whole lot in, occasionally pausing to spit out some offending piece of neck.

As nobody bothered to tidy up, relying on the odd pig to wander in and cart off the bits, most of the restaurants I ate in had a rather unpleasant layer of discarded meat covering the mud floor, combined with an extraordinary number of cigarette ends. According to one of the Chinese magazines left lying around Western hotel lobbies only 40 per cent of Chinese smoke, but from my observations of people in dormitories, cafés, temples and simply walking along the streets, I would have said the figure was at least twice as high – indeed, there was something almost manic about the way the Chinese smoked. Everybody chain-smoked, not just between courses but between mouthfuls, and particularly between the great rasping coughs, expectorations and spitting that were one of the most distinctive 'sounds of China'.

The result of these various habits was that 'sitting in cafés' meant kicking up a horrible pile of discarded meat, cigarettes and rubbish, while people sat around slurping, guzzling, coughing, and continually spitting out bones, gristle and phlegm. At some point the feeble bamboo roof would suddenly cave in, and a torrent of water would pour in until the breach had been hurriedly repaired, by which time I was usually back on my bike cycling in the rain towards the next café or restaurant.

The great consolation about the whole situation, which was on the whole fairly depressing, was that I could congratulate myself on the success of cycling alone and unsupervised in China, and I spent a lot of time imagining the stories I could tell of being the 'first white person' ever seen in X village. Unfortunately, even that was taken from me, because one day as I sat idly around, staring at the rain and contemplating the impact of raindrops on puddles, I was astonished to see two Western cyclists wearing the strange plastic gear I'd seen in France and Italy. They were covered with advertisements for European bike manufacturers and were ambling along, without luggage, giving no indication that they were in southern China and not out for a Sunday ride before lunch somewhere in Tuscany. After a few seconds I convinced myself that it was all a hallucination, and started thinking about where I should stay the night to sleep this worrying development off.

Suddenly two more appeared, followed eventually by an enormous party of twelve, all wearing the bright colours and chequered flags of professional cyclists, and none of them carrying luggage. I ran out to greet them, fondly imagining that they would be delighted to find out how I had coped with the twenty or so miles I had succeeded in cycling. I was wrong. The last thing they wanted to see was an individual cyclist, having paid vast sums to a West German travel agent to go on an organised cycling tour on the basis that it was impossible to travel alone.

It really was quite a revelation to find that there were other cyclists around, and I gloomily wondered whether China would turn out to be like Turkey, where every second village had a long-distance cyclist staying for a couple of days. Fired by a new urgency, I set off for the next town, which one of the German cyclists had told me was called Samshui and laconically dismissed as 'nicht gut'. It was a description which hardly did justice to the almost indescribable ugliness of the town, built like so much of Canton by a Soviet municipal town-planner in the 1950s. Large grey concrete blocks, complete with built-in dilapidation – cracks, damp, mildew and broken windows – stood pompously, if that is something buildings can do, on a strict grid pattern.

Shuffling around the corners of these buildings were little huddles of people all wearing the blue cotton suits commonly known as Mao suits, but apparently more accurately known as Sun Yat-sen suits. The only colour in the scene was in two posters which, like those at Canton railway station, featured happy, smiling peasants staring blissfully into the dim distance as they clutched huge baskets of shiny red apples or polished the new combine harvester. The sun shone brightly, the sky was blue, the birds twittered and the bees hummed, God was in his heaven and everything was in its element.

Except me. I still hadn't eaten or found a hotel, and however miserable Samshui was there was no alternative but to stay there. Armed with a couple of dumplings bought on a street corner, I approached one of the hundred or so people who were following me and asked, in my best Chinese:

'Dao fandian?' ('Where's a hotel?').

Everybody grinned at me.

'Fandian? . . . fandian? . . . fandian?' I asked, sounding more and more like Don Giovanni trying to seduce Zerlina.

They continued to grin.

I felt a little worried. I knew very well that the reason the West Germans had been told they couldn't cycle alone was because they wouldn't be allowed to sleep in the closed towns and cities, and it wasn't quite possible to organise a reasonable journey in one day between open cities, of which there were only about two hundred. I had no idea whether Samshui was open or closed, but was fairly certain that if it was closed the last thing I should do was to stand in the centre of the town with a large crowd staring at me, a situation which was bound to attract the attention of any passing policeman.

'Fandian? . . . fandian? . . . fandian?' I repeated, a little more urgently than before.

Nothing happened, except that the loudspeaker above us, which had been broadcasting what sounded like a nursery school rehearsing its percussion section, switched to presenting a lecture of some sort – presumably encouraging further efforts in pursuit of greater production or urging the need to sacrifice oneself for the national good. It wasn't until I heard this particular loudspeaker that I realised that Cantonese was the perfect language for delivering a hectoring sermon, possessing the right harshness in the way each word was stabbed out as if the speaker was being punched in the stomach, while simultaneously shouting angrily at us.

I appeared to be the only person in the crowd who was paying the slightest attention to the message, which was rather a waste as I didn't understand a word. After about five minutes' harangue, the broadcast went back to the nursery-school rehearsal and I resumed my repetition of the word 'fandian'.

They continued to grin at me. Eventually I drew a picture of a man lying in bed, pointed at myself and then at the man in bed, then pointed at the bed and shrugged my shoulders, peered intently in all directions, looked in my saddle-bag and generally tried to make it clear that I didn't know where I was going to sleep. To my relief it worked, although the hotel I was taken to – accompanied by about a dozen of the crowd – was set in a great lake of mud over which I had to carry my bike and into which I fell twice, covering my already soaked clothes with mud and confirming my jaundiced view of cycling in China.

I never found out for certain whether the building I stayed in was actually a hotel. It looked rather like a cheap copy of one of the restaurants on the Serpentine, complete with curved windows, terraces and even a concave roof. Half the building was on stilts above a shallow man-made lake, a design which had produced an extensive network of walkways, viewing platforms and even miniature gardens deposited in large concrete saucers dotted about the lake. I was led to a rather shabby wing jutting out on to the lake, and without registering I was sent off to a bitterly cold room where someone later brought me a tin bowl of hot water, a thermos flask and four small paper bags containing tea.

The only time I tried to explore the rest of the building, hoping to find a restaurant or something to supplement the two dumplings I'd had in central Samshui, I was headed off by two women who seemed to spend an inordinate amount of time either outside my room or sticking their heads round the door to see if I wanted any more water.

Sadly, they ignored the things I did want – somewhere to dry my trousers, something to eat and some form of heating – simply agreeing with me that it must be pretty uncomfortable to sit in a cold room in wet clothes without having anything to eat, but to cheer me up they'd refill the thermos.

The women were still offering re-fills at six-thirty the next morning, though as I had eventually fallen asleep I wasn't sure if they maintained their vigilant concern all night. In response to my groans and mumbled complaints at being woken so early they produced a book of invoices and clearly wanted some money. It was a big moment, as I had a pocket full of black-market renminbi; they were taken without complaint.

The relentless rain continued. Grey clouds hovered yards from the ground, the road surface was even worse than the previous day and all I had to wear were a pair of wet and muddy tracksuit trousers or thin cotton army-surplus summer trousers. After some thought I decided to wear the pyjamas I bought in Syria underneath my tracksuit, which would leave me with the thin cotton trousers for wherever I stayed that evening. I had more or less abandoned the thoughts I had had in Canton of wandering aimlessly about the south, and studied with desperation my large-scale Bartholomew's map for some sign of where I could find a decent hotel. Wuzhou was the next big town, but its reputation was pretty unpromising.

I set off miserably, and about forty miles from Samshui I came upon a huge, ugly building which immediately reminded me of the hotel opposite Canton railway station. It was covered with this unlikely slogan, written in English: 'The Overseas Chinese Hotel welcomes the world.' This sentiment was given a new twist inside, where a sign on the counter made the slightly unbelievable claim that: 'We have friends all over the world.'

It wasn't at all clear why the hotel had been built, as very few of the hundreds of rooms were occupied, and I didn't see any other Western tourists about. There were probably good reasons for this, as apart from a rather grotty lake there was precious little to see in the town, which I eventually discovered was called Zhaoqing. Obviously the Chinese government have great plans for the town, as a vast shopping complex was being built beside the lake, with hamburger bars, off-licences (selling only bottles of brandy), radio and hi-fi shops and places selling incredibly expensive souvenirs. Unfortunately, nobody was buying any of the goods, mainly because all the shops demanded Foreign Exchange Certificates and there were no foreigners to provide them.

I suppose there might be some amusement to be had in buying an amplifier in Zhaoqing – it might provide an amusing anecdote to tell in difficult silences at cocktail parties – but on the whole it was hard to imagine that sales would ever be more than negligible. Even if it were part of some great plan to build Zhaoqing up as a rival to Hong Kong, it seemed a little insensitive to flaunt such items in front of the local Chinese whose incomes would never stretch to include them.

At least, that was the impression I gained in the short distance from Canton to Zhaoqing, but in the frightfully friendly Overseas Chinese Hotel I picked up a handful of magazines, all pretty much the same but with different titles – *Beijing Review*, *Women of China*, *China Today* and so on. I felt that rather too much space was given over to articles on the brilliant success of a special economic zone (now closed), the phenomenal record-breaking production figures from a factory in Damian, and the huge increase in agricultural produce to make the magazines worth reading except as a cure for insomnia. Two photographs kept re-appearing – one of a combine harvester, the other of a woman dashing along on a Japanese moped and variously shopping, visiting her grandchildren or selling a few carrots at the local market.

Everybody interviewed in the articles accompanying these photographs banged on about the great success of the post-Maoist 'responsibility system', and how rural China was at last a prosperous and comfortable place to live. In one sense these magazines could be seen in the same way as the posters of ruddy-cheeked, smiling peasants I'd seen at Canton railway station and in Samshui – not really supposed to be the truth but more an indication of what life might be like one day if everyone pulls together.

Mao declared in 1942: 'There is no such thing as art for art's sake, art that stands above classes, art that is detached from or is independent of politics. Proletarian literature and art are part of the whole proletarian revolutionary nature.'

Assuming that the editors, writers and photographers of these magazines, and the painters of the garish posters, completed their work inspired by 'the proletarian revolutionary nature', then it isn't particularly surprising that they portrayed everyone as happy, smiling folk all leading wonderfully agreeable lives. But even they didn't dare to portray them as playing with videos, expensive Japanese stereos and German food-blenders, or quaffing French brandy – all of which were available in the bizarre shopping complex overlooking Zhaoqing lake.

More significantly, neither did any of the villages west of Zhaoqing look as if any of the villagers would ever be able to afford any of these items; the villages were devoid of any recognisable comforts or even any distractions from the struggle for a mean and primitive existence. They were just clusters of brown mud-brick houses standing forlornly in the centre of scraped, exhausted fields worked on by men with oxen, hand-steering the ancient ploughs through the mud. Trees, bushes and non-productive plants were allowed to grow only above a visible line which represented the limit of the Chinese genius for agriculture – a genius quite obvious in the intricate system of irrigation, of levelling banks on the side of the hills and manipulating a plough in the tiniest of spaces.

The result was that everything below a certain level (mainly paddy-fields) was the colour of mud at the time I saw it – except, of course, the great mass of blue cotton 'Mao' suits which everyone wore. Inside the houses there were usually just two rooms, unlit except by the daylight coming through the door and possibly one exposed light-bulb, and sparsely furnished with low wooden beds piled high with the familiar duvets found in every Chinese hotel, a crude wooden table with a bench pressed tightly against the wall and, if space allowed, a small chest for clothes. As a sort of *leitmotif* of Chinese village life, each house had a tin bowl used to carry hot water for washing from the communal boiler house, and each village had communal lavatories that stood in a central position as a collection point for the 'nightsoil' before it was spread across the fields – carried out in pails suspended from a shoulder bar and ploughed by a bare-footed man sploshing along behind an ox.

In the towns buildings were grander and rather barrack-like; long concrete corridors were lined with small concrete rooms sparsely furnished with metal beds, a table, possibly a chair and, again, the metal bowl for washing. And of course there was always the continual racket from some loudspeaker.

These loudspeakers started at about six o'clock and continued with a mixture of badly recorded music and the occasional lecture until about seven or eight o'clock at night. Apparently there were 100 million loudspeakers in rural China in 1975, which represented one loudspeaker for every six or so people. It was hard to believe that a prison could be worse – the constant intrusion; the lack of privacy; the awful accommodation; the dull, repetitive and humiliating work on the farm; and the discreet supervision through the 'units', to which every-one belongs and which provide all the necessities of life in return for work.

Yet despite this harsh existence, it is easy to see after reading of the wanton cruelty, cynicism and selfishness of the pre-revolution landlords and the various authorities that life has considerably improved. Statistics support this: before 1949 the average peasant lived to be only 22–25, whereas the average life expectancy now is 62 for men and 66 for women. Infant mortality has fallen since 1949 from 200 deaths per 1000 births to about 35–40 per 1000 today.

The fact that so much has genuinely been achieved makes it even stranger that the Chinese magazines, presumably with the blessing of the government, should try and portray the country as a wealthy place where all material wants are satisfied. It is an attitude reminiscent of the letter sent to King George III by Emperor Qianlong after Lord Macartney had visited Peking in 1793, accompanied by a glittering entourage and laden with numerous gifts, to plead for an expansion of trade with Britain. 'We possesss everything,' wrote the Emperor, 'and set no store by objects strange and ingenious. We have no need of your country's manufactures, and Our country possesses all things in abundance. Within Our borders We want for nothing. We thus have no need to import the produce of foreign barbarians and exchange Our own therefor.'

Two hundred years later the attitude has changed in that while the magazines pretend that all is well, impossibly inaccessible goods (all imported) are sold in fancy shopping arcades and, to aggravate the situation, in shops which require payment in a 'currency' officially only available to foreigners. It is a situation hard to reconcile with the 'whole proletarian revolutionary nature' – perhaps no longer the prime motivating force in Chinese internal affairs. On the other hand, the dual existence of the shops and magazines reflects the traditional Chinese inability to see foreigners as equals, but rather as either barbarians trying to steal the inherently superior Chinese civilisation or demi-gods bringing technological magic and intellectual cunning.

The villagers had a more straightforward reaction. Seeing a big-nosed chap with curly hair, a pink skin and long scraggy legs cycling on (by Chinese standards) an extremely high-technology apparatus, they naturally came over for a closer look. As in India, two aspects of my bike intrigued them most – the possible function of my water bottle and the front tyre, which must have been a third of the width of Chinese tyres. Unlike the Indians, though, who mostly showed a complete lack of interest at finding a white person in the village, the Chinese were as interested in me as in my bike – and particularly in my legs.

Following my first day's disastrous cycling, when I arrived at the cold hotel in Samshui with all my clothes wet and muddy, I had decided just to get cold and cycle in shorts. Legs were easy to dry, and I soon discovered that after a few minutes' hard cycling, they weren't that much colder than from cycling in wet trousers. They were also far more interesting to Chinese villagers, who seemed to confirm the rumour that the Chinese don't have body-hair by staring with wonder at the phenomenon of my hairy legs.

Had they confined themselves to gathering in large groups (up to 150–200 people) and staring at me, such incidents would have been almost unmemorable; in India even bigger crowds had surrounded my bike. But the Chinese took the matter further, and after a few minutes' contemplation, one or two would ask if they could touch the hairs. It was the best possible way to warm my legs up, massage my weary muscles and end the day's cycling.

The other advantage resulting from this unorthodox behaviour was that it greatly simplified the problem of finding somewhere to stay – it being a truism that a person who strokes another's legs will help find them a room. Usually I ended up in a cold room in one of the long barrack-style buildings that most towns seemed to have a number of – possibly accustomed to taking Chinese officials but totally unfamiliar with foreign gatecrashers. This was an ideal situation insofar as it meant that the 'receptionist' didn't know that Peking had regulations preventing non-Chinese from entering certain areas, but difficult in that their standard registration forms required, in addition to my name, age and sex, confirmation that I had my 'unit's' authority to be in the particular place.

Most receptionists succumbed to the pressure from the dozen or so leg-strokers who accompanied me to the 'hotel', and let me stay without creating any real difficulty – accepting either my passport or even my 'alien's travel permit', which listed a number of towns I had special permission to visit, in lieu of my unit's identification and permission. (About a hundred towns were 'open' as soon as one obtained a Chinese visa, and about another hundred if named on the alien's travel permit.)

As I cycled through China my accommodation began to develop a set pattern – an open city followed by one or two, occasionally even three, nights in closed towns before reaching another open city. I tried to choose towns that were some distance from a railway line, which I hoped would avoid the obvious danger of being put on a train, and that were large enough to have a couple of hotels yet small enough not to have a police force familiar with the rules against foreigners.

It was, however, inevitable that some receptionists would at least hesitate before finding me a bed, and on perhaps half a dozen occasions I discreetly pushed a ten-yuan note across the counter, which was about three times the official room-rate and on all but one occasion successful in overcoming the clerk's hesitation. The only time it failed, the clerk decided to call the police. It was an eventuality I was partly prepared for, and I had decided to claim firstly ignorance of the regulations, secondly that I did have permission and, finally, to argue that the regulations allowed me to 'pass through', which meant that cyclists should be allowed to stay overnight in closed areas as they passed between open cities. It was a pretty feeble argument, and even though the town – between Wuzhou and Guilin and I think called Laipo – wasn't on the railway I lost my nerve and marched out of the hotel, pretending to be deeply offended.

Such high-handedness had its dangers. Laipo had only one hotel, now closed to me. The police would presumably start looking for me and would quickly catch up if I tried to cycle away from the town. I approached a group of lorry drivers standing gloomily around a café, and asked them if they could give me a lift to Guilin, about sixty miles away and the next open city. They were obviously sympathetic to my predicament but, sadly, they were staying overnight in Laipo. I gestured urgently at their cabs – could I sleep in one of those until the morning?

Chinese hospitality doesn't allow a wet and obviously cold person to sleep in an unheated lorry cab. They helped me put my bike on the back, and we drove off in a convoy of three lorries to a factory about five miles outside Laipo. Once at the factory I was ushered into a large and absolutely filthy room furnished with six large burgundy-coloured plastic chairs and a low coffee table. The floor was covered with old chicken bones and cigarette ends. I sat alone in the room for about five minutes, wondering quite what was going to happen, until someone who was clearly important barged into the room, announcing with some hesitation:

'I have English . . . you dinner.'

I smiled anxiously, remembering the story in *The Water Margin* in which the hero, Lin Chong, arrives at an inn controlled by a band of robbers where the inn-keeper declares, 'If one guest comes along here and he has no money I let him pass on. If he has money and if he is to be treated lightly I only give him a sleeping draught, but if I am to deal with him more severely then I really kill him. His lean meat I cut into strips to make dried meat to eat and his fat I render and we burn it in lamps.'

I felt my money belt, filled with traveller's cheques, foreign currency, FECs and black-market renminbi, and pondered on the wisdom of cycling illegally in southern China, dodging the police, incriminating the lorry drivers and even doubting the 'proletarian revolutionary nature'. I kicked nervously at one of the chicken bones.

'Foreign guest . . . dinner,' said the grandee, with growing confidence in his English.

Two of the Laipo drivers came in, each carrying six bottles of beer. Surely I wasn't about to be pummelled to death?

'Drink . . . drink,' said the grandee, and shoved one of the bottles at me. So it was the sleeping draught after all. As I drank the beer I was watched with appropriate solemnity, and when I had finished another bottle was handed over.

'Drink . . . drink.'

It went on. Four bottles later two more men came in carrying plates of food. Chopsticks were presented.

'Eat . . . eat.'

I began pulling at the scraggy meat, still under the intense gaze of the drivers and the grandee. Plate followed bottle, bottle followed plate to an incantation of 'Eat . . . drink . . . eat . . . drink . . . eat . . . eat . . . drink.'

Eventually I could take no more – I had to go to the loo. After I had acted out a fairly obvious charade, a cry went up for the food and drink to be removed and the entire party trooped out to a shed in the corner of the factory yard. One half of the shed was elevated and had a narrow trench running along its full length.

'Yes . . . yes,' commanded the grandee as I looked balefully at the group, still intrigued by my every movement.

In due course we went back to the room with the armchairs, where we sat and smoked cheap cigarettes until at last the grandee rose and led me off to a dormitory. I felt dreadful the next day, the beer and cigarettes combining to dehydrate me and leave me with a dry mouth, awful headache, horrible aftertaste and absolutely no inclination to cycle up to Guilin. The grandee, however, had arranged for my departure, and after profusely thanking him for his kindness I set slowly and dejectedly off.

Another day of rain, clay roads, punctures and gloomy country would probably have sent me back to Hong Kong. In fact, it was to be the prettiest day's cycling in China, through an incredible landscape of sugar-loaf mountains, the road surrounded by massive monoliths looming out of the mist like hundreds of giant fingers punched through the ground.

More practically, the road surface had been tarmacked to provide a smooth passage for the dozens of tourist buses that drove down from Guilin to Yangshuo, the small village that has become a horribly commercialised tourist centre. For some unfathomable reason I was pursued by a collection of men and boys trying to sell me large and unrecognisable coins featuring a balding Chinese leader wearing ceremonial robes. When the coin-salesmen left me, other stall-holders began to thrust brightly coloured towels at me, about the size of those found on English pub counters but featuring – instead of brewery advertisements – garish and highly stylised images of the mountains, frequently with some slogan knitted into the towel such as 'The scenery of Guilin is the best under heaven' or, more prosaically, 'Guangxi Zhang autonomous region'.

The tacky commercialism of Yangshuo was nothing compared to the horrors of Guilin, a town no uglier than Canton but filled with people who perceive all tourists as rich fat-cats who can be overcharged, cheated and insulted with impunity. Some of these people run the Western-style cafés, others the black-market activities in train-tickets, currency exchange and Western cameras, radios and stereo walkmans. The rudest and most unhelpful of these street-dealers have been groomed for the China International Travel Service, an organisation which specialises in obstruction and pedantry. Guilin stands as a monument to their extraordinary behaviour – the graveyard of goodwill and international friendship.

I escaped from these bitter thoughts by locking my bedroom door and slowly reading through *Silas Marner*, *Cranford* and *Emma*, which exhausted my supply of novels but restored my sense of equilibrium. The return from nineteenth-century England to twentieth-century Guilin was painful. My attempts to buy a train ticket to Kunming were pathetically unsuccessful, and I became increasingly distressed by the assorted conmen who prowled through the streets, and oppressed by the sadly familiar grey concrete buildings and wide streets that make up modern Chinese towns.

Thoroughly shaken by the events in Laipo, I decided to try and get permission from the Public Security Bureau for my plan to cycle to Wuhan, about six hundred miles north of Guilin and where my guide book claimed I could get a ferry down the Yangtze to Shanghai. Foolishly, I cycled to the office; this inevitably attracted a largish crowd which, equally inevitably, attracted the public security officer's attention. I'd hardly started to list the places I wanted to stay in before he went out to investigate the commotion outside.

'You don't think you're going to cycle, do you?' he said when he came back.

'Yes, I've been told I can,' I lied, adding my own contribution to the prevalent illegality, lies and cheating in the town.

'Well, you can't.'

'Why not?'

'You can't.'

'But I'm cycling from Canton to Peking.'

'No.'

'I've cycled six thousand miles from London to Guilin and want to cycle through China to Peking.'

'No.'

'I've come from Canton to here.'

'No.'

'Oh go on.'

'No.'

'Creep,' I muttered, and stomped off.

Outside the police station three of the crowd examining the bike asked me if I wanted to change money, two more wanted to know if I was prepared to sell my bike and another was busy trying to remove my saddle. Compared with their determination and resolution, the public security officer seemed palely ambivalent. So, disguising myself in a woman's cycling cape – white with yellow and pink polka dots – and pulling a green balaclava helmet over my head, I crept unnoticed out of town and started out on the road to Wuhan.

13

A Yangtze Spring

On 4 April it stopped raining. For the first time I was able to cycle in China without water trickling down my back, and look at the scenery without having to squint into driving rain or finding that low clouds obscured the higher ground. I could cycle without splashing through puddles which soaked my socks and concealed hazardous pot-holes; I could even enjoy the sun in my face and the exhilaration of cycling on a fine spring day. Everything began to look more pleasant – the villages looked less like prison compounds and even the loudspeakers sounded less hectoring. Suddenly, trailing along behind a bullock-drawn plough didn't seem quite so dreadful, nor the communal lavatories so dismal. Instinctively I began to whistle the famous march from Chiang Ching's favourite opera, 'The night-soil workers are coming down the mountain.'

At first, as I cycled from Guilin up to Psingwan, I assumed that my new enthusiasm for China was caused solely by the change in the weather, and dreaded what I saw as the inevitable return to a damp gloom. After all, there were still the muddy paddy-fields which made everything look such an unpleasant brown; the work of the peasants was just as hard, using the same ancient techniques; the restaurants were just as squalid. But closer examination showed that the villages really had changed. They were no longer the bleak, mud-coloured buildings permeated with the oppressive feeling that much of life is an ugly, grovelling existence, but pleasant wooden houses built of old black wood with walls about a foot thick. The classic Chinese curved roofs, verandahs, balconies – even intricately carved wooden screens – were a pleasant reminder that Chinese architecture didn't consist exclusively of a bold functionalism.

The rooms were planned to create a series of interconnecting court-yards, with perhaps half a dozen rooms (nearly all bedrooms) around each of them. The roofs extended beyond the wall to create a sheltered verandah running all the way round the yard, and leaving a central hole for the fire-smoke to escape through. Beside almost every fire sat an old woman, stirring the contents of a pot or throwing in some vegetables or pieces of scraggy meat (that hadn't changed), while simultaneously looking after the hordes of children who dashed determinedly about.

Only the children's arms, which stuck out at right angles from their heavily padded bodies, distinguished some of them from rugby balls; one had the impression that if they fell over they would either roll rather unevenly into a corner or bounce back up again. As it would no doubt take hours to unravel the various layers, there was just one practical gap exposing the children's bottoms to the elements.

The number of young bottoms wagging in the sunlight suggested that the infamous one-child policy wasn't being strictly adhered to in this area, as the villages were so small that only a certain number of families could live there – indeed, the whole physical structure of the buildings, with only a few entrances through the outer walls of the complex, and the obvious interdependence within, suggested that just one extended family lived in the village.

Unfortunately, these pleasant, tight-knit communities didn't have any hotels, and I was forced to stay in Psingwan – another town built in the great Chinese tradition of grey concrete lumps. I had just finished all the novels I had with me, and it was too soon to start re-reading them, so I was forced to trudge around the town searching for distractions. I had my hair cut – the barber using a razor instead of scissors, but otherwise just like any other haircut; I tried on a blue cotton Mao suit; I tried on a green one; I bought some socks. After an hour or so I came across a group of people playing snooker on an old and dilapidated table they'd dragged out on to the street, and I was able to watch a game of coarse snooker for a few minutes. But in general it was a boring evening, and I trailed back to the hotel dreaming of one day staying in a really traditional Chinese building.

The one success of the evening was that on my way back I found a stall selling a selection of Panama hats, which introduced an incongruous flippancy into the sombre world of Psingwan. Trying one on, I practised doffing my hat to passers-by and issuing a jolly 'Nee-how'. It was a tremendous success and produced an infinitely warmer response than the more ascetic hatless 'Nee-how'.

There were other advantages in wearing a hat. Apart from giving me the irresistible urge to whistle, it made the general chaos of the world seem more ordered and even pleasant, encouraged one to stand

and face problems head on and generally induced a feeling of confidence, *joie de vivre* and *bonhomie*. Presumably this was because of the balancing and defining presence of the brim, which limits one's impression of the sky, normally a perpetual reminder of one's insignificance . . .

I continued to experience these rather extravagant emotions as I cycled north towards Hengyang and Changsha. The country had flattened out after the sugar-loaf mountains of Guilin and after about seventy miles became a barren plateau, with little sign of agriculture and no trees, bushes or natural vegetation. A scrubby, yellowing landscape stretched endlessly away, unirrigated and therefore impossible to farm – even for the Chinese, whose superior farming methods have always led to the 'sinification' both of minorities within China and invaders from the north who, having conquered, have often ended up adopting the Chinese mode of living.

The infertile land, and the consequent difficulty in finding enough to eat, inevitably meant that towns and villages were not only a long way apart but were fairly dismal places to cycle through, let alone live in. To further deflate my new-found enthusiasm, I found that the vast distances between cafés took even longer than normal as the Chinese, possibly in an attempt to generate business into the area, were tarmacking the roads – a process which involved digging up the entire road and slowly re-laying it, leaving the traffic to find its own way through the mess.

The road-works were an odd sight. For most of the time the surface was an unpleasant stony ground which forced the lorries to weave an eccentric route across the building site or, occasionally, in the muddy valleys, to try and struggle through a clay goo with wheels spinning wildly, churning up the road surface into a series of ruts and puddles. A further hazard to their progress was that everything except the final smoothing of the tarmac was done by hand, so there were great armies of men busily lugging shoulder-poles of stone underlay, sand or gravel to the road, or taking rubble away.

These conditions were not ideal for cycling. Apart from finding my wheels stuck in the mud or punctured by the stony ground, I was constantly having to dodge both the lorries, whose drivers were obviously used to cyclists getting out of their way, and the road-workers, who understandably thought it more amusing to chat to a Western cyclist than cart off a couple of baskets of sand. The only advantage was that everybody was so amazed to see me that hotel receptionists didn't bother to challenge my right to be in the area, but joined the crowd of well-wishers who would gather in my bedroom to stare appreciatively at my legs, play with my walkman and meditate on my bicycle pump.

Eventually I arrived in Changsha, the old capital of the state of Chu, whose people were always considered a superstitious, even lewd, lot by their contemporaries in the 'warring state period' (480–221 BC), apparently because they used wind as well as percussion instruments and became involved in shamanistic cults. Like all the Chinese towns I'd been to, there was no longer any sign of the ancient and interesting past, but instead yet more rows of large, ugly and inhuman concrete boxes which loomed oppressively over the wide and car-less boulevards and seemed designed to crush the spirit.

The much-despised Kuomintang regime was responsible for the destruction of old Changsha, preferring to destroy the town rather than leave it to the Japanese during the Sino-Japanese war of 1937–45. Since the Japanese were responsible for the destruction of Guilin, and the Red Guards responsible for the destruction of Wuzhou and any temples, pavilions and pagodas missed by the others in this strangely destructive trio, it wasn't surprising that cities like Changsha were somewhat lacking in interesting distractions.

Perhaps the main sight was the First Normal School of Hunan province, where the young Mao, who was born in the nearby village of Shaoshan, came to study and later teach. Predictably, the school has been decorated with large posters of almost dangerously happy peasants and steel-workers, whose bronzed and smiling faces stare keenly and lovingly towards an optimistic future. At the entrance of the building there was a large banner with one of Mao's slogans proclaiming: 'To be a teacher of the people, one must first be their pupil.'

Quietly reflecting on this 'thought', I examined the pond behind the school where Mao used to take his daily bath, and read of his walking holiday in 1917 through the villages near Changsha and of his two most influential teachers, Yang Ch'ang-chi, the professor of ethics and Yuan the Big Beard, the teacher of Chinese.

Inevitably, a suitably grand hotel has been built in Changsha to accommodate the great hordes of Maoist followers who flock to gaze reverently at this important revolutionary shrine. It seemed an appropriate reminder of the Maoist barriers between the local people and foreigners, when to talk to a foreigner was an offence, that Changsha was the one town I visited where I was forced to stay in one of these ugly great foreign-resident battleship hotels.

By obstinately refusing to accept one of the gaudy double bedrooms reserved for foreigners and insisting that because I was cycling in China

I should be given a particularly cheap rate, I managed to talk my way into the lowest accommodation category I ever achieved – that of 'ordinary Chinese'. The financial savings were considerable, but the cost in terms of loss of privacy, discomfort and overcrowding made these savings almost certainly uneconomic.

I was put in a dormitory containing six beds, but occupied on my arrival by fifteen people who sat on the edge of the beds watching a television. Of these fifteen at least ten were chain-smoking, which filled the room with the sweet smell of Chinese tobacco and encouraged the coughing, the loud and uninhibited expectorating and finally, the slow spitting – almost dribbling – of the phlegm on to the floor which I had come to dread.

On my journey from Changsha to Peking I came across quite a few television sets in Chinese hotels, and soon learnt that the only way to turn the thing off was to remove the fuse or cut the wires. This set, however, was the first I'd seen since the one on the train from Hong Kong to Canton, apart of course from those sitting in the bizarre shopping centre in Zhaoqing. For some unimaginable reason a pro-gramme was being shown on the training given to hotel staff for foreign hotels, in particular the trials and tribulations of a group of six barmaids being taught to mix cocktails.

Pictures of mopeds and combine harvesters in magazines, posters of smiling workers celebrating a bumper harvest or record-breaking production figures, brandy and videos in the Zhaoqing shopping centre, Panama hats in Psingwan, and now this latest shock – mixing cocktails in Changsha! The whole of China seemed to exist on fantasy, or was it me slowly going mad?

I stared helplessly at the green, yellow and pink concoctions shown on the television and looked around the room at the blue-suited men puffing away at cigarettes, apparently overwhelmed at the sight of the television and with at most some tea-leaves in their plastic shoulder-bags. Emerging from my dumbfounded stupor I asked if any of my room mates would like to join me for a cocktail, assuming that some-where in the vast hotel complex there was a bar. They looked aston-ished, almost incredulous, that anyone could actually want to drink one of the horrible things on the screen. Perhaps it wasn't a programme on the training of barmaids after all, I thought, but a denunciation of deviant Western behaviour. In any event, they tapped their tea-mugs and pointed at the thermos beside the television.

I decided to go alone, and after half an hour spent wandering around different lobbies in the various buildings of the complex I managed to find a reasonably swish bar. A uniformed receptionist stood at the door, possibly to keep Chinese out of this Western den of iniquity, or possibly to keep jeans and training shoes out in the manner of the more pretentious Western establishments.

'Good afternoon, sir,' she said as I walked in. 'Welcome to our bar.'

'Thank you,' I said, as she escorted me to a table.

I was left alone for a few minutes, and contemplated the merits of a 'Peking Pick-me-up' or a 'Changsha Charlie'. In due course a waitress approached me, raising her eyebrow in an engaging if slightly under-rehearsed New York manner.

'Nee-how,' I said, showing off my Chinese. 'Do you have any cocktails?'

She looked bewildered, smiled and then arched her eyebrow again.

'Do you have any cocktails?'

'Cakes?'

'No. Cocktails. It's a type of drink.'

'We have just tea or beer. Or cakes.'

The receptionist stepped forward to give the waitress some moral support.

'What sort of a drink is it?'

'A mixed drink . . . er, brandy with coconut milk, cherries. Slices of lemon and umbrella-shaped swizzle sticks.'

The receptionist looked almost angry.

'We do not sell that sort of thing. We have tea or beer.'

'It's all right, thanks,' I mumbled, and started walking back to my room.

Somewhere in one of the courtyards I was interrupted by a gloomy Western tourist.

'Bloody horrible, isn't it?' he pronounced.

'It does seem a bit much,' I agreed.

'Thirty-two bloody yuan a night.'

'No cocktails.'

'For nothing.'

'Have them on Chinese television.'

'There's not even any hot water. The plug's been nicked. Bloody horrible.'

At last, a kindred spirit. We walked along in silence, reflecting upon the iniquities a tourist in China has to suffer.

'Don't suppose this dump's got a decent restaurant, do you?' he asked.

'Hm . . . pah!' I observed.

We trudged off into the town, scowling at the hideous buildings, glaring at the badly stocked shops and refusing to obey the red pedestrian signs at traffic lights, a pathetic gesture of nonconformity. Eventually we found a restaurant where, demoralised by the dismal walk, we allowed ourselves to be shunted into one of the horrible, kitsch annexes reserved for foreigners – an attempt by the Chinese to protect the local population from the Non-Revolutionary Westerners, and the NRWs from the usual squalid concrete floors, vinyl-topped tables and peeling walls. Unfortunately, the result in Changsha was a quite ghastly combination of velvet flock wallpaper, silly oil lamps in the centre of the tables and the brashest carpet I have ever seen.

The information that there was someone else in China who thought Changsha was, to use his perfectly expressed phrase, 'a dump', and who wasn't interested in where Mao used to bathe or the influence of Yan the Big Beard on contemporary China, was the most tremendously cheering news and in a strangely supportive way helped me not just to suffer the further horrors in silence, but even to secretly relish them. In a new and grimly determined mood I began a childish campaign of disruption – removing the fuses from the televisions, replacing the hot water in the thermos with cold, introducing myself as the English representative of the 'Friends of Lin Biao Movement' (the man who was accused of attempting to assassinate Mao), and even trying to expectorate and spit in a more savagely obtrusive way than the Chinese.

It was a campaign that started badly and got worse. After lying in bed heaving with exaggerated coughing fits I realised that the only person I was keeping awake was myself, and all the Chinese were up at the crack of dawn, sitting morosely on their beds, smoking, coughing and spitting. I scowled at them as I became more and more despondent. Outside I could hear the rain pouring down; I looked at my watch – it was five to six. Regretting the time spent making foul, guttural noises, I pulled my duvet over my head and tried to go back to sleep.

At six-thirty two cleaning maids came in and told me to get out of bed. I stuck seven fingers out from underneath the duvet and rolled over; at six-forty the cleaning maids came back with someone wearing a blue jacket with two more pockets than the maids. The new arrival stood authoritatively over my bed and told me to get up. I cursed myself for not knowing the Chinese for seven, and angrily shoved seven fingers at the three of them, and jabbed at my watch.

'Mayo,' the supervisor calmly declared, and demonstrated that the two maids wanted to tidy up and, most importantly, fold the duvets.

'Who's the hotel for?' I cried. 'The chambermaids or the guests?'

'Mayo,' he repeated, obviously not understanding my English.

I continued to rant on, knowing full well that I had lost the argument but determined to have my say, however futile it might be. In due course the maids were instructed to remove the duvet and I was forced to get up, muttering bitterly about the strange values and false priorities of Chinese hotel management.

Irritably I pedalled off into the rain, pausing briefly to examine the exhibited entrails of the first-century woman who married the Marquis of Dai and whose tomb was discovered at the nearby site of Mawangdui. I stomped out and resumed cycling, finding the jar containing Lady Dai's entrails a suitably grim image to retain of Changsha.

The rain continued. The roads deteriorated and I became increasingly disconsolate. Even having my legs stroked failed to revive me – how on earth was I going to get myself out of this rut? Shanghai, I thought. Surely Shanghai would be fun. I'd even read of a jazz club in Shanghai, of discos, of good restaurants selling more than spinach and noodles. There was the Bund, perhaps the most famous thoroughfare in China, lined with old European and American office buildings. And even if Shanghai turned out to be boring, then I could take a ferry either back to Hong Kong or north to a town within easier cycling distance of Peking, the Forbidden City, the Great Wall and, most importantly, the Trans-Mongolian Express out of China, and home.

After two days of utterly boring cycling I arrived in Yeuyung, another in the interminable chain of dreary grey concrete towns. Fortunately I had been able to swap my Eliot, Gaskell and Austen novels with some of my disillusioned friend's collection, and I buried myself in my hotel room reading about South American shamanism and more of nineteenth-century England, escaping from the austere existence all around me until I could arrange my ferry ticket for the trip down the Yangtze.

Despite my disaffection with Chinese 'low life' and my long-standing aversion to discomfort, I meanly decided to economise on the first leg of my journey to Wuhan, maintaining that it was unnecessary on a twelve-hour boat journey to buy more than a 'deck'-class ticket. It was a stupid decision – twelve hours crouching on a greasy corridor floor, being stepped over by the grander inhabitants of the fourth and third classes and not even within sight of the luxurious second class (in an absurdly token gesture the Chinese had abandoned the nomenclature 'first class'). Worst of all, I couldn't find anywhere to eat, so I arrived in Wuhan hungry, uncomfortable and thoroughly fed up.

Wuhan was the first city I visited in China that had been destroyed not only by the Japanese and the Red Guards but by the Americans as well, yet another element in the forces responsible for the destruction of old China. The result was that scarcely anything remained of the old architecture of the city, and one was supposed to trail around admiring the Monument to the Martyrs of the 7 February General Strike or the Yangtze bridge, designed in 1957 by Mao Yisheng and 1670 metres long on eight pillars. One could end a thrilling day at the point where Mao Tse-tung made his 'world famous' ten-mile swim down the Yangtze in July 1966 in defiant contradiction of the rumours that he was too old to lead the country.

I plodded around, ostentatiously raising my Panama and bawling 'Nee-how' to anyone I passed, until even that diversion seemed inappropriate. The Yangtze, like so much of China, tends to discourage such frivolous behaviour as one is within continual sight of relentless work. Just beyond the point where Mao went for his swim, a coal barge was being emptied – eight men equipped with the ubiquitous shoulder-pole formed a human chain from the barge to the warehouse, lugging the coal up in two baskets suspended from the ends of the pole. Behind them, actually on the river, a junk battled its way upstream, powered by two tattered sails and helmed by a thin man hanging against the weight of the rudder, like an antiquated windsurfer. Looking out across the river, the overwhelming impression was of junks, barges and sampans, fuelled in part by the wind and river currents, but chiefly by human sweat.

Inevitably, throughout Wuhan there were more of those cheerful posters, this time featuring merry dockers and industrial workers staring into the sun and holding spanners in triumph, and in the background the dramatic outlines of cranes, power-station chimneys and miniature paintings of welders and men working on conveyor belts. These scenes of 'glorious heroes of the revolution' included a painting of a grand liner alleged to run between Wuhan and Shanghai – bunting flew from its masts, happy people threw streamers from the deck and jolly sailors resplendent in gold-bedecked sailor-suits stood like Popeye fore and aft.

To my surprise, second-class life on board the ferry to Shanghai was almost as much fun as the poster suggested it might be. Three stewards installed me in isolated magnificence, my cabin protected from the sweaty hordes by several locked doors and the vigilance of two women whose job appeared to consist solely of the none too arduous tasks of refilling a kettle to ensure that I had enough hot water, and opening the door for me when I set out on my semi-regal tours of the more deprived areas in third, fourth and 'deck' classes. For the first day I sat in an armchair, the cabin door open, and stared wistfully at the distant shores – my only regret the absence of a cane to match my Panama. My meals and copious amounts of beer were brought to me in my cabin, if I used a towel it would be immediately replaced, if I put a book down someone would pick it up and put it away, and if I wanted a cigarette someone would be there to light it.

This luxurious treatment ended at three-fifteen in the morning of my first night on board, when a large Japanese party loudly and clumsily boarded the ferry; trunks crashed against doors, and several passengers barged into my room, turned on the light and shouted to their tour leader that there was someone in bed. At about quarter to four a man wearing a grey flannel Mao suit came slowly and meticulously into my room, removed my Panama which was lying on his bed, handed it to me and lit a cigarette. Shortly afterwards he began to cough . . . and cough until gradually he eased and jogged the nasty, irritating phlegm from his throat. He rolled it around his mouth and then, leaning forward, let it dribble on to the floor. I was transfixed, scarcely capable of leaning far enough out of bed to see if my shoes were all right, and pinched myself to make sure that it had really happened and wasn't some hallucination from a Chinese nightmare.

'Turn out the lights,' I croaked when I found that it was all real.

He smiled paternally at me, and offered me a cigarette.

'Ching, ching,' I said, pointing at the lights.

He nodded, smiled again and removed his trousers, to reveal a pair of turquoise tracksuit bottoms. Eventually, I had to get up to turn the light off, thereby interrupting his early-morning reading as he sat in bed wearing his bizarre turquoise tracksuit, smoking and apparently enthralled by the contents of a comic.

By six this strange man was up again – smoking as always and pacing up and down in the small gap between our beds. At half past six one of the stewards came in to explain that, starting with breakfast, I would have to have all my meals in what turned out to be an observation room furnished and decorated in the garish Changsha restaurant style. The sudden influx of people, led by the Japanese tour party, had exhausted the kitchen facilities, and I chewed disconsolately on a cold fried egg served with a small pork cutlet and potato crisps, followed by plum jam on fried bread.

Thoughts of escaping this situation by disembarking at the next port were dismissed when, on returning to my cabin, I discovered that the man had gone, leaving in a touching gesture a packet of cigarettes on my pillow. For the remaining two days to Shanghai, I remained alone in my cabin, the door closed and the armchair facing the spare bed which I used as a footrest. Occasionally one of the stewards would knock at the door to remind me that I was expected in the observation room, where I smiled weakly at the Japanese, hurriedly ate my food and raced back to the privacy of my armchair, stirring only when someone pointed out the European outline of Shanghai.

Like Calcutta, Shanghai was built by imperialist interests in the pursuit of trade, both towns being established on the banks of suitable rivers by massively expanding the small fishing villages that previously existed. The merchants, bankers, shippers and diplomats attracted by these opportunities for fortune imported with them the grand, confident and assertive architecture of nineteenth-century Europe and America, and in Shanghai at least reduced all contact with the local population to the barest minimum – summed up by the famous images of fat businessmen being hauled along by rickshaw-boys and the notorious sign in the park: 'No dogs or Chinamen allowed'.

It was strange, then, to find that of all the cities in China Shanghai seemed to have suffered least from the various destructive forces that had ravaged other cities, and that a place which was a fishing village until 1843 should have an older appearance and a greater sense of atmosphere than, for example, the two-thousand-year-old Changsha; stranger still that the town which heralded the start of the Cultural Revolution and the destruction of the 'Four Olds' (old ideas, old culture, old customs and old habits) with the publication of Yao Wen-yuan's article in the Shanghai paper *Wen-hui Rao* should retain so much architecture from a humiliating period of capitalist and imperialist domination.

For whatever reason, the old buildings have survived, and immediately conjured up images for me of the town's past – the secret societies, gambling dens, drug addicts, prostitutes and poverty, existing side by side with exclusive gentlemen's clubs, large Western mansions, grand hotels and the general paraphernalia of the Roaring Twenties in Shanghai.

This atmosphere had affected the inevitable crowd of 'travellers' gathered in the Pujian Hotel, the only central place to stay that offered the unbeatable combination of cheap beds and a willingness to accept renminbi. In place of the heavy lassitude that normally gripped these gatherings, there was a rare delight, even excitement, about the luxuries of Shanghai – the apple pie and ice cream, the lemon-meringue pie, the jazz club in the Peace Hotel, the discos, the excellent restaurants and the kissing couples in the Whangpu Park. There was even a bookshop selling English paperbacks at a rate which made them cheaper than they would have been at home – at last an opportunity to stock up with some escapist literature for the long nights to come when I would eventually return to staying in villages on the long ride north to Peking.

For Shanghai, though, I simply wore my Panama at a more jaunty angle, and even bought a particularly nasty red tie to wear in the jazz club and discos. There I succeeded in wasting a large amount of time on the pretext that, by listening to old Judy Garland and Louis Armstrong numbers played by a no-more-than-competent Chinese jazz band, or dancing to bad versions of Western disco music imported illegally from Hong Kong or Taiwan, I would end up with a better understanding of rural China, bop bop de-woo.

14

Shanghai and the Chiang-nan

Into these halcyon Shanghai days came two strangers. The first, an Irishman who brought with him tales of Chinese prostitution in Canton and Peking, wished to prove to us and to himself that the 'Shanghai girls' were the best in Asia. His insidious presence slowly infected the group of friends who collected in the jazz club, where he could be seen playfully sticking beer cans up the waitresses' dresses, and along the Bund at night, where he would taunt the innocence of the young lovers and offer some revolting service of his own.

The second stranger was an American, who opened his stay with this question:

'Er, like, huh, do you, like, Europeans feel any, y'know complex about, huh, like, y'know the European, I mean like total eclipse of, huh, Europe by the US of A?'

'No,' we told him.

'D'ya know watta mean?'

'No,' we told him.

'Well, like y'know, er, all the innovations in, huh, culture and technology, right, well I mean, just everything's innovated in the States.'

We drifted in some dismay to the Peace Hotel for a restorative apple pie and ice cream, only to find the Irishman energetically pursuing another woman. To have to watch this distressing scene immediately after meeting the absurd American was a sobering experience; melodramatically, we agreed that the pleasures we had found in Shanghai – the jazz, the discos, the unusual sense of a Chinese *dolce vita* – were now gone, never to return. Better then to leave the corpse to others who would know what to do with it, while we moved on elsewhere.

Three of my companions left within hours of the Irish and American arrival – two going by ferry back to Hong Kong, the other by train to Suzhou. Through some strange masochistic urge I had committed myself to staying in China for another four and a half weeks, having almost recklessly reserved a hard-seat berth on the Trans-Mongolian Express from Peking. At the time I'd made the booking I was perfectly happy to spend the extra time in China, in Shanghai if possible, and had convinced myself that my memories of the grotty bedrooms, the unmade roads and how harsh and unspiritual life was away from my Shanghai haunts were exaggerated.

After much consultation two of us decided to try and get a ferry south to Ningpo, from where I could cycle back north through Shaoxing, Suzhou, Hangzhou, Wuxi and, finally, Nanjing on the Yangtze, where I could see how much time I had and from where I could feasibly cycle to Peking without jeopardising my train reservation home. Ideally, I would be able to loiter around this small corner of China, known as the 'Chiang-nan' and renowned for its traditional concentration of literary, artistic and intellectual activities. This had apparently moderated the destructive impulses of the Cultural Revolution, and was supposed to have produced a pleasant, relaxed atmosphere in which people read and even wrote books, sketched and painted or just sat in Chinese gardens reflecting on the harmonious juxtaposition of trees, rocks and water.

To get to this wonderland I needed the help of the China International Travel Service, an organisation which I feared on past performance would tell me that the ferry was either suspended from operating, full, closed to foreigners, didn't exist or was for some other reason impossible. In Shanghai, however, the CITS office were quite unexpectedly helpful: not only had they booked my Trans-Mongolian Express ticket without complaint, but they even wished me a pleasant trip. At first their behaviour seemed almost sinister, but slowly I had become accustomed to asking their advice on where the acrobatics were, what was on at the cinema and where I could find English newspapers.

This unusual behaviour meant that I took the address they gave me without any feeling of suspicion, only to feel devastated when the address turned out to be that of a warehouse. I trudged back to the CITS office.

'Hello,' said the clerk, smiling in a friendly way. 'Did you get your tickets?'

I felt again the awful sense of panic that maybe 'reality' in China was a meaningless concept – the posters in Wuhan showing the silhouettes of hundreds of cranes against a glorious sunset, when immediately beneath them were men hauling baskets of coal from a barge into a warehouse by hand; the photographs of combine harvesters and mopeds where none existed; the brave descriptions of a city being the ancient capital of one of the earlier Chinese dynasties, when there were scarcely any buildings left that had been built before the 1940s.

Surely the clerk knew she had sent me to a warehouse, that the address was wrong. What was I to say – tell her that I had the tickets and avoid an argument, or say the boat was full? I ended up doing neither, but stood silently gawping at her.

The impasse was broken by the Irishman, who staggered past the counter with some girl squealing under his left arm.

'Are ye all right, Chrissy boy?' he called, before barging into the hotel lift. It was an incident which reminded me of the importance of leaving Shanghai.

'I didn't get the tickets,' I announced. 'You sent me to a warehouse.'

'Yes, of course. The ticket office is in the warehouse,' the clerk replied, still smiling sweetly.

I asked her for a piece of paper with two questions written in Chinese: 'Where can I buy tickets for the ferry to Ningpo?' and 'Two second-class tickets to Ningpo, please.' Armed with this piece of paper, I went back to the warehouse.

Just inside the main entrance two men sat around a crate of cabbages quietly smoking a cigarette. In the far corner, a man was lying on a tarpaulin having a quick snooze. Beneath a ramp leading to the first floor there was a stack of wooden pallets. There was absolutely no sign of a ticket office – nobody carrying bundles of luggage, no groups of passengers sitting around waiting for the ferry to depart, no signposts even in Chinese to suggest that the building was anything more than a rather down-at-heel warehouse.

Feeling a little embarrassed at the stupidity of my question, I shoved the bit of paper at the two men smoking cigarettes. It turned out that they couldn't read. Sportingly, one of them went over to wake the man on the tarpaulin, who grunted, yawned, stretched and blinked incredulously at the written question. In due course he grunted again, pointed upstairs and held up eight fingers before tapping his watch. Another night in Shanghai.

At quarter past eight I was back at the warehouse. An old woman was sitting on the crates by the ramp, encouragingly surrounded by a huge pile of bundles, plastic bags and boxes of oranges. I showed her my question. She nodded and pointed upstairs. On the first floor two men were unloading a crate of what looked like flour. Up, up they pointed.

On the second floor there were three long queues for ferry tickets. Wondering if it was all a hallucination, I joined the Ningpo queue, and after about forty-five minutes reached the window and handed across the request for tickets. The clerk studied it:

'Mayo, mayo,' he said eventually. ('No, no.')

'Mayo to you,' I said, adding the Chinese for the CITS to support my application. 'Luxingshe, Luxingshe.'

'Mayo.'

'Luxingshe . . . Ningpo, Ningpo.'

We grew angrier and angrier with each other. The rest of the queue pushed forward to witness this strange chorus of 'Mayo', 'Ningpo' and 'Luxingshe' across the counter, until at last, in despair that they would never get their tickets, someone behind me went off to get a policeman.

After hearing the clerk's version of events the policeman grabbed me and marched me downstairs, to the delight of all those held up in the queue and with complete disregard for my repeated cry, 'Luxingshe, Ningpo.' The old woman tutted as I was dragged past, no doubt reflecting sadly on the wickedness of youth and unconcerned about where I was being taken to.

Once away from the warehouse the policeman relaxed his grip and even seemed open to the suggestion that I should just be sent on my way with the Chinese equivalent of a clipped ear. But unfortunately, he was evidently so unused to exercising his initiative that he dithered to such an extent that we ended up in a secured room somewhere in the bowels of the ferry terminus building, both of us a little uncertain about what would happen next.

The situation was obviously very unsatisfactory. I couldn't speak Chinese, he couldn't speak English. I felt quite strongly that my behaviour hadn't warranted this incarceration, particularly when it was at the instigation of China International Travel Service that I'd gone to the warehouse in the first place. In some despair I pointed to the bit of paper still held tightly by the policeman, and urged him to accept it was 'Luxingshe'.

He stared at the message for a short while before suddenly rushing out of the room, leaving me debating whether to make a dash for it or stay and see how the situation would end. Idly, I peered out of the window to see if there was any escape that way, and it was as I began to test whether the window-handle worked that another man, wearing a rather incongruous peaked naval hat with an anchor sewn in the centre of the peak, wandered in and asked in English:

'You wish to go to Ningpo?'

I confirmed that I did, adding that it was all the Luxingshe's fault and that I didn't want to go if it was inconvenient.

'Wait here,' he ordered, unimpressed by my demeaning subservience. He stalked out, to return a few minutes later with two tickets and the arresting officer.

'Be here at five o'clock tonight,' the man with the peaked cap said. 'He will take you out' – a contemptuous reference to the policeman.

It was an inauspicious start to the long-anticipated return to life on board the luxury of second-class Chinese cruisers, so fondly remembered from my trip down the Yangtze: the attentive service, the private cabin, the observation room, the armchairs, the opportunities to sit and reflect or just stare into space watching the sky pass by. However much I had romanticised it, the Yangtze cabin had been infinitely more comfortable than the squalid little room we were put in, with two bunks practically touching at one end, and a rather narrow plastic-covered bench to sit on. The cabin was already half-occupied by two Chinese heavy-smokers, complete with a fantastic number of parcels.

'Don't worry,' I said, 'it's all a mistake.'

'I doubt it,' said a despondent Don, the Australian who had decided to come with me down to Ningpo. 'Hey you, put those bloody things out,' he told the Chinese who, possibly deliberately, took the statement as a request for a cigarette.

'Come on. Let's go to the observation room,' I proposed, anxious to defuse the situation and feeling more than a little embarrassed by the dramatic difference between my description of the spacious, luxurious cabins we could expect and the over-crowded hole that we found ourselves in.

There was just one person in the observation room – a distinguished-looking Chinese woman dressed in a long black silk gown buttoned at the front from her knees to her neck. She sat, or rather perched, on the end of a bed that had been specially made up for her, occasionally fanning herself with an intricately carved wooden fan painted with a scene from the Guilin mountain ranges.

'Nee-how,' I said, and doffed my Panama.

The woman looked at us with disgust – a middle-aged Australian in a rather tatty corduroy jacket and ostentatiously heavy working-man's boots and me, in dirty tracksuit trousers and a thin red sports shirt bought off a black-market barrow in Hong Kong and in imminent danger of falling apart. It was obvious that our appearance caused her acute distress, and swallowing hard she looked away before reaching with her left hand for a small silver bell that lay beside her pillow.

Within seconds of her tinkling it, two heavies dressed in white uniforms with blue piping and shiny brass buttons came rushing in and bundled us out. It was the second time in twelve hours that I had been ignominiously manhandled by Chinese officials, and on both occasions I had no idea why. There was a certain irony in this situation, given that for most of the time I had spent in China I had been travelling illegally, yet I only seemed to encounter difficulties when my activities were actually authorised by CITS.

Don was more robust. 'What the hell do you think you're doing? This isn't some bloody feudal state – get her out of there. We've paid for it. And I told you to put those bloody things out,' he said, referring to our cabin-mates' cigarettes. With an infuriating smile they offered us a packet of biscuits.

At three the next morning we were woken up – our cabin had to be tidied up before we arrived at Ningpo at five. We stood sullenly in the corridor, watched with some contempt by one of the white-suited heavies who had earlier ejected us from the presence of the lady in silk. By six o'clock we were outside the 'Foreign Guest Hotel', another of the large, grey, oppressively inhuman buildings into which the Chinese try and force all foreign tourists. The one in Ningpo stood on the edge of the industrial estate, and we stood, waiting for a room and watched the sunrise through the smoke and pollution from the factories.

After about five hours' sleep, the memories of our gruelling ferry journey had faded a little, and I felt prepared to explore what I was sure would be another example of the worst of 1940s architecture. I was wrong: the centre of Ningpo was a pleasant group of white-washed two-storey houses, shaded by plane trees and surrounded by parks, canals and ponds. Even more extraordinary, these amenities weren't cordoned off or appropriated for some silly exhibition of papiermâché swans, as in the Mandarin's Garden in Shanghai. In Ningpo, people actually sat and did nothing, without loudspeakers blaring at them or brash posters exhorting them to achieve higher production levels. Nor were they deadened by the soulless architecture of the Sino-Soviet school.

Things became even better as I cycled from Ningpo to Shaoxing, where I had arranged to meet Don, who was going by train. Spring had at last arrived, and I was able to see China at its most beautiful – the sun causing mist to rise gently over the ancient canals, over the curved roofs of the small houses clinging to the canal banks, and over the elegantly arched stone bridges. Emerging from this misty and delightful scene, a man wearing a wide-brimmed straw hat gently herded ducks from one canal to another.

Shaoxing was even nicer than Ningpo, the town criss-crossed with canals and two thousand bridges, the centre a tightly built mass of the small white-washed houses nestling under trees that I'd seen in parts of Ningpo. As usual, only one hotel was allowed to take foreigners but, most unusually, it was an absolutely delightful building. There were three large courtyards surrounded by a wooden two-storey building, the upper tier with an old wood balcony running around it, and in the centre of each of the courtyards there was a fountain and pond. Just outside the hotel was the Ling Feng Peak, a small hill crammed with a disproportionate number of peaks, caves and rocks and a waterfall.

Before dinner on my first night I set off to explore this Peak, and to try and find the Zhenji (true tranquillity) Temple and the Chang-chun (eternal spring) Cave. I failed to find these two, but clambered to the top and admired the view of the town – the setting sun creating a yellow haze over the curved, tiled roofs, further diffusing and softening the already unobtrusive, even harmonious buildings. Only the rather dilapidated nine-storey pagoda and the occasional flashes of sunlight reflected off the canals or paddy-fields could really be individually identified, scarcely disturbing my sentimental thoughts about the fusion and serenity of Chinese life.

Walking back to the hotel, quite overcome by these romantic feelings, I came across six workmen trying to lift some large and heavy tree trunks on to a barrow. Almost choking with feelings of common humanity, I offered to help and, in the process, lost my watch. At the time, uncertain whether I'd left it in my hotel room, and in any case reluctant to shatter my mood of good will, I carried on, sure that it would turn up.

Once back at the hotel, however, I was no longer capable of maintaining such a sanguine approach. Somewhere north of the Mediterranean I had discovered that the only way I could keep pedalling was to make myself cycle until half past the hour, then rest for a period of no more than ten minutes, and in general race against the clock to try and reach a particular town ahead of some highly arbitrary schedule. Worse, since I'd started cycling in China, where there were scarcely any signposts (and none that I could read), I relied solely upon my watch as a means of estimating how far I'd travelled, assuming an average speed of nine miles an hour, and, more importantly, how far I had to go.

After the highly embarrassing fuss I'd made in Alleppey over the loss, or assumed loss, of my bicycle pump, I was particularly anxious to deal with this latest setback in a calm and rational manner – to try and avoid the entire Shaoxing police devoting itself to searching for my watch, when I could easily buy a new one in the town. But not a reliable Swiss watch, I thought; nothing in Shaoxing would be like the watch I'd lost – one I'd had for fourteen years. None would have the nice little separate dial for the second hand which I'd become so attached to over the years. No, I thought, it was more important to me to get my watch back than to avoid causing the Chinese police a headache.

I went to tell the English-speaking receptionist that I wanted to telephone the police about a lost watch. His face went white – a re-minder, perhaps of the days when old, discarded razor-blades would follow tourists around China, sent on by hotel staff frightened of being dismissed for dishonesty.

'You must see the manager,' he stammered. (The only stammer I heard in China.)

The manager arrived.

'You have lost your watch?'

'Yes. It's all my fault. I went out for a walk . . .'

'So you didn't lose it in the hotel.'

'No, probably not. I think I lost it when I helped the workmen.'

'What?'

'I helped some workmen lift some logs on to a barrow.'

'You helped workmen? Why did you help workmen? It is better that you do not help workmen.'

I began to get rather irritated by this uncomradely talk, so soon after my rehabilitation with the 'common humanity' school.

'Well, I did, and I lost my watch, and now I want to report it to the police.'

'First we must look for your watch. Perhaps we will find it.'

The three of us plodded off, feebly shining torches over the road, no one realistically expecting to find it. The tirade against helping the workmen continued, interrupted only by the sight of them sitting exhaustedly beside their barrow.

'There they are,' I cried and rushed up happily to exchange our 'Nee-hows'.

The manager bustled up, and quickly put a stop to such friendly overtures with a noticeably aggressive attack, in Chinese, against the group. They obviously denied whatever charges she had laid before them, an impression confirmed when the manager turned to me and announced that they had said they hadn't stolen my watch. All six of the workmen, understandably angry about this unwarranted accusation, shoved their own watches at me – expressing their contempt at any suggestion that they needed to steal mine.

My heart sank at the tactless way this had been handled, inept in any circumstances, but especially so in a country where the whole gamut of social relations rested on the Confucian ideals of moderation, order and harmony, and particularly on a reluctance to cause others to lose self-respect and prestige – in other words to lose 'face'.

'Can't I just report it to the police station?' I asked the manager as I smiled weakly at the workmen in an attempt at conciliation.

'The police station isn't open until Monday.'

'I shall wait until Monday then,' I announced, delighted at this unexpected information about the once-feared Chinese police force. In future I could always cycle at weekends, avoid detection and retain my energy for clambering up and down the Great Wall.

For two days I drifted around Shaoxing, hitching lifts on passing barges by standing at the edge of bridges and sticking my thumb out, even helping to unload the occasional barge if I had been given a particularly long lift. I also spent a lot of time sitting in my bedroom doorway and watching the life of a Chinese courtyard.

At eight-thirty on Monday morning this idyll was disturbed by the arrival of two police officers, both in their early twenties and both fairly inexperienced at hard investigative questioning, asking at the end of my long account of the incident whether I'd found my watch. I realised that I was unlikely to see my watch again when, after about half an hour, they announced that they were going to start their investigations without a description of the watch they were looking for. I would have let them go, but I needed a certificate to claim on my massively expensive insurance policy. It took me a further hour and a half to explain the basics of insurance before they would give me the certificate, time utterly wasted as the insurance company subsequently refused to pay out on the policy on the spurious grounds that I hadn't had the watch valued before I lost it.

Cycling without a watch was as bad as I had expected, a helpless, undisciplined floundering about China trying to establish new criteria to force me on, and avoiding the temptations of the various tea stalls and grubby restaurants I passed. Nothing presented itself – if I allowed myself to stop after the fifteenth canal, for example, I invariably ended up sitting self-indulgently for hours, watching the barges and punts skim up and down, or focusing idly on the activities of one of the duck-herds who 'walked' their ducks from one canal to another, controlling them by twitching a stick in front of the herd.

In Canton province I would, no doubt, have stuck with this languid approach to cycling, finding in it some quite unjustified proof of my empathy with rural China. Between Shaoxing and Hangzhou, however, a new urgency was required if I was to succeed in cycling all the way to Peking. Eventually, I was forced on by the chronic absence of anything to eat or drink in the cafés – a remarkable state of affairs in the lush and fertile land of the Chiang-nan. All around me there were domestic ducks, pigs and chickens; every house had a little vegetable patch behind it, and on some of the rivers and canals there were elaborate 'Chinese fishing nets', which I hadn't seen since Kerala in southern India.

I couldn't even get a cup of tea, despite the area being famous for one of the finest varieties of green tea – Lung-ching (dragon's well). Every café I stopped at between Shaoxing and Hangzhou gave me a tin mug of hot water, and insisted that it was the 'Lung-ching chai' that I had ordered. It was an extraordinary situation, and strengthened my nervous fear that in China one had to suspend disbelief, and temporarily enter some strange fantasy world where black was white and two plus two equalled five.

It wasn't the first time that I had been given hot water. In some places the people obviously couldn't afford tea, in others it was just a hangover from the Cultural Revolution when everyone drank water as an expression of their solidarity with the poor Chinese peasant, and a demonstration of their belief that an ascetic peasant's existence was intrinsically superior to other ways of life. In these places, though, it was made abundantly clear that one was drinking hot water, indeed the whole object was to announce to all the world that it was hot water, and not socially divisive tea.

Perhaps, like the Shanghai warehouse which turned out to be the ticket office for ferries to Ningpo, the hot water really was 'Lung-ching' tea, or perhaps the tea was like the Shaoxing Chia Fan Chiew – the rice wine claimed to be not only one of the most popular wines in China but possibly Shaoxing's most famous product, yet mysteriously unavailable even in the foreigners' hotel and in exchange for Foreign Exchange Certificates, normally the best way to get hold of any of China's 'most popular' products.

I felt the same sense of existing in a fantasy in Hangzhou, where as I booked into my hotel I stood beside an American paying for further accommodation in the dormitory. I watched as he paid eight yuan a night for a bed, and after he had gone I asked the clerk for a bed at the same price.

'We have no dormitory.'

'You've just put that American in the dormitory.'

He studied his register:

'There are no Americans staying here.'

'Please . . . please. I've just seen you register the American, and you put him in the dormitory.'

The clerk was silent – a Sinologist would no doubt say that I had left him with no opportunity to save 'face'. I went off and sat in an armchair for a few minutes, declaring that I was prepared to wait for a bed in the dormitory, which I knew existed, to become free.

'We have double rooms at fifty-three yuan. That is all,' warned the clerk, staring sulkily at his register.

'I'll still wait,' I said and picked up a magazine.

After about five minutes the clerk declared that he had found a room at twelve yuan a night.

'Thank you, but I'd like a bed for eight yuan in the dormitory.'

'The beds in the dormitory are nine yuan,' he said irritably, as if angry that I'd tried to cheat the hotel out of one yuan. I went off to an empty six-bedded room, where I reflected on the incomprehensibility of Chinese behaviour, too dismayed by my lack of understanding to draw any satisfaction from the reduction in the room rate.

The next day I was up early, hoping to see the sunrise over the West Lake, which, surrounded by mountains, trees, gardens and old pavilions, mansions and pagodas, is Hangzhou's great contemporary attraction. In my current mood of disbelief, it would not have surprised me if I'd failed to find the lake at all; indeed, I half expected to find myself being manhandled by some policeman or soldier if I even asked where the lake used to be. Such scepticism was unjustified, however. I watched the sunrise, the red and yellow streaks reflected in the lake, and a few cyclists pedalling gently along the shores, their pace suggesting an ease with the world which would soon be shattered by the loud-speakers, the expectorations and the general noisy frenzy of Chinese life. As I watched, I saw first dozens and then hundreds of Chinese begin their dawn shadow-boxing exercises, swaying gently between the reds and yellows of sky and lake. It was an image that was worth preserving so, racing back to the hotel, I packed and left Hangzhou quickly before it was shattered.

Ever since the end of the sixth century, anyone travelling from

Hangzhou to Suzhou would have followed the course of the Grand Canal, and would probably, as I did, consider hitching a ride on one of the hundreds of small vessels that chug slowly between the two cities. Presumably, given enough time, it would be possible to hitchhike on barges and small tugs all the way to Peking. Unfortunately, though, it was faster to cycle along the well-made roads that ran alongside the canal than to be heaved along by little more than a small sail and two men punting. In any event, the weather was absolutely beautiful, and cycling under the shade of my precious Panama was a joy.

At the end of the second day I arrived at Suzhou, another Chiang-nan town divided by canals and waterways, with trees shading the traditional one- and two-storey houses – either white-washed or with wooden fascias. The town used to have about a hundred gardens, mostly privately owned and designed to provide retired court officials, merchants and landowners with somewhere to lead the contemplative life. Supposedly 'microcosms of nature in harmony with man', these extraordinary combinations of pavilions, water, trees, flowers and the hollowed, carved and twisted rocks have now been hi-jacked by the Chinese fetish for loudspeakers, which shatter the tranquil environment as they blare out commentaries on how the gardens helped people to study, entertain and examine such phenomena as the rising of the moon.

Despite the awful spitting and expectorating, the continued pushing and shoving to get into the pagodas and gardens and the obstruction and lies of CITS, I was beginning to see what a civilised people the Chinese could be – how good-humoured, courteous and graceful. This glimpse into their character gave me new optimism as I cycled north from Suzhou to Wuxi, and on to Nanjing and the Yangtze.

15

Fame in Xuzhou

Seventeen hundred years ago, when the city was already 700 years old, Zhu Geiling described Nanjing as 'a crouching tiger', and the hills to the east of the city as 'a curling dragon'. Nothing about present-day Nanjing conjures up such evocative images, as it was destroyed during the Taiping Rebellion in the 1850s and again by the various forces of destruction during the 1930s and '40s. The hills are now renowned for the Sun Yat-sen mausoleum, and the town for the Jinling Hotel (the highest building in China and the one place I saw which had a permanent crowd of gawping Chinese outside, staring up at it) and, most importantly, the Yangtze river bridge, started in 1960 and finished, with the help of 50,000 volunteers, in 1968 – a statistic which might help to explain the city's overwhelming pride in the bridge, a two-tier object devoid of any beauty or particular engineering brilliance.

Unfortunately, Chinese pride in the bridge meant that there were several armed soldiers wandering around, making sure that nobody planted a bomb, painted any slogans or otherwise spoiled the sanctimonious atmosphere. They strutted about, shoving stray members of the vast crowd who were taking photographs of each other back on to the massive pavements, supervising the parking of the dozens of coaches, climbing ladders to observe the general scene from the watchtowers and preventing cyclists from cycling outside the narrow cycle lane, a lane which was for the most part already occupied by the mass of Chinese tourists.

One can imagine that after undergoing the extensive army training that China requires of its soldiers, and no doubt dreaming of glory on the Russian, Indian or Vietnamese frontier, to be asked to guard the Nanjing bridge must seem a bit of a disappointment. And one can just about imagine the perverse pleasure to be gained in upholding the most trivial of rules relating to the bridge – especially when they were being violated by a Western cyclist, pedalling merrily along outside the confines of the cycle lane without any apparent regard for the seriousness of the offence. In retrospect, I realised there had been a change of tone in the voice booming out over the loudspeaker, from a soothing incantation of the bridge's statistics to an angry tirade against something or other, but I had absolutely no idea that the tirade was directed at me. I cycled slowly on, the voice getting steadily more hysterical, until finally one of the soldiers engaged in dealing with the orderly parking of the coaches was instructed to stop me and, presumably, told that he could use force if it proved necessary. He stepped across my path and, grinning savagely, pointed his rifle at me.

Despite having experienced a similar incident on the Turkish–Syrian border I still found this sort of behaviour somewhat alarming, and came to a rather inelegant halt. The soldier, ignoring my plight, began to point wildly at the loudspeaker, at the division between the cycle lane and the normal road and finally, accusingly, at me and my bike. The end result was that I was forced to push my bike along the pavement at the fast pace set by the soldier, and escorted across the bridge. Adding a farcical note to the whole affair, the wind caught hold of my Panama and blew it into the Yangtze, an accident which initially appeared to me a major disaster, although it had the slight advantage of convincing the soldier of my fallibility and absence of malice.

Freewheeling down the hill away from the bridge, I took further comfort in his obvious lack of interest in the fact that I was cycling out of Nanjing and off into the hinterland of central China despite the fact that there were no 'open' towns within cycling distance. This was encouraging, as sitting gloomily over a map in my Nanjing hotel I had only found five 'open' towns on my proposed route to Peking. For some reason I felt particularly nervous about this route, as cycling across the flattest and most exposed part of China without permission somehow seemed more daring than cycling through the hills of southern China. But now, although I'd lost my beloved Panama, I'd gained renewed confidence – and in any case the Panama was beginning to get a little battered.

Within about half an hour of leaving the bridge, my new confident, sanguine attitude was reinforced by another bizarre confrontation with a Chinese authority. Pedalling along happily, I suddenly came upon a roundabout, with a motorway the other side leading to the town I wanted to go to, Liuhe. After the potholes, dirt tracks and single-lane roads of southern China, I was sure that I was hallucinating, and cycled two circuits of the roundabout before standing on one leg with my eyes closed in an attempt to re-establish reality.

When I opened my eyes again the motorway was still there, but it was only after a considerable time that I fully accepted its existence. Normally there are few things less pleasant than cycling on long, straight roads with heavy traffic flying past at great speed – dangerous, noisy, repetitive and enormous distances between cups of tea. But such considerations didn't apply in the present situation – the motorway was the only road which went directly from Nanjing to Liuhe and any detour would add at least forty miles to my journey. Furthermore, I was in a hurry and, most importantly, I wanted to have a cup of tea in a Chinese service station. I set off up the hard shoulder.

'Paaaarrppfff,' screamed a police whistle, the shock nearly causing me to fall off my bike.

I was torn between two conflicting responses – to carry on in a demonstration of my adamant disdain for policemen whistling at me, or to pull over meekly.

'Paaaarrrpppffff,' came a second blast, if anything louder than the first. I decided that in view of the gun-toting soldiers at the bridge, and the unpleasant experience I had already had of being fired at in Turkey, it would be prudent at least to turn round and have a look at the formidable character capable of obtaining such noise from a tin whistle.

About twenty-five yards away a policeman was hanging out of an open-sided traffic turret, his face red from blowing the whistle, his arms waving wildly in the air. Although I couldn't see any gun, it was fairly obvious that he would take a dim view of my cycling on. I smiled, reached for my Panama and suddenly remembered that it had gone at the bridge. Despondently, I waited for the policeman to climb down from his vantage point.

He marched towards me, shouting.

'Nee-how,' I said. 'Dao Liuhe?' pointing up the motorway.

'Mayo,' squeaked the policeman, his buttons about to burst in his indignation. 'Mayo, mayo.'

'Mayo Liuhe?' I produced my map. 'Dao Liuhe?'

The policeman stared with an expression of benign incredulity. In due course he took my map, stubbed his finger against the character for Liuhe and asked:

'Dao Liuhe?'

This confused me, as I thought the question meant 'Where is Liuhe?' and the officer seemed to be asking 'Are you going to Liuhe?' If he was right it explained why so many people looked puzzled when I asked them whether they were going to X or Y. I tied a knot in my handkerchief to remind myself to ask the next bilinguist I met.

'Dao Liuhe?' the officer repeated, unimpressed by my reflections.

'Hao. Hao,' I declared.

The officer turned and began to study the numberplates of one of the lorries that lumbered slowly past. Suddenly, he rushed on to the slow lane and, whistling madly, ordered the driver to stop.

'Dao Liuhe?' he cried, which seemed to confirm that I had indeed been misusing the word.

'Mayo,' the driver bawled back.

The third lorry stopped by the policeman was going to Liuhe, and the driver was prepared to give me a lift, if I didn't mind sitting on the machinery loaded on the back. Once I'd found a comfortable position and thanked the policeman for his quite unexpected help, the lorry lurched off and we chugged gently along the motorway. For the first few minutes I stood in the wind, keenly observing the surrounding countryside, determined not to lose my relationship with Chinese soil. After about fifteen minutes, though, I decided that it was too cold to be worthwhile, and so I nestled into a corner of the lorry, which was shaded from the wind but offered no view of where we were and the country we were passing through.

In any other situation, the prospect of sitting on the back of a lorry with just the sides of the trailer and the sky to look at would have seemed not merely boring, but a complete waste of time: a pandering to the much despised obsession with getting from A to B; a denial, in fact, of the whole motivation behind cycling in China. I peered over the side; there was a field, there was a bullock with a man in a blue cotton suit and straw hat plodding along behind it, there was a crude restaurant probably selling spinach and onions fried in oil and ginger. In the distance I could see a small copse of trees, but otherwise I stared bleakly across a harsh landscape without hedgerows, without trees, without birds, without variety. Suddenly, I was determined to abandon cycling and hitch-hike the remaining 500 miles to Peking.

Had there been any clouds they would have rolled away, had there been any birds they would have twittered and had there been any bees they would have hummed. I imagined myself in the Imperial Palace within two, at most three days – clambering along the Great Wall, exploring the Temple of Heaven, the Hall of Supreme Harmony, the Palace of Earthly Tranquillity. Liuhe convinced me. It was another of the hundreds, thousands, of dull provincial towns with the regulation concrete blocks, the car-less dual carriageways, the grotty restaurants and the dusty and uncomfortable atmosphere. I celebrated my decision with several mugs of hot water, a selection of stuffed dumplings and another spirited rendition of 'The night-soil workers are coming down from the mountain'.

In due course, once the excitement had subsided, I set off for the outskirts of Liuhe, in search of a suitable spot to hitch-hike from. Having parked my bike I stood expectantly, waiting for the first lorry to take me on my way to Peking. Within seconds, two passing teenagers stopped to inspect the strange phenomenon of a Western cyclist hitch-hiking.

'Nee-how,' I said cheerfully.

'Uh,' they grunted, a little wary of such an odd sight.

Such circumspection didn't concern me, and while they studied my legs, nose, hair and dérailleur I peered intently towards Liuhe for the first lorry to appear.

A few seconds passed and another six people gathered around me. Two others turned up, leaving their bikes in the middle of the road. Three men pushing handcarts decided to stop and see what was the cause of the obstruction. After about two minutes I was surrounded by at least forty people, their number steadily growing and the road rapidly becoming blocked by the collection of push-bikes, carts, converted prams and mini-tractors that make up the normal traffic on Chinese roads.

I rushed around, frantically trying to clear a route through the barricade and get rid of some of the crowd in a desperate attempt to make it clear to the lorry drivers that someone was trying to hitch-hike, and not deliberately blocking the road. In the distance I could see the lumbering movements of a lorry trying to negotiate its way through the usual bumps and pot-holes of 'non-motorway China'. It growled its way slowly towards us.

'Quick, quick,' I cried. 'Dao Tianchang. Dao Tianchang.'

The crowd looked amused and did nothing either to get themselves out of the way, or to help clear the bikes and other obstructive clobber.

'Quick, quick,' I shouted again, and began to haul the bikes off the road, an utterly futile exercise as the space was immediately occupied by another cyclist.

'Mayo,' I shrieked, becoming embarrassingly hysterical – wildly pointing at the approaching lorry while simultaneously pushing bikes to the side of the road. A deep 'paarpff' came from the lorry.

'Quick, look. Brrmm, brrmm, brrmm, brrmm,' I said, impersonating the lorry.

'Paarpff,' hooted the lorry.

No one moved, except the lorry driver, who was hanging out of the cab window yelling at the impassive crowd. Eventually, the lorry was forced to stop, and started slowly inching its way through the tangled mess of bikes and carts. I waded my way through towards the cab, still hoping that I might get a lift, though the closer I went the more impressed I became by the fury written all over the driver's face.

'Dao Tianchang?' I cried.

The lorry driver glared at me, might even have waved his fist. Dejectedly I trudged back to my bike, to interrupt the clumsy experimentation with my gears and dérailleur and watch the lorry ease its way through the blockade. Once it had gone, I miserably accepted a cigarette from one of the crowd before cycling off to try from a less populated spot – if one existed. The immediate prospects were discouraging: stretching ahead in an apparently never-ending torrent of people were great lines of cyclists, pedestrians, cart-pushers and bullock-herders – all clearly capable of forming a large crowd of curious bystanders.

The obvious solution, which was just to keep on cycling, was too depressing after my fantasies of reaching Peking in two days. The decision to hitch-hike had drained me of all my energy and caused my back, bottom and legs to ache horribly. It didn't matter that this was obviously a lazy psychological reaction, that I ought to relish the prospect of cycling through the Chinese countryside on a lovely spring day. Unfortunately, the moment I stopped a crowd started to form. I began to get desperate, scarcely believing that I had set out from Nanjing that morning looking forward to arriving in Peking in about a week's time and cheerfully carefree about cycling there, and quite refusing to accept that just minutes before I had been in Liuhe humming and whistling refrains from 'The night-soil workers'.

I struggled on, finding even first gear unbearably exhausting but too dispirited to fall on to the ground to attract a crowd of potential leg-strokers. Cycling on, listening for the approach of lorries, was a slow process – in two hours I managed to travel just ten miles according to one of the rare, and frequently unreliable, road signs. Eventually, some salvation appeared: a lorry-drivers' café with three lorries parked outside, two of them facing towards Tianchang.

To my relief one of the drivers agreed to take me, and after a quick mug of hot water we set off. Predictably, all my pains eased away, and I rather rudely began to study my map to see how far I could get after Tianchang. Ten minutes later the driver stopped the lorry and produced five dry, salty and utterly unappetising pieces of bread. He handed me two, which I chewed at for a few minutes before dropping them as discreetly as possible out of the window. I sat there gently tapping the outside of the door as he devoured the disgusting bread, which he followed with great swigs from an old army water-bottle. Finally, he produced a packet of foul-smelling cigarettes and proceeded to smoke three in a row.

After the third, by which time I was getting thoroughly fed up with our prolonged standstill, the driver leant towards me, gave me the most sickly grin and began to stroke my legs. In dozens of southern Chinese villages I had found such behaviour a relaxing, even pleasant, way of ending the day. But there was something about this particular man which suggested that his intentions were less innocent than those of the curious villagers – the funny look in his eye, the revolting leer of his lip, the unpleasant groping and the excessive smoking. It was still difficult to be sure, after the familiar sight of men walking down the road holding hands, or helping each other to wash in the primitive boilerhouses used as bathrooms. I had had so many disorientating experiences within China that I suddenly lost confidence in my ability to perceive a homosexual advance.

The driver's hand went higher and higher up my leg, his leer becoming more and more pronounced. I couldn't think what to do, not wishing to make any unfounded allegations or misinterpret a perfectly innocent act, or, most importantly, jeopardise my lift to Tianchang, but on the other hand I didn't want to spend the rest of the day locked in a homosexual embrace. I tried to recall a half-forgotten magazine article, or was it a television programme, on homosexuality in China. It had spoken of the way in which the great social pressures of ancestor worship and the importance of maintaining the family name encouraged heterosexuality, and had even suggested that at various periods in post-revolutionary China homosexuals had been executed.

But then I remembered the old Ming dynasty euphemism, 'playing with the flower in the back chamber'. I looked again at the driver, felt his absurdly high hand and decided that unless I moved fast the situation might become irreversible.

'Mayo,' I snapped, and threw his hand away. 'Tianchang. Tian-chang.'

We wasted still more time arguing, without any agreement in prospect. Finally I tired of the pointless argument, decided that Tianchang wasn't worth it and dramatically stormed out of the cab – an exit which lost some of its impact when I had to climb up on to the back of the lorry to retrieve my bicycle and panniers.

For a few miles I cycled along with the lorry providing an unwanted escort, trailing in its wake with the driver yelling various Chinese insults – presumably along the lines that if I was going to wear shorts I should expect the consequences. In due course he drove off, leaving me to continue wearily north, unlikely to reach Tianchang that night, let alone fulfil my ambitious plan to get to Xuzhou, the first 'open' city north of Nanjing.

I ended up in a village dormitory immediately reminiscent of the cold, damp rooms of southern China. The light bulb didn't work, the tap I was allowed to use was behind a restaurant's kitchen and supplied only cold water, the duvet was damp and I had to pay a premium before the receptionist would allow me to stay. Locking the door against the curious villagers, I tried unsuccessfully to find the World Service on the highly expensive radio I'd bought in Hong Kong. I gently fell asleep to the soothing American accent of Radio North Korea droning on about 'US imperialism . . . workers . . . peasants . . . glorious . . . smash . . . US imperialism . . . forward . . . struggle . . . solidarity . . . people's . . . democratic . . . struggle . . . oppression . . . smash . . . liberate . . . US imp . . .'

Resigned to continuing cycling for the last few hundred miles to Peking, I tried to enjoy them, finding some peculiar pleasure in the sight of the latest gang of road-workers carting building equipment around, their little loads of gravel, mud and sand collected in baskets hanging from their shoulder poles. I even began to enjoy the bumpy ride across the potholes and the view across the bleak northern plains planted with wheat, cabbages and potatoes, the occasional field of rape adding variety to the otherwise uniform impression of green, brown and dirty blue cotton suits.

Eventually I arrived in Xuzhou, another ancient city reduced to the familiar collection of concrete municipal buildings. I was forced to stay in the 'South Suburbs Guest House', perhaps the most pleasant of the chain of concrete monolithic hotels built in the post-revolutionary period of Sino-Soviet friendship. Its purpose was to house the various mining specialists who were asked to advise on how to increase coal productivity, principally through the introduction of machinery. Appropriately, a bright poster featured a jolly miner staring into the sun against the usual background of high-technology equipment.

The receptionist in the 'South Suburbs' was astonished, even distressed, that someone totally unconnected with the mining industry wanted to stay at the hotel. Despite my assurances that I would much rather be in Peking or, if forced to stay in Xuzhou, at one of the other hotels, we agreed that circumstances were such that I had to be given a room.

'I think the hotel is too expensive for you,' he dismally concluded.

'How much is it?'

'Eighty yuan,' he replied in an ashamed and apologetic way.

It would have been hopelessly impolite to have tried to reduce this price by my usual tactics of sitting on a sofa pouting, or histrionically pacing up and down the hotel lobby shouting 'Pah' at intervals, or aggressively accusing the receptionist of lying because I had only just met someone who was staying at an infinitely cheaper price. Forced to negotiate with someone in a civilised manner, respecting them as nice, friendly people 'just doing a job', I suddenly realised that I didn't know how it could be done – China had made me accustomed to contrived and artificial confrontations, to stupid posturings over some ridiculous and invalid 'principle'. Feeling thoroughly second-rate, I mumbled that eighty yuan was rather more than I usually paid.

'What do you normally pay?'

I began to panic. Since Canton, I had always bullied my way into dormitories and hotels, or bribed my way into village institutions. The result was that my average expenditure was about seven or eight yuan a night, which because I paid in renminbi meant that I paid the equivalent of about four Foreign Exchange Certificates per night – somewhere around one-twentieth of the nice receptionist's starting position. One-twentieth . . .? I began to question whether I could afford to be pleasant. What was a reasonable figure? I remembered the advice given to me in Aleppo about dealing with traders in the covered bazaar – offer a quarter, don't offer more for at least five minutes, and if you leave, never go back.

'Twenty yuan a night.'

The receptionist looked surprised.

'So much? That must include your meals?'

'Um, yes.'

So we settled on twenty yuan, to include an evening meal.

I had a bath before dinner, reflecting on the false economies I had subjected myself to while in China. Out of the bath, and lying on the comfortable bed wrapped in three large white towels, I switched the television on, switched it off, rang room service and ordered some tea. The telephone rang – I was like a small boy with a new toy, unable quite to believe in the room's magical powers and expecting to wake up at any moment and find some expectorating and smoking horde staring at my hairy legs. The phone continued to ring, saving me from having to pinch myself back into reality. At last, I picked the receiver up. It was the receptionist:

'Hello. You have cycled from England to Xuzhou?'

Iran, Pakistan, Bangladesh, Burma, Vietnam . . . all flown over. Ferries from Italy to Greece, Greece to Turkey, the backwater trip in Kerala, the Yangtze from Wuhan to Shanghai, train from Madras to Calcutta, even hitch-hiking from Nanjing to Liuhe.

'Yes,' I lied.

'Our local television company would like to interview you.'

Fame at last! Carefully smoothing my hair, straightening my eyebrows and putting on my cleanest tee-shirt, I swanned down to 'meet the press'. Half a dozen men stood beside a Japanese van, all of them looking desperately bored.

'Nee-how,' I cried.

One or two may have grunted, but most just looked rather cross that they were having to do such an inconsequential story. The receptionist came out, transformed in a pair of white trousers and a pink blouse.

'Will you stand by your bike?' he asked, and checked his appearance in the van's windscreen.

The half dozen men began to play with their Japanese camera, obviously barely familiar with how it worked. In due course they managed to get the thing focused on me and the receptionist, and one of the men began to bawl out some instruction on how the interview was going to proceed – his questions and my answers would both be translated by the receptionist. We all nodded, and the 'director' pulled a grubby bit of paper from a pocket and yelled out (after translation):

'Are you enjoying your stay in Xuzhou?'

'It's very nice. AFTER CYCLING 13,000 KILOMETRES FROM ENGLAND it's a great relief to find a comfortable hotel, because it's pretty tiring CYCLING TO CHINA FROM ENGLAND.'

'Do you like the "South Suburbs Guest House"?'

'Well, it's very comfortable and relaxing which is what, er, I want after CYCLING FROM ENGLAND.'

'In what ways do you prefer China to other countries you have visited.'

'It's very interesting to see how a quarter of the world's population live, um, and to compare China with, for example, India, both countries with large rural populations, both poor with little industry and technology, and to see how each country tries to develop. I think . . .'

The receptionist tapped me on the arm.

'Thank you,' he said. 'Now will you go in and have your supper, because the restaurant closes soon.'

I crept inside, forcing myself to repress the faint tremors of excitement about appearing on television, about how close I was to reaching Peking and the great sense of anticipation about catching the Trans-Mongolian Express home. After my disastrous hitch-hiking experience I had stopped thinking about such matters, almost frightened that something would go wrong on the remaining miles to Peking, scarcely believing that in five, maybe six, days I would never have to wake up in the morning worrying about where I was going to be that night, about how many miles I should try and cycle or where I was going to be in three days' time.

The road north from Xuzhou to Qufu discouraged any speculation about actually stopping cycling. Like so many roads in China, it was being re-laid, though the process had caused such disruption that, most unusually, motorised traffic was prevented from using the road by a large mound of earth. The result was an extraordinary, eerie silence – no engines, no birds singing or farm animals crying out, but just the faintest sound of spades digging into the ground and basketloads of road-making materials being poured on to the ground. The method raised the absurd image of Western engineers selling advanced technology for producing coal and being driven in imported buses along roads built by hand or, in an even more vivid contrast, driving past the queues of coal-workers pulling by hand the small carts laden with coal produced by modern methods.

Again I felt the pecular sensation that reality in China was somehow a relative concept, capable of being manipulated by excluding tourists from 90 per cent of the country, forcing them to stay in exclusive hotels, eat in special restaurants, and use special money – and then repeating *ad infinitum* that China was a beautiful, modernised country with a happy, ordered people enthusiastically using modern technology for the further development of the country.

In some ways this imposition of an 'order' on society, where the individual becomes subsumed within the natural workings of the state, reflects the traditional theories of, firstly, Chinese animism, in which man's actions were affected by the spirits of land, wind and water, and where improper conduct by man could throw the world out of joint; and, secondly, of Confucius, who classified five relationships between people and insisted on submission, loyalty and (the complementary virtue to loyalty) decency. The classification, the numbering and the strange reliance on theoretical logic continues: the Chinese work for the 'Four Modernisations' (defence, science and technology, industry and agriculture), have 'Five Loves' (work, people, neighbours, science and public property) and 'Eight Antis' (intellectual, western, bourgeois, 'capitalist roader', revisionist, traditional, Confucian and imperialist) and have fought against the 'Four Pests' (sparrows, rats, mosquitoes and flies).

In Qufu, the birthplace of Confucius, the population must have minds of rubber. Official attitudes towards the philosopher have varied from the 1970s 'Movement to criticise Lin Biao and Confucius', a time when all the statues of Confucius were systematically smashed, to the 1980s, when his ancestral home has been restored and converted into a museum packed with crowds lovingly peering through the red wooden screens at the interior and listening without complaint to the inevitable loudspeaker broadcasting a commentary and the unusual sounds of Chinese music.

The strangest feature of the town was that nobody seemed to think these violent changes in policy more than just a change in fashion. It must take an almost superhuman stoicism to enable people to dismiss the extraordinary anarchic violence of the Cultural Revolution, in which 100 million people were adversely affected, in terms as unemotive as 'a mistake' or 'the wrong principles'; to live in grotty houses in soulless environments, eating a repetitive diet of vegetables and small slivers of meat, and subjected constantly to crude propaganda from loudspeakers, posters, magazines and art generated by the 'revolutionary proletarian spirit', and yet seem totally unconcerned by the daily hardships of their unspiritual and unimaginative lives.

In this state of confusion I progressed steadily towards Peking, inspired not so much by a feeling of elation that I had achieved (more or less) what I'd set out to do, but by relief that I would soon be out of the Chinese countryside. Appropriately, when I eventually reached Peking I had no idea that I had done so. From Tianjing onwards the road signs stopped using the character for Peking that I had on my map, no grand banner declared a welcome to the capital of the People's Republic, and no spectacular monument stood out to suggest a capital city.

I stopped at a bus stop to ask the whole queue:

'Dao Beijing?'

A few people tittered, some looked embarrassed, some looked away.

'Dao Beijing?' I repeated.

The queue realised I was being serious. 'Here,' they pointed, their fingers pointing at the ground.

'Beijing? . . . Beijing?' I pointed at the ground, and looked around me, my face obviously revealing my disappointment.

In the distance, across the motorways and underpasses of central Peking, I could see the Peking Hotel. I cycled off towards it, wondering if it had a dormitory or would accept renminbi, and reflecting bitterly that I felt no sense of elation, merely relief that in ten days' time I would be on the Trans-Mongolian Express.

16

Peking and the
big green train ride

Somewhere in one of the dozens of Chinese magazines that were left around the tourist hotels I had seen a satellite photograph of the centre of Peking. Similar photographs of, for example, London are never particularly interesting – one can identify the Thames, and possibly Hyde Park, but essentially one is looking at a mass of dots and un-coordinated squiggles only recognisable because one already knows what they are. The photograph of Peking was extraordinary because in the middle of the city an enormous square imposed an order on the surrounding chaos. That square was the Imperial Palace.

An earlier photograph, taken before 1967 and the campaign to 'des-troy the old to establish the new', would have shown a larger square surrounding the Palace – the old city walls. The relationship between the walls and the Palace was in Simon Leys' words 'the projection in stone of a spiritual vision; its walls were . . . not so much a medieval defence apparatus as a depiction of a cosmic geometry, a graphic of the universal order.'

Those walls, the old city gates, and vast areas of the heart of the city were ripped down during the Cultural Revolution and replaced by endless highways, underpasses and row after row of bleak, hideously ugly office blocks staring solemnly across the wide empty roads at equally ugly buildings just visible at the other side of the road. Perhaps the most damning comment on the aesthetics of contemporary Peking is that among the more attractive buildings is the Soviet embassy, normally one of the most ghastly buildings in any capital city.

There are, however, little oases of beauty around Peking, identified by the guide book and map I bought at the Peking Hotel as the 'Five Musts': the Imperial Palace, the Summer Palace, the Temple of Heaven, the Ming Tombs and the Great Wall. In general, though, the rela-tionship between these ancient buildings and their modern surrounds is negligible, so much of old Peking having been destroyed. Strangely, modern Chinese literature seems proud of the destruction, and almost excited by what is described as an ingenious juxtaposition of new and old. The *Official Guidebook of China*, for example, describes the southern end of Tiananmen Square thus: 'Here the walls that once surrounded the Imperial City have been replaced by an underground subway and a broad avenue of fourteen- to sixteen-storey apartment houses. Standing majestically over this scene, as it has since the fifteenth century, is the beautifully restored Qianmen Gate.'

The result of the Gate being surrounded by high-rise blocks of flats is of course that, far from 'standing majestically over the scene', it is crushed by the ugly, dreary buildings around it, and it is difficult if not impossible to imagine it without the unimaginative little subway entrance, the flats, the Monument to the Heroes of the People and the Mao Memorial.

The Mao Memorial, which looks like a pretentious swimming pool, stands in the centre of the ancient square between the Qianmen and Tianmen gates. What little nobility the building has derives entirely from its monstrous imposition on the grandeur of Tiananmen Square. Even in China no one appears to be enthusiastic about the cloddish design of the Memorial, though one is supposed to squeal with delight at the fact that it was built within ten months by a huge army of volunteers apparently imbued with a revolutionary and spontaneous enthusiasm for the Great Helmsman.

However, most people would probably prefer to be able to stand under Qianmen Gate with the old walls intact, and gaze across at Tianmen, the ancient entrance to the Imperial Palace, without the view being obstructed by the awful bulk of the Memorial Hall, and an absurd obelisk which calls itself the Monument to the Heroes of the People. The obvious solution is to knock them both down, or perhaps compromise and move them to somewhere like Tianjin, where such monstrosities would look and feel more at home.

Behind the walls of the Imperial Palace an infinitely more subtle and humane architecture emphasises the ridiculous pseudo-grandeur of the buildings outside. A wonderfully harmonious series of courtyards, palaces and halls were built on a human scale, their names an attempt to convey the atmosphere the architects tried to achieve: the Palace of Heavenly Purity, the Hall of Earthly Peace, the Hall of Literary Glory, the Hall of Exuberance, the Palace of All Happiness, the Palace of Concentrated Beauty, the Hall of Preserving Harmony and, at the centre, the Hall of Supreme Harmony. It wasn't clear why the Chinese authorities considered that installing crackling loudspeakers every fifty yards improved the atmosphere, or even whether they were conscious of the irony in a broadcast description of, for example, the Hall of Preserving Harmony. As always, at any one time at least half a dozen people were loudly expectorating – their harsh and intrusive behaviour emphasised by the beauty of the place they were in and the smell of cheap tobacco instead of jasmine or oriental flowers, which one might feel to be more appropriate.

For the Chinese there might be some justification in behaving like this – the Palace became known as the Forbidden City because entrance was forbidden to all but the Emperor's family and attendants, so their behaviour might be deliberately disrespectful, a snub to the ousted dynasty and its demands for demeaning subservience. This explanation does not of course excuse the equally revolting behaviour of the Western tour groups who barge up to the very foot of Tianmen, pile out of their minibuses and march round under the hectoring command of their tour leader. It is just unlucky if one is in the way, or standing where they want to stand: a great scrum of camera cases and elbows simply shove all obstacles aside, particularly anyone who might be trying to glean some free information from their expensive guides.

Buffeted by the tour groups and the Chinese crowds, and subjected to the constant racket from the loudspeakers, the tour leaders and the blocked-up throats, I found it impossible to experience the 'physical sense of happiness' and harmony that I had read about. And the same intrusive and distressing behaviour succeeded in spoiling the Summer Palace and even the Great Wall.

To make the Great Wall overcrowded is the most remarkable achievement: as the dozens of tour leaders constantly told their parties, the Wall runs 3945 miles between the Himalayan mountains and the Yellow Sea; it's the largest construction built by man and can be seen from outer space with the naked eye; 235 million cubic yards of rammed earth and rubble form the Wall's core and 79 million cubic yards of brick and stone its outer shell; designed differently, it could have girdled the world as a dyke 8 feet high. Why then, does everybody have to squeeze into the reconstructed section at Badaling, clamber up with hundreds of others and be constantly pestered by salesmen with a selection of 'I've climbed the Great Wall' sweatshirts, wide-brimmed caps and pocketfuls of old coins which they claim originate from the Ming dynasty?

Unfortunately, I wasn't prepared either physically or mentally for a clandestine walk along the Wall, despite the enormous temptation to walk from Badaling to the coast, about 200 miles away at Shanhaiguan. In any case I had other infinitely more boring distractions to occupy me – obtaining my visas for the Trans-Mongolian Express, and trying to establish whether, and if so how, I could put my bike on the train back to London.

This necessarily required me to waste an inordinate amount of time with the Peking office of China International Travel Service, to whom no form of obstruction or irritation was too low or too mean. No known methods have succeeded in obtaining from them information which can honestly be described as truthful, helpful and clear, though some people claim to have entered their offices without being abused, cheated or ignored. After an almost interminable period when my attempts to attract the attention of the staff were ignored, I was finally asked to stop leaning on the counter and to say what I wanted.

'Is it possible to put my bicycle on the train to Moscow?'

'What sort of bicycle?'

'It's a Western bicycle.'

'You are not permitted to bring Western bikes into China.'

'I have my bike in China, and I want to take it home. Do you know if it can go on the train back to Moscow?'

'No.'

'Do you mean it isn't possible, or that you don't know?'

'You must ask at the railway station,' and the clerk concerned went back to his methodical copying out of the Chinese railway timetable.

I accordingly went to the railway station, where I was told that all enquiries by foreigners were dealt with by CITS. For two days I went to and from the station and the untrained brutes, slowly spiralling down into a state of gloomy lassitude. A Chinese-speaker wrote down my questions in Chinese, and provided little blanks which could be ticked if, for example, I *was* able to take my bike, how much it cost and when I had to deliver the bike to the station. I presented the note at the station, and rushed back clutching the treasured scrawl to my chest to find that the ticket clerk had simply written: 'All foreigners must negotiate with the International Travel Service.'

In the end I solved the problem by persuading a hardware shop to unwrap two cardboard boxes from some Japanese washing machines and give them to me, along with some lengths of string. After my charade, the production of my railway reservation ticket and a promise to show them the bike when I was next going past, they agreed to the donation and I spent most of my last afternoon in Peking carefully dismantling my bike, tying it together in the smallest possible form and wrapping the whole in cardboard.

I had no real idea whether I would be able to get this parcel on board. Asking other tourists who had travelled on hard-sleeper (the equivalent of third class), I was too dismayed at their description of conditions on the trains to think seriously about adding a bike to the overcrowded corridors, lined by three-tier metal bunks and sub-divided by a wire mesh. My protests that the Chinese couldn't be so inhumane as to allow people to travel in such conditions for six days were dismissed as naive by those who had already spent four days in hard-seat (fourth class), without even the comfort of a bed, from the far north-west to Peking.

Needless to say, CITS refused to describe the hard-sleeper compartments and I spent a week listening to appalling rumours of life on the Trans-Mongolian: of how the restaurant always served the same meal; that it always ran out of food by Irkutsk, so unless one took masses of food starvation beckoned; that the meals had to be paid for in foreign currency, taken at such a bad rate of exchange that the railway fare was nearly doubled; that the heating never worked; that there were loudspeakers in every compartment, playing 'The East is Red' all the way to the Mongolian border, the 'Internationale' throughout Mongolia, and Russian folk songs from Irkutsk to Moscow; and that there was never any beer, wine, vodka or champagne.

It was difficult to ignore these rumours as, in common with most other cities, nearly all the Western tourists in Peking on individual visas were herded together into a cheap dormitory establishment about fifteen minutes' cycle-ride south of the Qianmen gate. If Fethiye was my first experience of the long-suffering, weary 'Asian traveller', the dormitory in Peking was my last; its atmosphere combined the Turkish and Indian sense of great timeless wanderings in search of the 'real' Turkey/India/China with an intense anger, almost hatred, that Peking required such conformity with the despised tour groups. If one couldn't get away from the tourist part of the Wall then it wasn't worth visiting, and the people who whiled away their hours in the hotspot of the Peking Hotel (referred to as the 'Beijing Fandian' by the really experienced travellers) were selling their souls to mass tourism. Small cliques gathered in the most obscure cafés in a desperate quest to be the first white face in the area. They would sit smugly in the corner of various tatty restaurants, chewing at some impossibly recherché dish and reading translations called *Modern Chinese Fiction*.

Although at first my membership of these groups was guaranteed (I had been away from the materialist West for more than nine months; had, by cycling in China, embarked upon something illegal; and had pledged myself to the graphically portrayed discomfort of hard-sleeper on the Trans-Mongolian – indeed, had even adopted the fashionable regret that foreigners weren't allowed to travel hard-seat), I ultimately blew it all by accepting some invitations to lunch and dine with what were perceived as some of the last bastions of privilege and capitalist complacency, the diplomats at the British Embassy.

The common view of the Foreign Office is, of course, that of brainy chaps wearing odd socks and wandering around translating Tolstoy from the original into ancient Greek. Not so in Peking, where everyone gets red in the face rushing around on bicycles. Obviously whoever allocates overseas postings assumes that someone who liked cycling at university or who had been seen disappearing down Whitehall on a push-bike would find themselves happy in Peking, where everyone cycled. We chattered away about dérailleurs and spoke specifications, and on one occasion we pedalled back to the Embassy bike shed in convoy. I was slightly disappointed that there wasn't a fleet of tandems – each with a Union Jack fluttering from the front wheel, a Chinese driver and a passenger on the back wearing a bowler hat, pin-striped suit and completing *The Times* crossword – but possibly government cuts prevent such ostentation.

The only thing these cycling diplomats had in common with the gloomy travellers were dark and pessimistic fears about the standard of hard-sleeper accommodation. Didn't I know that de-luxe was only about £250 from Peking to Berlin? I did, but hard-sleeper was exactly half. People winced in sympathy, and were clearly considering fore-warning their colleagues in Moscow about the disease-ridden specimen that would arrive, half-starved, dirty, smelly and miserable in six days' time.

Both the diplomats and the travellers were wrong, however, and strangely enough the Shanghai CITS, who had been so un-characteristically helpful, were right when they assured me that there was no need for me to travel in anything superior to hard-sleeper. There turned out to be four berths in the compartment, each containing a comfortable bed with pillow and duvet which, although scarcely interesting in itself, made the warnings I had been given seem absurdly alarmist. Above the corridor, a luggage space could have been designed solely for the purpose of taking bicycles disguised as parcels. The only difficulty was that because of my junketings with the diplomats I had only had time to buy a dozen cans of beer and so was heavily reliant on the restaurant car.

My anxiety about the fate of my bike meant that I had arrived at the station ridiculously early in the hope that I could establish whether or not there was going to be any problem. Instead, I was ordered into an appalling waiting room reserved exclusively for 'foreign friends'. It succeeded in amalgamating the very worst elements of the foreign rooms in restaurants, the more pretentious hotels and a caricature of a cheap and nasty Chinese restaurant in the West. Incredibly, they didn't even play something fun like 'The East is Red', but a tape, probably smuggled in from Taiwan, of unidentifiable Western supermarket musak.

In a sudden panic I became confused between this Chinese impression of Western life and the reality – a terrible fear of being greeted at home by compulsory musak, continual game shows on television and waiters in the seediest restaurants all wearing black ties, calling me sir and constantly asking me if everything was all right. I thought I recognised the musak – an unspeakable combination of Johnny Mathis humming Viennese waltzes and Christmas carols to the accompaniment of an electric organ.

The nightmare passed, and in due course the train pulled into the station and we élite foreigners left our privileged environment for the comfort of the train. Each carriage had two men looking after the heating and bedding and ensuring a supply of hot water for tea. Both wore the universal blue cotton suits and puffed endlessly at the usual cheap cigarettes; after the horrors of the waiting room their plain appearance restored my sense of equanimity and I sat in my compartment waiting to see who, if anyone, would be travelling with me.

I think I assumed that I would be sharing with some of the 'Asian travellers', and that I would have to explain my meetings at the embassy before analysing Mao's agricultural reforms and Deng Xioaping's abandoning of 'the faith'. I certainly didn't expect an elderly German academic; and I was so sure he was in the wrong section that I ignored his angry questions about whether I intended leaving my large and mysterious parcel in the luggage rack, and suggested he move up to de-luxe, which I thought was at the front of the train.

His exposition on the merits of travelling on a low budget was interrupted by the arrival of a third passenger, an Irishman living in Australia. He was obviously furious that he was expected to travel in the same compartment as someone holding a British passport, and resolutely refused to speak to either me or the German; he sat in the corner either glaring at us or reading books by Sven Hassel. Fortunately, he was on the train with an Australian friend, and after a few hours the two of them left their compartments and stood morosely in the corridor, blocking everyone else's way and muttering abuse at anyone who went past. We later discovered that they intended getting off the train at Irkutsk, which, though two days away from Peking, still left four days before we reached Moscow when we could leave the compartment without fear of getting mugged.

The German, who turned out to be a professor of physics teaching in New York, was obviously placed in a difficult situation – he could either sit in silence, speak to someone who carried bicycles around wrapped in cardboard or try and talk about Sven Hassel with the Irish mugger. He turned to the Irishman, who had put the book down to stare gloomily out of the window. The cover of the book featured an SS officer apparently being attacked in mid-air by an eagle.

'So you have a book on Germany. May I see it?' asked the professor.

There was a nasty grating, gurgling sound which was at the very least ambivalent, so the professor shuffled towards the Irishman, who immediately snatched up the book and pressed even closer into his corner.

The professor turned to me.

'Have you been cycling in China?'

I confirmed that I had, as part of my journey from London to Peking.

'How did you get across Iran?' he asked. It was a question which was obviously going to follow me around for an indefinite period, and expose me to constant accusations that I had cheated, failed or done anything other than behave sensibly. I told him that I had flown.

'Probably very sensible,' he replied. I couldn't believe it at first, but then he repeated it. Immediately I knew that I was going to enjoy this chap, and taking him by the arm I suggested we ought to have lunch together.

From Peking to the Mongolian border the restaurant car was provided by the Chinese, through Mongolia by the Mongolians and from the Soviet–Mongolian border to Moscow by the Russians. Inevitably a number of other rumours were spread about – that there was no restaurant through Mongolia, and of course the familiar stories about the Russian restaurant only accepting foreign currency on the rare occasions when they were both open and supplied with edible food. After eating the Chinese food everybody seemed to cheer up a bit, as it delayed by another day the moment when we would have our last decent meal, and most thought they could survive without food from Mongolia to Moscow.

Another significant reason for the general good cheer was that we were passing through Chinese and Soviet-controlled Mongolia on a comfortable train and not by camel, foot or bicycle. The dry, infertile land was no doubt suitable for the hardiest of sheep and the most lovingly tended grain, and that it was a hard life where no time was free for amusements and distractions was obvious enough from the train and didn't need closer examination. Every time I looked out of the window and saw another squat collection of stone and mud huts, and the little groups of people wrapped in enormous padded jackets, stamping to keep out the cold, I felt another great surge of happiness that I was no longer cycling and wouldn't have to try and find some spartan room to sleep in, suffering the constant intrusions from curious Chinese as I lay shivering and trying to work out where to go on to the next day.

My only worry as I went to bed that night, shortly after we'd crossed the border and into Soviet-controlled Mongolia, was my failure to conceal a titter when the Mongolian guard had stared at the Irishman's passport for a while and then asked, in a superbly thick voice, if it was really a British passport. I tried to pretend that I'd sneezed, but it was obvious that he knew what I'd done so I had to sleep lightly that night. In a small gesture towards peace I left a copy of a Flann O'Brien novel I'd swapped in Peking lying on the side of my pillow, and to try and support my sneezing charade I blew my nose a lot and even tried a couple of dummy sneezes. The Irishman, however, continued to make his strange growling noises and stared menacingly out of the window.

North of the Chinese–Mongolian border we began to be conscious of two aspects of life which continued together until the Urals: the first was the emergence of colourfully painted wooden houses looking like elaborate doll's-houses, each with a verandah round it and, beyond that, a vegetable patch. The second was the appearance of Russian soldiers on all the station platforms preventing us from taking photographs of trains, station buildings and, particularly, the soldiers themselves. By the time we reached Ulan Bator several people had worked out how to take these photographs without getting caught. It required the cooperation of the blue-suited Chinese railway guards, which, once they realised that this would annoy the Russians, was easily obtained. For some reason all the windows and doors on the train were locked, and we had to be let out at the stations by the guard. Normally, he quite understandably didn't think that anyone would be in a great rush to leap out on to a cold platform patrolled by thuggish armed soldiers, where there was rarely any food or drink and almost nothing to see. It was a view shared by the thuggish soldiers, who had learnt that the whistling of the train as it pulled into the station meant nothing, as all the dilatory guards still had to let the passengers off before the soldiers had anything to do. The solution to the photograph problem was to persuade the guard to open the door as we pulled into the station, whereupon we would all jump off and take loads of photographs before the soldiers ambled out on to the platform.

At Ulan Bator this was made worthwhile, as overlooking the station were two enormous paintings of Gorbachev and a rather stupid-looking man who was presumably the President of Mongolia. After staring across the beautiful but unphotogenic Gobi desert for the last few hours, the sight of these paintings was almost unbearably exciting for the dozen or so photographers among us, who clamoured to be allowed off to sprint over and get their pictures before running back to the train and hiding their cameras. Very few stopped to ask why they were risking the wrath of the thugs in order to take a photograph which was probably obtainable on request from the Mongolian embassy.

A number of other passengers actually thought it unfair to tease the poor Russian soldiers who had been sent out to Ulan Bator. They felt that even off-duty soldiers would probably come and meet the Trans-Mongolian express, as it might well be the highlight of the week in the depressing collection of factories, blocks of flats and large, bleak super-markets that stretched from Ulan Bator to somewhere west of Dresden.

Apart from the battalion of Russian soldiers who came along to meet the train, it was saddening to see the whole of the British embassy staff hanging around two Range Rovers parked on the enormous parade ground between the railway station and the posters of Gor-bachev and friend. The widely held view on the train was that they came along every week in the hope of someone donating an old novel, magazine, newspaper or box of chocolates bought in the Peking Friendship Store.

Picking up two copies of *Time* magazine which an Italian-American had finished with, I shuffled across and asked if they would help to kill the long Mongolian nights.

'Oh, it's not so bad here, y'know,' shrieked a woman. 'We're playing bridge tonight, and there are some lovely walks.'

'But why do we need an Embassy here?'

'Keep an eye on the Russians,' she cried, as though it were like refereeing a lower-sixth hockey match. 'And put up passengers who fail to get back to the train in time.'

I looked back, saw the Chinese guard waving his flag anxiously, and just heard the faint bell over the station tannoy. After China I had become so immune to the sound of loudspeakers that the inconsequential ringing of a bell and someone mumbling in Mongolian and Russian that the train to Moscow was about to depart no longer registered at all. It suggested that at least one of the apocryphal stories from the Trans-Mongolian might be true – that people did end up on Mongolian or Siberian stations without luggage, ticket, passport, permission or train.

However, I managed to get safely back on to the train and we rattled on across the infertile landscape. This was flooded with melted snow, with a few hardy reeds beginning to appear at the edge of ponds, but basically there were just the same coarse clumps of grass that gave a green tinge to the northern extremities of the Gobi desert. Occasionally we would see a horseman or two, dressed in thick, colourful woollen smocks and wearing incongruous Russian leather boots. The Chinese would probably have half-killed themselves providing irrigation for these areas, and one would have seen the familiar blue suits splashing across some muddy field. In Mongolia, and later Siberia, the land was left fallow and the only signs of progress were the number of chimneys belching black smoke, the size of the refining tanks and the height of the dilapidated skyscrapers in which the workers lived.

Increasingly, time and distance began to seem meaningless – one looked forward to a station nine hours away in the hope of buying some cheese on the platform, remembering stations because someone either got on or off; we arrived at Ulan Bator after lunch, so the Russian border would be reached some time after dinner. Watches and clocks were useless – everything on the train ran to Moscow time, except the restaurant car which operated a quite unfathomable system of opening and closing without announcement, precedent or logic.

Crossing Mongolia, the train began to change from a microcosm of China – blue cotton suits, the distinctive smell of Chinese cigarettes, the smell of Chinese cooking and the powerful sense of overcrowding – to a subtle blend of the more distinguished Mongolian citizens visiting Moscow and Russians returning from their God-forsaken colony. Both sets of passengers began a peculiarly relentless celebration over the approach of the Soviet Union – not the exuberant drunkenness I'd expected, but a weary, obsessive over-consumption which began with carafes of brandy at breakfast and went on all day, with vodka brought with them on to the train and champagne and more brandy bought on the train and stations. The restaurant car, which in China had closely resembled one of the garish 'foreign sections' of Chinese restaurants, changed into something like a small-town saloon; small groups of two and three crouched around a bottle, their heavy, jowly faces falling slowly and inevitably towards the table.

The train began to smell of these pickled drinkers, of spilt vodka, cigarettes stubbed out in alcohol, body odour and the strange combination of tinned pilchards, gherkins and red cabbage which seemed to form their main diet. The Russians stopped bothering to change out of their pyjamas (rather like track-suits) and stood dourly in the corridors, their almost uniformly overweight bodies reeking of excessive alcohol, cigarettes and vinegar.

At the end of the second day we crossed the Mongolian–Soviet frontier, and groups of soldiers wandered along the train searching some compartments, ignoring others, confiscating an innocuous cassette and one of the old *Time* magazines, but not even interested in my curious brown parcel. The train stood still for some time while the engine was changed, and the passengers queued up on the freezing platform to buy roubles from another little doll's-house, built from thick wooden planks colourfully painted in reds and greens.

By the morning we were at Lake Baikal, and we breakfasted as the train trundled slowly round the icy surface, pine trees and snow covering the huge mountains that surrounded the lake and one or two fishermen who, with typically Russian dour determination, hacked holes in the ice to fish through. A grey, cold, steely sky seemed to guarantee that spring would never arrive at Lake Baikal.

From Lake Baikal we began a massive tour of enormous industrial complexes located in the midst of an agricultural wasteland, one minute crossing an unpopulated taiga – flat, frozen swamp sustaining a few pine trees and bushes – the next in the centre of a bizarre high-rise city, with large, shabby blocks of flats surrounded by floodlights, smoky chimneys and huge steel-works and chemical-processing plants. Irkutsk, Krasnojarsk, Novosibirsk and Omsk, the great cities of Siberia, 500 miles apart from each other and all striving to present the least appealing aspect.

The distances became almost overwhelming, and began to explain the permanently bleak attitude of the Siberians, surrounded by an unimaginably vast area of cold, useless land and forced to live on pilchards and cabbage. Our carriageful of Westerners, tacked on at the back of the train, became a silent, reflective place, where little was said other than the occasional anguished exclamation that anyone could live in such a place. The Chinese, reduced in number to just two carriages by the time we reached Novosibirsk, crammed into a few compartments and smoked and played cards all day, trying to retain throughout Siberia the illusion that China was outside and that the next stop would be Nanjing, not Omsk or Petropavlovsk. The Russians carried on drinking.

On the fifth day we crossed the Urals, for some the eastern limits of Europe, but still 1000 miles from Moscow and 2500 from London. There was another day on the train before we reached Moscow, yet as we passed the famous obelisk at the summit of the Urals, engraved with 'Asia' and 'Europe', people were already beginning to discuss accommodation in Moscow, which train they would catch to Berlin or Warsaw, and where we would be able to find a shower and eat something other than pork, fried eggs, fried potatoes and the peculiar substance described as 'chicken' on the train menu.

The next morning, our last on the train, most people were packed and ready to leave at least six hours before we were scheduled to arrive in Moscow, and stood staring out of the window asking whether Jaroslav was a suburb of Moscow. The German professor paced up and down, wearing a tie for the benefit of the Swiss friend he was to stay with, and the rest of us debated whether to sleep on Byelorussia Station and see something of Moscow, or rush straight on to Berlin, unable to face another two or three nights without a shower.

The sight of Red Square, the Bolshoi and the streets of nineteenth-century mansions as we crossed Moscow in a taxi to the station for the West convinced most of us that two nights in the station waiting-room and a little more accrued dirt were worth it. In what seemed, after months in China and India, to be a sort of dream world I went with two other train passengers to a wine bar to eat caviar and drink two bottles of Hungarian wine, paying with roubles bought on the Moscow black market. It was with a strange sense of disbelief that we realised that nobody in the wine bar was throwing chewed bones on to the floor, that nobody was expectorating, spitting or smoking between mouthfuls, that people weren't all wearing the same clothes, and that they didn't stare at the sight of three Western tourists. It was fantastic, and we practically danced back to the station along the silent streets, uninterrupted by loudspeakers.

The police woke us up at six o'clock with the warning that the station was about to be cleaned, and the request that we book on to the train to Berlin leaving that evening. It seemed reasonable – Moscow stations were as uncomfortable as any other country's, and the eight days since the last shower were beginning to take their toll. The heady excitement continued for the rest of that day: the Kremlin, the churches, the civilised restaurants – all so irreconcilable not just with Chinese life, but with the awful Soviet life in the industrial towns across Siberia.

In due course we began searching for some vodka and food for the journey from Moscow to east Berlin, a mere twenty-four hours away on a train supposedly without a buffet car – another scare story which turned out to be quite untrue. Again there were no complaints about my taking my parcel into the compartment, no challenges at the Polish or East German borders, no comment as I passed through the underground from east to west Berlin and from west Berlin through to Holland.

Only at Harwich did I get any complaint:

'You got a ticket for that, mate?'

'No, but I don't need one, do I, it's a bike.'

'Cor, so why you got it all wrapped up, then? You ought to bleeding well cycle it, mate, do you a lot more good than going by train.'